The Writer's Essential Tackle Box

Getting a Hook on the Publishing Industry

Lynn Price

First UK edition

Proudly published in 2010 by
Snowbooks Ltd.
120 Pentonville Road
London
N1 9JN
www.snowbooks.com

Paperback ISBN: 978-1-906727-543

Printed and bound in the UK by J F Print Ltd., Sparkford

A catalogue record for this book is available from the British Library.

www.snowbooks.com

To all the wonderful authors

Who serve as my inspiration

Contents

Section 2

The Submission Process 239

Section 3:

Publishers 307

Section 4:

The Writer's Survival Style Guide   337

Introduction

Gone Fishin'

"Honey, don't hold dinner; I'm going fishing!" You gather up your tackle box, your shiny, new rod and reel, goofy hat, and vest and head out the door. Upon arriving at the fishing pond, you're stunned at the crowd of people standing around the shore.

"How am I ever gonna attract a fish with all these people?" Looking at all the other poles and all the other fishermen, you begin to wonder if your rod and reel is shiny enough.

Well, publication is a lot like fishing. Since there are more writers than agents and editors, you need the best equipment. Your fishing pole has to be top of the line, and your tackle box must be filled with the most effective bobbles, bellsinkers, lures and hooks. Are you aware there are over 800 different styles and sizes of fishing hooks? There are Jig Hooks, Spinner Bait and Trailer Hooks, Worm Hooks, Octopus, Kahle and Siwash Hooks. Some are weighted and some are swim bait. How does one choose the right equipment? Research.

Understanding how the industry works; why we do things the way we do, how books sell, and the reasons why manuscripts are rejected are vital pieces to having a properly filled tackle box. And that is the purpose of this book. *The Writer's Essential Tackle Box* introduces you to some of the top names in the industry and takes you on a behind-the-scenes tour of our side of the pond while answering all of your publishing questions.

Knowledge is power, and whether you've just signed a deal with Random House or you're beginning your writing career, there is probably something about this industry you wished you knew. This is no longer a world of "if you write it, they will come." Writers need to be savvy about the industry in order to make the best and most informed decisions of their literary careers, and this book is tailored especially for you.

So come on and get your fishing pole and tackle box. We're goin' fishin'.

How To Use This Book

I've organized *The Writer's Essential Tackle Box* into sections for quick and easy reference. This cuts down on knowledge meltdown and brain overload.

Section 1: "Casting the fly rod" showcases interviews with industry professionals and explores what happens before, during, and after the publishing process.

Section 2: "Forget the bait, pass the Pepto Bismol" is devoted to the daunting submission process and defining the elements that go into a snooze-free cover letter and synopsis. Also discussed is how to write an effective bio. This distinctive point of view of my side of the pond will help you better understand our frustrations and our, "Halleluiah, I think we got us a winner!" moments.

Section 3: "Chumming the Waters" deals with defining the many types of publishers currently populating the industry; what they can and can't do for you, and why. This section finally answers all those questions about the differences between vanity, Print-on-Demand (the printing process vs. the business plan), trade publishers, and everything in between.

Section 4: "The Writer's Survival Style Guide" contains a four-part Manuscript Autopsy which is based on my collection of the most common mistakes I see in manuscripts that invariably result in their untimely demise—the rejection. This isn't meant to be a replacement for *The Chicago Manual of Style* or the Strunk and White books (which should be in every writer's possession), but more of an uncomplicated and straightforward reference guide that serves as writer's metaphorical wrap on the quill for POV switches, dialog tags, voice, paragraph transitions, adverbs, comma usage, character and plot development, etc.

Section 1

Interviews

"Casting the fly rod"

Our particular pond is filled with many different kinds of fish; cover designers, distributors, website designers, book reviewers, agents, publicists, event planners. Since this is all about making your fishing rod as shiny as possible, it's important to hear what these fish have to say. I went to the most experienced fish in the pond willing to share their expertise in the goal of making you the prepared, equipped, and organized fisherman at the pond. I present you with some very cool fish.

1: Agents -
Why Do I Need An Agent?

Nearly every writer I talk to knows they need an agent and understands these marvelous gifts from heaven are instrumental in securing the best possible deal. But, too often, those writers have instant visions of Random House dancing in their heads, and this is often where reality and fantasy collide.

Not every writer is Random House material, but that doesn't mean they aren't publishable. There's a difference. The large publishers look at submissions knowing they require a higher sell-through of their titles to remain viable and profitable. Literary agents walk on Reality Lane every day and are in the best position to advise their clients as to where they fit in the publishing game and whether they have big time possibilities or perhaps a home with a smaller boutique publisher. The agent will submit where they feel their client's work has the best shot, and believe it or not, the criteria aren't always about money.

There's a great deal that goes on in the background of manuscript submission, and I thought it could be educational to show an editor's perspective regarding agents' importance.

Good agents:

* **Form relationships with all kinds of editors with big and smaller houses.** They do this by being organized and knowing

what each house publishes before they query. The agent who wastes my time is someone I'll remember the next time they query me, and I'll be more likely to let their submission rot on my desk for a while. A good rule of thumb to remember when looking for an agent is that writers are agents' clients, but editors are their customers. The smart and successful ones cultivate relationships with many editors. We send dirty jokes back and forth to each other, and we get together when we're in each other's cities. Funny how we're always the ones to pick up the bar and dinner tab, though. Go figure.

* **Know how to sell their client's work.** They accomplish this by writing mouthwatering cover letters that make me want to shove everything off my desk and dive right into it. They don't rely on the synopsis that the author provided, but rather, they write their own. Why? Because they know what we short-attention-spanned editors want to see.

* **Are organized.** They have professional proposals and queries. Face it; this is a game of selling, so it makes sense to have the best sales pitch possible. The savvy agent includes the synopsis, reasons why the manuscript is marketable, defines the readership, and lays out their client's marketable assets. If an author claims to have blurbs from big names, the agent makes sure the author comes through. An agent should never promise anything to an editor unless it's in the bag. To come back to the editor with egg on their face gives the impression of pulling a bait and switch in order get the work reviewed. Whether it's accidental or not, it smacks of pulling a fast one, and our elephant-like memories will store this for a long time. Redemption is unlikely.

* **Protect their image.** In order for an agent to remain on top of their game, they make legit and solid sales on a regular basis. This is good for their clients and also enhances their reputation. They're an open book and list their clients and sales on their website. They

advertise their sales on Publisher's Marketplace and other venues. They don't sell their clients off to Print-on-Demand companies, nor do they advertise that they've done so. This would damage their credibility and reputation.

* **Protect their client.** Flying solo is not a good idea because authors have no idea how to protect themselves during contract negotiations. I've heard hundreds of stories where an author took their contract to their attorney, who said it was great, only to find out down the line that they gave away half their rights. That's because authors need to consult with a literary attorney. Or better yet, an agent.

There are other times when a manuscript has made the rounds without a bite, and, sometimes, an agreement is struck that will allow the author to attempt to find a smaller publisher on their own. In these cases, the good agent outlines the potential dangers—no POD companies or vanity presses—and, in turn, agrees to serve as their consultant. This is an unenviable position for the agent because, by this time, the author is very motivated to be published and is vulnerable to making some tragic decisions. It's vital that they listen to their agent's advice. If an author is determined to be swallowed by a POD company that could take their book to Nowheresville, the agent has little choice but to drop them because there's no longer a meeting of the minds.

I have seen instances where an agent listed the "sale" on their agency website, and it created a backlash with their reputation among editors. It's too bad because, invariably, those reputations were taking an upward swing due to some solid sales. In order for an agent to be taken seriously by editors, their reputation should be unimpeachable. Authors may not see this as being a bad thing. But editors do, and that's who they're selling to.

* **Aim high.** This is in keeping with establishing a good rapport with editors on all levels. Manuscripts normally travel through several layers of publishers. You have your A Team—these are the mega

houses. The B Teams are the mid-level houses and imprints. C Teams are the smaller boutique publishers who have solid distribution but smaller budgets, smaller print runs (4,000—10,000), and produce fewer books per year. Good agents go through all these levels. They never start at the bottom and stay there, nor do they necessarily start at the top and stay there.

I love working with good agents. They've already culled through the slush pile, send me manuscripts they feel I'll be interested in, and they know my tastes. They bend over backwards to make my job as easy as possible because I'm their customer. Because of this symbiotic relationship, they have the ability to get things read that I'd more than likely reject had the author submitted them. Even though I still accept unagented work, I can see why a lot of my editor friends have an agent-only policy.

Authors must do their homework

* **Check their client list.** If an agent hides their client list, ask yourself why. What are they hiding and why? The scammers that have stumbled across my desk tell me they are protecting their client's privacy. From what? Publishing is a showy business, and the idea is to get one's name out there, not hide it.

* **Check their sales.** If they hide their sales, again, ask yourself why. Agents are, in a sense, a public relations machine, and they grow in stature by publicizing their clients and sales. Check those sales. Are they to Print-on-Demand or vanity companies or are they to solid publishers? How recent are those sales?

* **Check the proposal they're sending out to editors.** Do they rely on your synopsis (which may be good, but theirs should rock), or have they rewritten it into a mouthwatering slice 'o love? Have they discussed your promo plan with you? Have you both discussed and defined your readership? Have they gone through titles that are competitive to your book? If they haven't, then you have to consider how well they can sell you to an editor because we're

going to ask for these things. We editors are in a buyers' market and have our choice of a plethora of great works. It's your agent's job to ensure you're sitting on the top of the heap so we'll pay attention to it.

* **Are they charging you?** If they are; find the door and make a break for it. Normal agent fees such as mailing and Xeroxing comes out of royalties after the sale is made. They should never charge you a fee just to read your work.

Lastly; yes, it's hard to find an agent. Finding an agent that's right for you isn't unlike shopping for a car. Both take research and knowledge of the industry. You've labored over your manuscript, tweaking it to within an inch of its life, so doesn't it make good sense to take equal care in finding a legitimate agent? Consider incorporating some of these pointers into your own sales pitch to agents. And good luck!

The interviews of these talented agents will help you learn the do's and don'ts of agent fishing.

Andrea Brown

Andrea Brown is President of the Andrea Brown Literary Agency, Inc., established in 1981 in New York City. It was the first agency to represent both children's book authors and illustrators and the agency has sold over 2000 titles to just about every publisher. Now based in California, the agency has seven agents, was rated number one in juvenile sales in 2007 by Publisher's Marketplace and has had six titles on the top ten of the New York Times Bestseller List in 2008. Andrea is the Director of the Big Sur Writing Workshops, a Board Member of the San Francisco Writer's Conference and is author of WRITERS' AND ARTISTS' HIDEOUTS: Great Getaways for Seducing the Muse.

Contact Info:

Andrea Brown

Andrea Brown Literary Agency, Inc.

1076 Eagle Drive

Salinas, CA 93905

Email: andrea@andreabrownlit.com

Website: http://www.andreabrownlit.com

Author of:

Writers' and Artists' Hideouts: Great Getaways for Seducing the Muse (Quill Driver Books)

What does an agent do? Why do authors need an agent?

A literary agent should be an author's best friend—and partner.

Publishing a book takes a team effort and it begins with the agent/author relationship. First, an agent needs to recognize talent and commercial viability. Then, the agent should help an author polish the manuscript to make it as perfect as possible. An agent should know the markets, what the editors and publishers want and need and then submit the manuscript to as many editors as possible. Hopefully, the agent should then negotiate a good deal and contract for the author, hold the important rights such as film, foreign and merchandising if the project warrants those and then be the intermediary between the author and the publisher. If the author hates the cover or the copyediting job, it is best to have an agent complain, so the author can continue to have a good, close working relationship with the editor. An agent also must help an author plan his/her career, help with financial issues, promotion and sometimes even babysit.

Authors need an agent these days if they plan to have more than one book published, or, if they don't have a relative/friend who is an entertainment or publishing lawyer. Editors prefer to deal with agents who know what to ask for and what to expect.

Most authors have designs on being published by a large publisher with a 50,000 print run. Why do agents submit to a smaller publisher who does smaller print runs?

Sometimes a book is better off with a smaller press, especially if it is a niche book or a regional book. Agents usually know if a book will sell to Random House or not. The idea is to be well-published, and often a smaller press will keep a book in print longer, know the niche markets to sell into and be a better place for a project. It is easy to go back to print, but not so easy to recover a career if too many books are printed and not sold.

Do agents submit to publishers who accept unagented work? If so, then can't the author do this for themselves just as easily? What are the advantages to looking for an agent in this respect?

Some agents only submit to big publishers and others submit to anyone likely to buy a particular book, but it isn't only the sale that matters, it is the whole big picture and that is why a serious author needs an agent these days.

What should authors look for in an agent?

I often say it is easier to get divorced from a spouse than from your agent. You can file a legal document and be divorced but once a book contract is signed, it becomes a three-way contract with the agent listed as "agent of record." As long as that book is in print and it could be decades if an author is so lucky, the agent is tied to that book and receives the monies, statements, etc. So, it is crucial for authors to be careful in choosing the right agent. Authors need to do their research, study lists, referrals, talk to writers, go to conferences—everything they can do to get names of reputable agents who might be right for them. Don't go with someone brand new unless they are part of an established agency. It doesn't matter where the agent is located—what matters is if they have sold any books like yours to real publishers. And make sure, besides trust, you find an agent who you can talk to, likes email if you do, and someone you can work closely with over the long haul.

How long after querying an agent should I wait for a reply?

After a query, give it 4-6 weeks and then check in. Sometimes rejection letters are lost in the mail, or emails don't go through and you can wait months when it was a no. And submit to more than one agent at a time to save time; just let the agents know it is a multiple submission. Do not call and bug the agent. If you haven't heard anything in two months, assume it is a pass.

What input do you need from me when preparing to submit my work to publishers? Do I write the synopsis?

Plan to supply the agent with a proposal, synopsis, as many chapters as the agent requests or, even better, a complete manuscript. And a good title.

My agent charged me reading, mailing, and processing fees. I'm $500 in the tank, and I still haven't seen a publishing contract. Is this normal?

Some agents do charge a "marketing fee" or some such fee up front. We don't; most reputable agents do not. Unless an author wants his manuscripts sent Fed Ex, the agent should pay for the marketing costs of doing business.

How long should authors stay with an agent?

Authors should stay with their agent as long as the relationship works. Conversely, authors should never sign any agency agreement that gives a time limit. An author should be free to leave and terminate when he/she wants to; but the author shouldn't be too hasty. Just because an agent has not sold your book in the first 6 months of the relationship, it doesn't mean the author should terminate. Only if the agent does not respond, give feedback, direction or list submissions, then the author should look elsewhere but the author should give an agent a fair shot after they have invested time. Agents won't take on clients they don't believe in or feel they can sell. And, new agents will be wary of an author who jumps ship too quickly.

How many publishers will my agent query before they give up on me?"

This varies for each book. Sometimes it takes us two or three years, and thirty rejections to place a book.

Do authors need to provide a promotion plan? Will it help convince an agent to accept their work if they do?

Some agents insist on a promotion plan, especially for non-fiction. Sometimes now for fiction, too.

Do agents sell foreign rights as well, or is that a separate agent?

Some agencies sell foreign rights in-house, some use foreign agents in other countries, some don't sell any at all and this is a question to ask when interviewing agents. But not every book will sell in foreign countries and if you get a big six-figure deal, the publisher might want to keep those rights.

Do you get involved in many auctions? And is the result always for more advance money, or are there other parameters you consider?

We do a fair number of auctions each year, and mostly an auction gets a big advance. But there are other considerations and sometimes we don't go with the biggest offer, but the best offer, which might include a big marketing/advertising budget as well.

Do you have personal relationships with all the editors you submit to? Is that how they sell manuscripts?

All agents have personal relationships with editors, some more than others. It is certainly one way of selling books but not the only way, and many of our books are sold to a first-time editor. Sometimes we'll submit a manuscript to a personal editor friend who will then pass it on at the house to an editor who will truly love it.

"What kind of an advance can I expect? After all, that's why I got an agent."

Who says you will get any advance? Authors should not have any preconceived idea about money. I hope that is not why you are writing. You should write, as Isaac Asimov said, "for the same reason that I breathe—because I have to." Some new publishers are trying a different model of paying big royalties with no advance. Sometimes we get $2500 and sometimes we get $500,000. It is best to be surprised.

My agent told me I needed to edit my manuscript. Won't my publisher do this?

Editors will edit, but they don't have the time these days to edit a manuscript that needs a lot of work. Manuscripts do not get sold if they aren't really polished. That is why I started the Big Sur Writing Workshops, so writers could really work on polishing their manuscripts to perfection to sell. That is why there are so many book doctors and freelance editors helping writers now.

Do you help promote a client's book once it's published?

We do help with promotion ideas/plans but don't have the time or knowledge to really help. There are publicity professionals who do that, and often we tell authors to plan to use some of their advance to find a publicist to work with, or to use for their own promotion efforts with bookmarks, cards, etc.

What are your biggest frustrations when working with a client?

Biggest frustration is unrealistic expectations and grandiose ideas. Writers need to keep an open mind.

What steps should authors take to ensure you will review their work? What elements do you look for in a query letter?

Above all, writers must appear to be professional and courteous. If we see that a writer had done his homework, checked out our clients, recent sales, interests, we are more inclined to ask to see their work. Query letters should be short—two paragraphs are all we need. The first paragraph should have the genre, word count, brief pitch or plotline, and a bio or relevant credits in the second paragraph. Writers really should work hard on polishing their query letters. And always attach the first page of text so the agent can see your writing, even if it says "query only," on submission guidelines. Agents need to see your writing.

What changes have you seen in the publishing industry, and do those changes affect how and where you submit your client's work?

Changes are happening all the time. I became an agent because in 1981, while editing books at Alfred A. Knopf (part of Random House), I saw contracts go from four pages to eight pages. I saw that writers needed more help and representation. Nowadays contracts can be eighteen pages long, and it seems there is a new clause popping up every other month. Houses get bought and sold, editors leave, markets and trends change, so don't write for any trend. Write what you love, read, and care about. Don't write unless you have something to say to people. We are a successful agency because we have adapted over the past twenty-seven years, and try to help our clients adapt to stay relevant and published.

What is the most important thing for writers to know about agents?

Writers should know that just because an agent takes on a manuscript, it doesn't mean the mss will sell. Many of them do, but not all. We aren't in the miracle business and the publishing business can be fickle. Authors must remember that an agent has many clients, not just them. Courtesy and patience go a long way in creating a wonderful working relationship.

Rita Rosenkranz

Rita Rosenkranz founded Rita Rosenkranz Literary Agency in 1990 after a career as an editor with major New York houses. Her non-fiction list includes health, history, parenting, music, how-to, popular science, business, biography, sports, popular reference, cooking, spirituality and general interest titles. Rita works with major publishing houses as well as regional publishers that handle niche markets. She looks for projects that present familiar subjects freshly or lesser-known subjects presented commercially.

What does an agent do? Why do authors need an agent?

Optimally, an agent is the author's primary advocate. The agent helps shape the proposal (so that it is clear how the proposed work is different from and better than the competition) or work of fiction, finds a publisher, negotiates the contract, sells subsidiary rights to the work, intervenes when there is a controversy (whether it be over an editorial question or the publisher's promotion plans), weighs in with an opinion (e.g., the book cover), monitors the publishing process and steers the author's career book by book. Many authors don't know how to manage all these concerns on their own; when a representative is there to intervene, the talent can concentrate on the creative process.

Most authors have designs on being published by a large publisher with a 50,000 print run. Why do agents submit to a smaller publisher who does smaller print runs?

Most large houses require a minimum first printing for the publication to meet their overhead requirements. To simply keep it in the catalog and store inventory is costly, and the book has to have a large enough anticipated audience to be worth a big publisher's investment of time.

Smaller or regional presses can be a better match than the larger houses for certain niche projects where the initial printing will be modest even though, ultimately, the evergreen[1] market results in regular reprints and respectable overall sales. I have many examples of books that started out with a 5,000 first printing but over time proved their sturdiness by continuing to sell from year to year. Some of these books require updates, but if the publisher keeps tabs on the book's content and the market, the author will revise the work from time to time.

I stay up-to-date on many smaller publishers' lists and have a sense of their regional or niche interests. Sometimes when I have not been able to place a book with a large house I will look to a smaller publisher. For some books where I understand the market is small but renewable—again it might be a regional book—I might still take the work on because the subject interests me or I simply believe the work will prove itself over time.

Do agents submit to publishers who accept unagented work? If so, then can't the author do this for themselves just as easily?

I believe some of the smaller houses I submit to work with unagented authors. At times I am brought in to negotiate a contract after the author has found a publisher on his own. I've sold a number of projects to university presses, which also work directly with authors. I would like to think I get a better overall contract thanks to my detailed negotiation. This is not to say authors can't negotiate hard on their own, but, generally, it is easier for an agent to step in as an advocate for the author. Publishers understand that this is the agent's role.

Nearly every author wonders if they are "big New York publisher" material. Do agents immediately know where a manuscript fits in the publishing food chain?

I have a game plan in mind from the outset—an immediate sense of the prospects for a work—whether that means major publishers or smaller houses. For most projects I hope for a big house but have backup smaller

---

1   A book that sells year after year and remains in print

houses in mind, too. This game plan is one part science and one part art. My instincts are honed by my experience with previous projects, my conversations with colleagues—agents and editors—my keeping tabs on recent publicized deals and the market.

What should authors look for in an agent?

I advise authors to "know thyself," because there is a spectrum of agents with different personalities, strengths, level of experience, connections to the film world, etc. Depending on the author's publishing history and/or ambitions, she might benefit more from a well-established agent, whereas another author will connect better with a hungry, new agent. Do you want a New York-based agent? Some—but not all authors—do. Some authors prefer to have an agent close to where they are based. Will the author be working with the agent or mostly with an assistant or intern? What are the agency's commission and agency charges (and is there a cap on charges)? I advise authors to review the questions listed on the Association of Authors' Representatives' (AAR) Website to help determine the best fit.

My agent charged me reading, mailing, and processing fees. I'm $500 in the tank, and I still haven't seen a publishing contract. Is this normal?

The AAR prohibits reading fees but does allow for mailing, messengering, and copying reimbursement. (Some agents will send manuscripts electronically—and many editors prefer this approach because it reduces or eliminates any copying charges. Generally the author is responsible for copying when hard copies are generated.) Any allowable charges and how reimbursement is handled should be clear in the agency agreement. Agents approach reimbursement differently. Some will send an invoice on a regular basis, even before the publishing deal is made. Others might wait to be reimbursed from the book's advance or from royalties.

How long should authors stay with an agent?

Under the best circumstances, the agent/author relationship builds book by book, and the author feels well served at each stage. But if the agent doesn't handle an author's new genre or if the agent doesn't want to move forward with that project but the author is intent on publishing that work, then the issue might be forced, and it might be time to move on. So much depends on good chemistry, faith, perhaps the history of the author and agent. Usually it is good to have a conversation to understand the agent's intentions—especially if the agent and author have worked together for a long time and the author has had success with the agent. If the agent is losing steam on a project after many months (or years), the author likely will know this, and it's appropriate for the author to come to terms with the next step. It might be appropriate to move on if there is a personality conflict, regardless of the reason.

How many publishers will my agent query before they give up on me?

Before signing an author, I make it clear how many prospective publishers there are for the project. This is a case-by-case situation depending on the obvious (and not so obvious) candidates for a work, the author's financial requirements, and the overall durability of the relationship—in part determined by both the author's and agent's stamina and patience. I have had several successes where I have told an author that I have only one publisher in mind and asked, "Are you game?" and hit the target with that one submission. My watermark is 42 submissions after three years. I attribute this to the author's faith in me, my sustained interest in the project, and the fact that the author ultimately did not mind having a small publisher for her project. There are many inspiring stories about the long road to publication, but that often requires the strength of will to stay the course once it's clear gratification won't be instant.

Do authors need to provide a promotion plan? Will it help convince an agent to accept their work if they do?

In the case of non-fiction proposals, I do like to see a promotion plan to understand the author's marketing strengths. Publishers will want to know this too. A promotional plan often will note the part the author's Website, email list, speaking circuit, promotional outreach—perhaps tried-and-true for previous books—and connections to media will play in the promotion of their book. Perhaps the book's publication can be tied to an anniversary or holiday.

Do agents sell foreign rights as well, or is that a separate agent?

This is different from agency to agency. Some have in-house staff, some use co-agents abroad, some use domestically based co-agents who sell foreign rights. They will either sell directly to a foreign publisher or use a co-agent to sell to that territory. Foreign rights agents have an understanding of the international appeal for a work, keeping in mind which categories are popular abroad at that time. Foreign rights agents might sell on the basis of a proposal or more likely wait for galleys or even a finished book before they make the deal. Sometimes an agent will sell rights abroad first to prove international interest that can lead to a U.S. deal.

What does it mean when a manuscript is taken to auction?

When an agent thinks the project will command interest from multiple publishers, she can raise the bar by putting a project up for auction. The agent will set rules for the auction (what rights are being offered, when the agent needs to hear back from the editor, whether there are "topping" privileges, etc.). It is important to note that most projects are not auctioned.

Do all agents have personal relationships with editors? Is that how they sell manuscripts?

An agent depends on her relationships with editors and the access that provides. When you've had success with an editor, it's easy to build on that relationship with new projects. That said, I'll sometimes reach out to new editors by email or phone if I'm handling a new category or need to go beyond my set checklist of editors. I'll hope that my years in the industry and the strength of the material help streamline that connection. Perhaps I'll name a title I represent in a category they handle or I'll name a colleague who has done business with them, hoping to secure an instant connection.

My agent has submitted my manuscript to everyone with no bites. I've decided to go with a Print-on-Demand publisher. Will she help with contract negotiations? If not, why?

I suspect many agents would not be in favor of a Print-on-Demand publication and would not be interested in reviewing the contract. There is no advance from which to get a commission so there would have to be a different arrangement for payment to the agent. Generally, POD publications do not help a career. If a POD book does not do well because the author has not promoted it successfully, the book isn't likely to interest a new publisher. Simply having the work in book form does not make it more attractive to a mainstream publisher.

What kind of an advance can I expect? After all, that's why I got an agent.

A book's advance is determined by size of market, author's track record and ability to promote the work, how popular the category is at that moment, if there is more than one interested publisher, as well as other considerations. Typically a publisher's profit and loss statement, and the advance offered, will be influenced by the estimated first printing (which is subject to change at the time the book goes to press), the estimated retail price (also subject to change), the estimated page count, whether there are illustrations, etc. While agents can make ballpark guesses, we are not the ones making the offer and there is no way to know what the advance will be until the process plays out.

My agent told me I needed to edit my manuscript. Won't my publisher do this?

As much as the editor will edit the work, in order to increase the odds to generate an editor's interest it is best to submit the cleanest proposal or manuscript possible. This process can change from agent to agent. Some offer general editorial advice. Some will edit the work. Others will recommend outside editors who will work with the author closely and be paid by the author. The agent's hands-on involvement might be determined by the amount of editing the work needs.

Do agents help promote the book once it's published?

This differs from agency to agency. Some authors hire outside publicists. Some agents use their contacts to complement a publisher's and author's efforts. Some agencies now have in-house publicists.

What are your biggest frustrations when working with a client?

It's easiest for me to do my best work when an author is dependable, respectful of deadlines, proactive in terms of generating publicity for themselves and promotion of their books, thanks to their speaking circuit, podcasts, etc. The more I am preoccupied about these points the less time I will have for higher level efforts, for instance, discussing the author's next book project. Also, too often I am making excuses for delays in the publishing process—for instance in getting contracts or payment of advances to the author—and it can be frustrating to spend so much time on what should be automatic.

What steps should authors take to insure their work will be reviewed?

I have found that well-crafted proposals—that make clear the book's intentions, how the book is different from and better than the competition, how well the author is paired to the subject, and the author's ability to promote their work—often generate quick interest from multiple agents. Agents read their mail, are always scouting for new and interesting talent. I advise authors to send out their best work—work they are proud of and that they feel expertly expresses their point of view. I find that sometimes authors work very hard on their work and simply get tired and decide to send out the proposal even when, in their heart, they are not sure about its strength. They might contact me shortly after the first submission and ask to submit an improved version. This tells me that the author is still honing and sent out the project prematurely. I don't want to stigmatize a submission for this reason, but it does seem wasteful.

What changes have you seen in the industry, and do those changes affect how you submit your client's work?

Almost all categories are crowded, and it has become increasingly difficult to make a work stand out. I can get more easily excited about a project when I know the author is impassioned about his work, has great insight into a subject, perhaps has spent many years researching the subject and has unearthed new and fascinating material on it, and proves in the sample chapters a strong ability to harness the information to make it readable and useful for an audience that is identifiable (where there is an understanding of the demographic of the readership and the popularity of the category thanks to comparative titles).

Most proposals are interchangeable; they don't have a distinctive, fresh point of view or an author who can carry the project past the clutter in the marketplace. Occasionally, I am disappointed when I see a great idea, but I don't believe I can sell it with that author. The author doesn't have a good enough résumé, and I expect publishers to reject the work for that reason. As a result, the promotional strengths an author brings to a work can both help launch a work and help that work endure. While I am drawn first to the project's concept and content, I have a special appreciation for authors who intuitively understand the promotional needs of the industry and who capture that in their proposal. I enjoy it when an author captures my attention with a subject I hadn't realized interested me. They are opening a new world to me with their work, and that makes my own work worthwhile.

Do you show your clients the final proposal before you begin submitting it out?

I feel obligated to not only show the author the last draft of the proposal before it goes out (they might see something in need of tuning that I missed) but also the cover letter in case there's inaccurate info, or perhaps new info to add.

Laurie McLean

Laurie McLean is an agent at Larsen Pomada Literary Agents in San Francisco. She represents adult genre fiction (romance, fantasy, science fiction, horror, westerns, mysteries, suspense, thrillers, etc.), as well as children's middle grade and young adult books. She looks for great writing, first and foremost, followed by memorable characters, a searing storyline and solid world building.

For more than twenty years Laurie ran a multi-million dollar eponymous public relations agency in California's Silicon Valley. She is wise in the ways of marketing and publicity, negotiation, editing and a host of other business-critical areas. She is also a writer herself, so she can empathize with the author's journey to and through publication.

Contact information:

Email: laurie@agentsavant.com

Blog: www.agentsavant.com

Guidelines: Preferably emailed submissions of the first ten pages and 2-page synopsis

What does an agent do? Why do authors need an agent?

At the most basic level, a literary agent is an author's business partner. An agent locates a publisher interested in buying an author's writing and then negotiates a deal. But a literary agent is so much more than that.

An agent is:

* A scout who constantly researches what publishers are looking for

* An advocate for an author and his or her work

* A midwife who assists with the birth of a writing project

* A reminder who keeps the author on track if things begin to slip

* An editor for that last push before submission

* A critic who will tell authors what they need to hear in order to improve

* A matchmaker who knows the exact editors for an author's type of writing

* A negotiator who will fight to get the best deal for an author

* A mediator who can step in between author and publisher to fix problems

* A reality check if an author gets out of sync with the real world

* A liaison between the publishing community and the author

* A cheerleader for an author's work or style

* A focal point for subsidiary, foreign, and dramatic rights

* A mentor who will assist in developing an author's career

* A rainmaker who can get additional writing work for an author

Most authors have designs on being published by a large publisher with a 50,000 print run. Why do agents submit to a smaller publisher who does smaller print runs?

Not all books are bestsellers. Not all manuscripts get published. And bigger is not always better. Small publishers, university presses, and niche/specialty houses might be the perfect place for a particular book. The small horror genre publishers, for example, have done a fantastic job for this market segment. With tiny print runs (100-500 copies), ornate special editions, and well-written novels that would never have shouldered their way into the miniscule mainstream horror market, these "indie" publishers, like their counterparts in film and music, play an integral role in providing opportunities to writers along with providing a steady stream of excellent books for their readers.

Take this book for instance. Will it be a bestseller? Who knows? It's possible. Does the author have something of value to impart to new authors? Absolutely. Ingesting a wide variety of sage advice and informed opinion from diverse voices keeps our minds lubricated and fertile. Who wants a dry, inflexible mind, right? By choosing an indie publisher that concentrates on transformative non-fiction, the writer receives a less-daunting (but still not trivial) entry point into publishing, direct access to passionate professionals on all levels, and marketing and distribution support targeted directly to the appropriate audience. Does the author receive a six-figure advance? Not likely. But not impossible. The job of the small, independent publisher, as I see it, is to provide the critical-dissenting-opinion-fresh-idea-groundbreaking-discovery guys and gals a chance to be heard.

Do agents submit to publishers who accept unagented work? If so, then can't the author do this for themselves just as easily? What are the advantages to looking for an agent in this respect?

In a nutshell, you'll probably wind up with a larger advance, more favorable contract and all-around better deal worth more than the fifteen percent you'll pay an agent if you let a professional hawk your manuscript or proposal to a publisher. Plus, editors tend to move your submission further up in the pecking order if it comes represented by an agent whose opinion and knowledge they value. The reason unagented submissions are collectively called a "slush pile" could be because the daunting weight of all that roughage squeezes the enthusiasm right out of the harried editor! By the time they get to the unagented submissions, their goal is to hurry through them and reject, er, I mean process, them as expediently as possible. Would you rather have your work considered by an editor during the mandatory Thursday afternoon "Dream Crushing" session, as it's called at one mid-level New York publisher, or on the SONY eReader of that same editor who becomes so engrossed in your work on the way home she misses her stop? I choose door number two.

Nearly every author wonders if they are "Big New York Publisher" material. Do agents immediately know where a manuscript fits in the publishing food chain?

Knowing where a manuscript fits should be part of any good agent's knowledge base. A good agent knows which editors want what material. And even better, a good agent knows what they don't want.

Like relationship building in any industry, information sharing and mutual respect are keys to getting the job accomplished. When an agent recognizes the perfect storm of excellent writing skills, exceptional storytelling talent, and a direct fit into the market, a tingle goes up the spine. I get giddy. I love it when I know exactly which four editors will go ape over a particular romance novel. (Non-fiction agents must also consider the author's platform or fan base, but I'll let the non-fiction agents talk about that.)

However, what about those cross-genre novels or exploratory writing that don't fit a particular mold. When an agent loves a book but doesn't know exactly where it might find a home, one of two things happen:

The agent, regretfully, passes on offering representation but asks to see future work. He or she might even guide the writer to some degree if the work shows that much promise.

The agent will step outside her comfort zone and explore unfamiliar options (smaller publishers, university presses, etc.) to get a book published. This is much rarer than option I simply because agents are also business people and have bottom lines to attend to. But most agents love good books and sometimes this passion will overrule ease-of-sale issues if they truly believe the project has potential.

What should authors look for in an agent?

An author should interview an agent as they would a publicist, printer, or any other business partner and not be star struck to the point of accepting the first agent who offers representation. I believe an author should find an agent with the following characteristics:

* Integrity

* Wisdom

* Knowledge (different from wisdom)

* A strong work ethic

* A personality fit (this becomes even more important as your career develops)

* A personal commitment to their profession (they should be developing their career too!)

* A professional relationship with you (not just a friend, but a partner)

How long after querying an agent should I wait for a reply?

The length of time between receipt of a query, reading of same query and reply to the author depends heavily on an agent's style and his or her workload. It can be anywhere from minutes for an email query to a young or aggressive agent, to six months in extreme cases. My best advice is to check the website of each agent you submit to and discover their usual response time. If you can't find the information there, you can always email or call and ask. Or check **www.agentquery.com** or **www.litmatch.net** for such information.

I try to reply to email queries within a week and mailed queries within a month. Although when I get super-busy with client deals, unsolicited submissions take a big back seat and my reply time lengthens. If an agent hasn't replied in eight weeks, it is perfectly acceptable to drop them a line using whatever process you used to query them originally and inquire about your submission. Sometimes queries get lost in the mail or in cyberspace. Don't assume anything. Submit, wait eight weeks, then inquire.

One further point; at the query stage of the process it is not necessary to grant any agent exclusivity. The idea is to spread your query far and wide to an appropriately targeted list of agents. If an agent asks to read the full manuscript, then you might consider offering them an exclusive. But only if the agent requests it and only for a month or less.

What input do you need from me when preparing to submit my work to publishers? Do I write the synopsis?

I handle adult genre fiction (romance, fantasy, mysteries, science fiction, horror, westerns, suspense, etc.), children's middle grade (ages 9-12), and young adult (high school) books. From you, once we'd agreed to work together, I'd need a polished manuscript, a brief (1-2 pages) synopsis that reads like a movie trailer instead of a chapter-by-chapter summary (boring!), information on any editors who are familiar with your work, and an idea of your short-term and long-term career goals.

My agent charged me reading, mailing, and processing fees. I'm $500 in the tank, and I still haven't seen a publishing contract. Is this normal?

An agent is entitled to reimbursement for nominal out-of-pocket fees incurred in the process of attempting to sell your work. Some agents, myself included, consider postage, phone charges, copying and other out-of-pocket expenses a part of doing business and do not charge our clients for these costs. Other agents ask clients to reimburse their exact charges or they add a processing fee.

Know the expense reimbursement policy of the agency whose services you are hiring BEFORE SIGNING A CONTRACT! If it isn't stated in writing in the contract, put it in as an addendum.

If you can't live with what an agency charges for expenses incurred on your behalf, don't sign the contract.

And. . .

. . .NEVER EVER pay an agent reading fees. This is the big tip off that they are not legitimate.

How long should authors stay with an agent?

You should stay with an agent for as long as the relationship continues to work for both of you. As long as the agent still loves your work and continues to actively pitch it. As long as you keep producing new work that your agent can try to sell.

Part ways if your agent has ceased pitching your writing to editors, if you've taken a hiatus from writing, or if your work styles have become incompatible. No hard feelings. Don't let them develop. It's a small world, this world of publishing. Manage your career with savvy, courtesy and honesty. Don't get mad. Simply move on.

The reasons behind your writing not selling, or not selling for as much money as you think you deserve, are not always obvious.

You may have written the most compelling vampire novel ever penned. But perhaps the fickle public has moved on to shapeshifters, meaning your vampire novel is now long in the tooth (sorry, I couldn't resist). Or you've written a fantastic story about an all-girl wizard's school only to be eclipsed by J.K. Rowling. Maybe every publishing house already has its epic Southern family novel, or Iraq War memoir, or Mayan 2012 thriller. The point is, some works take longer to sell than others, and you can't compare.

Since I come from the world of business, I highly recommend that you track your agent's successes and failures selling your work. If you're not satisfied, talk to your agent. Be honest. Don't whine. And realize it can take anywhere from a few phone calls to several years to sell a project. Have patience. Understand the process.

My best advice? Begin working on your next novel or proposal and try to ignore the glacial pace of the publishing industry.

How many publishers will my agent query before they give up on me?

This is another "it depends" answer. I once queried 93 editors for one of my clients before I told her I was switching from aggressive to opportunistic pitching—basically putting her novel on the back burner. She went back to writing, and I sold her next book in six weeks. The reason? The second book was there at the right time to catch a trend in young adult romance exactly when a new imprint was emerging and casting a wide submission net.

I've sold a three-book series in a bidding war that lasted four days from first reading to done deal. It's also taken me 13 months to sell a delightful Hispanic middle-grade novel. There is almost no rhyme or reason to this, but you have to keep plugging away.

As long as I feel I can sell a client's book, I'm going to keep trying.

Do authors need to provide a promotion plan? Will it help convince an agent to accept their work if they do?

Ever since the publishing mega-mergers of the 1980s, it has become essential for authors to become proficient at marketing to advance their careers. Publishers try to squeeze every facet of their business—from author advances to distribution costs—to remain profitable. It gets tougher every year. Marketing is crucial to the success of a book. But aggressive, expensive marketing is usually reserved for best-selling authors. Since bestsellers fund the rest of the unprofitable books published by any one company, this is a smart move. But it also means that if you want to do a ten-city book signing tour, place an ad in *Publishers Weekly*, or distribute bookmarks to every Barnes and Noble and Borders in the U.S., you have to foot the bill yourself.

The good news is that the marketing departments at the major publishers have witnessed the success all kinds of authors are having with Internet-based publicity and are leveraging these tools themselves. One publisher won my client's YA book because they were offering mobile initiatives, author blogs, Myspace and Facebook pages for authors, a downloadable e-book version of her book, extensive online contests, giveaways and promotions, and YouTube video book trailers. To me, this was more valuable than an extra couple thousand dollars on the advance.

So, yes, create a promotion plan that is heavy on websites, blogs, podcasts, email lists, YouTube video trailers, etc., and you'll be on your way.

Do agents sell foreign rights as well, or is that a separate agent?

Larger agencies have a foreign rights agent or department and sell foreign rights themselves for their clients. Smaller agencies, like ours, team up with a co-agent who specializes in foreign, television, movie or dramatic rights. Before you sign away your foreign rights, ask your agent about the strength of the agency's rights capabilities versus the publisher's rights departments. If you let the publisher keep any secondary rights, it means you will only see extra money in your semi-annual royalty statements, and then only if you've earned out your advance. If your agent retains the rights and aggressively markets them, you get 85% of every deal your agent can make. That can add up fast.

Talk a little about auctions.

Auctions occur when multiple publishers want to buy the same book, hopefully yours. The agent manages the auction where each publisher bids on the book, and the book goes to the highest bidder at a pre-ordained deadline. Auctions are the highest form of flattery, in my opinion, and bode well for how strongly the publisher will push your book once it's published.

Do all agents have personal relationships with editors? Is that how they sell manuscripts?

What I love about the publishing industry is that the writing trumps everything. I can be best friends with an editor, but he or she will still not buy a property from me if it isn't superbly written and just right for their list.

Agents and authors need each other. This means they must work together—and the closer the better. Since we all love books, it is easy to form a friendship based on a common bond, so yes, agents and editors have both personal and professional relationships of varying degrees. But if a book isn't right for a particular editor, it is assumed that they will reject it. And the friendship remains intact.

My agent subbed my manuscript to everyone with no bites. I've decided to go with a Print-on-Demand publisher. Will she help with contract negotiations? If not, why?

Once you decide to self-publish, you have taken yourself out of the traditional publishing process for that book, in my opinion. I will not even look at a self-published or POD book unless the author managed to sell at least 5,000 copies by himself. Other agents don't share this viewpoint. They will look at self-published books. But my experience in genre fiction is that editors don't want to see self-published books unless they are selling like hotcakes. And if that's the case, the publisher will find you, trust me.

My advice to those of you who choose POD as a publishing mechanism is to find a literary attorney to vet the POD contract. Then market the heck out of your book.

What kind of an advance can I expect? After all, that's why I got an agent.

Advances against royalties, the really big check that you receive when you sign the contract (perhaps split in halves or thirds depending on the publisher) can range from zero to hundreds of thousands or millions of dollars. My personal experience in genre fiction and children's books has ranged from $5,000 to $50,000. Only best-sellers or potential bestselling books earn million dollar advances from publishers.

My agent told me I needed to edit my manuscript. Won't my publisher do this?

Editors at publishing houses are overworked and underpaid. They are tasked with acquiring profitable books, cleaning and polishing with a light editing cycle where they advise the author on changes to be made, copy editing, marketing and shepherding the book through the production process. Editing is the author's responsibility.

Do agents help promote the book once it's published?

Most agents do not help you promote your book beyond a phone call or email brainstorming session where they point you in the right direction. They sell the book for you and then turn you over to the publishing team for editing and promotion. When your next book is ready, they'll sell that one for you, too.

I have 25 years of experience in publicity and marketing, so I enjoy brainstorming these activities with my clients. This is rare in the industry, but I figure the more successful an author is, the more money I make, too. It's an investment. Besides, it's fun!

What are your biggest frustrations when working with a client?

How long do I have here for an answer? Just kidding.

I don't have a lot of client frustrations—which is weird because most of my clients are new authors or established authors desiring a change in their career.

New authors don't understand the publishing process yet so their expectations are often out of whack—and so are a lot of their questions. But an honest patient relationship smoothes out most of these speed bumps.

What steps should authors take to insure their work will be reviewed? What elements do you look for in a query letter?

Generally, the publisher will send reviewers Advanced Reader Copies (ARCs), which are uncorrected proofs of the forthcoming book, months before the book is due to hit the store shelves. The author can suggest online blogs or review websites that the publisher might not know about, but generally the publisher will know who should get an ARC for an advance review. The author can then spend his or her time being interviewed on blogs or other online venues, and in magazines, etc.

Query letters?

My colleague, Michael Larsen, says that queries should show the HOOK, the BOOK, and the COOK, and I like that. It's simple to remember and a great way to structure a query.

The HOOK is the brief tantalizing phrase about your book that will excite the reader enough to want to buy it and read it. A high concept pitch that offers concentrated excitement.

The BOOK is an expansion of the hook that gives more depth and builds on the promise of the hook so that the agent knows there is a story behind the hype.

The COOK is about you, the author. Hit the highlights of your writing credentials. Mention any famous author endorsements or awards you've won. And put it last in your query letter, not as the lead. Agents want to know about the book first, then the author.

What changes have you seen in the publishing industry, and do those changes affect how and where you submit your client's work?

The biggest change in publishing that I've noticed over the past five years is the digitalization of pitching, publishing and promoting. The Internet, e-books, podcasts, blogs, email, websites, mobile device outreach, and more are being embraced with such fervor and rapidity, it is mind-boggling. Especially when you understand that the publishing industry has not changed very much in a hundred years!

Pitching:

Three years ago, not one major publisher would accept a submitted manuscript via email. All of them had to be printed and mailed. Then the publisher paid to return the package if it was rejected. Expensive! Last year things began to shift and approximately half of the editors I pitched requested that I send manuscripts to them via email. This year I have not sent out one hard copy submission. Everything goes out to a publisher as an emailed attachment. They download it to their eReader, and off they go. So much simpler, more efficient, and green!

Publishing:

Have you seen the variety and sheer number of books that are being offered in e-book format? Amazon's Kindle program offers e-books the same minute that hard copy books become available for purchase—at lower prices in many cases. E-books are still not mainstream, but they are rapidly moving in that direction.

Promoting:

If you don't have an author website, you are not taken seriously anymore. Same thing with a blog, or a shared blog. The days when authors could write and let the publisher promote their work are OVER. The good news is that once you learn to navigate the new frontier of web-based marketing tools, it is cheap to do and a lot of fun.

What kind of groundwork would you like the writer to do before querying you?

Research me by reading the agency website, www.larsenpomada.com, and my blog, www.agentsavant.com. This will tell you what I'm looking for, give you insight into my personality and show you what I've been successful selling.

Understand what literary agents can and cannot do for you. Mike Larsen has written the definitive book on agents called, *How to Find a Literary Agent*. Buy it, borrow it, or pick it up at the library. This is a fabulous tool that will educate you on the agenting profession and how we can help you build a career as an author.

Understand the publishing process and commit to it. I am looking for authors who write at least one book a year for at least ten years. A rule of thumb in genre fiction is that it takes five novels to build a significant fan base. Jim Butcher's Harry Dresden series didn't take off until book 5. Laurell K. Hamilton scored big on book number 9. I want a commitment from my clients that they are in it for the long haul. I'll make the same commitment back to them.

Is it harder to sell an author who has no platform?

I don't handle non-fiction, so the concept of a platform (which is an established audience formed by workshops, organizations or other publics and built in advance by an author who is an acknowledged expert and a public speaker) is less important to my clients. But I still encourage my authors to do book signings at "cons" specific to their genres (e.g. World Horror Con, World Fantasy Con, Comic Con, Romance Writers of America conference, Romantic Times conference, etc.). I also like them to blog to build a public persona.

It's important for the agent and author to have a good working relationship, e.g. finding the "right agent." How can authors prepare for this?

It helps when you enter a relationship to know what you want to get out of it—and to be able to articulate this to your agent business partner.

Do you want someone who will hold your hand or a shark who will get you the last dime possible from a book contract? They're not usually the same person.

Do you want an editing agent to help you polish your work prior to submitting to editors? Or do you want a strict business-oriented agent who will concentrate solely on pitching your work and negotiating deals on your behalf?

Do you want someone who's fun to work with or do you prefer a no-nonsense, results-oriented personality?

Once you build a profile for what you want in an agent, you improve the probability that the agent who becomes your partner will work out well long-term.

What is the most important thing for writers to know about agents?

Agents are humans, not gods. They should be pursued as business partners and evaluated as such. They are critical to your success in the publishing world, but if you cannot interest an agent in your work, you can always self-publish, self-market, and prove yourself that way. Agents need writers as much as writers need agents.

Do you require fiction work to be completed before authors query you, or can it be unfinished like nonfiction, where authors query having only completed the first few chapters?

Authors need to have their manuscript completed, edited and polished before they query me. Unlike non-fiction, first time writers need to show agents and editors that they have what it takes to finish a full-length novel and then edit and polish it.

When they query me, I ask them to email the first ten pages. From that I will see whether they have great writing chops and can hook a reader into the story from the first word. I also ask to see a 1-2 page synopsis. If I like the first ten pages, I'll read the synopsis to see if the story holds up all the way through to the ending. If I like the synopsis and first ten pages I'll usually ask for the whole enchilada. THAT'S why the entire novel has to be in tip-top shape before they query me.

Because this process doesn't take that long and if I'm hooked by the partial and the author responds to my request for the full with, "Well, I'm not quite done yet, but I think I'll be finished writing it within two months," I totally lose interest. If a writer doesn't even know that much about the publishing process, how are they going to be savvy enough about the marketing of their work to compete in this dog-eat-werewolf business!

Peter Cox

Peter Cox became a literary agent after a successful career as a writer. Working with his wife and writing partner, Peggy Brusseau, they collaborated on 27 books, mainly published by Bloomsbury and Random House in the UK. Many of them were UK bestsellers, and one—*Linda McCartney's Home Cooking*—became a major international bestseller.

Peter's background is in advertising and marketing. "I had three very traditional literary agencies representing me while writing," he says, "and I wasn't really happy with the degree of service and attention I received from any of them. Redhammer, my own agency, was created specifically to look after the unmet needs of authors—not the needs of the literary agent. I believe we are the prototype of the literary agency for the 21st century. We already do a lot more for our clients than most agencies, and as the publishing industry goes through today's seismic changes, I think our way of doing things will become more and more relevant and attractive to authors."

Peter's clients include the worldwide bestselling children's author Michelle Paver, U.S. Senator Orrin Hatch, television journalist and former Member of Parliament Martin Bell, OBE, science writer Brian Clegg, children's author MG Harris and former deputy editor of the *New York Post* and Britain's *Sun* newspaper, David Yelland. Redhammer is recognized by the Association of Authors' Agents.

Peter, Redhammer Management is based in London, so you have a unique perspective as to the differences between American and British writing styles. What are those differences and do you sell those stories differently?

That's a huge question, but the basic answer is Yes, I do sell those UK and U.S. authors quite differently. The principal differences are cultural. For example, edgy or experimental work has traditionally been easier to sell in the UK rather than in the US—one reason for this is the perceived price of failure is a lot higher in New York than in London. Writing styles themselves principally differ for cultural reasons, too, but I'm bound to say that good writing is surprisingly universal in its appeal. I'm always much more aggressive in my selling stance in New York compared to London—another cultural difference.

If you sell an author to a foreign country, does this impact the author's ability to promote their book? And will publishers consider that a liability?

It depends. Publishers invariably ask about the author's "platform"— whether they have good access to a numerically-significant group of potential buyers, and whether they can attract the right sort of media to reach buyers at launch time. Sometimes, and I'm mainly thinking of non-fiction here, the subject matter of the book dwarfs any consideration of the author's platform. And let's not forget that most media is very international these days, not just the Internet, but the easy availability of satellite media tours, which save the publisher the expense of physically bringing a foreign author over for the book's launch. However, the name of the game these days is maximum return on minimum publishing investment, so a publisher will naturally prefer an author with a good existing platform (which may well include being local to the market).

Most authors have designs on being published by a large publisher with a 50,000 print run. Do you submit to smaller publishers who do smaller print runs, or are you more selective of the authors you sign?

I'm very split on this. My natural preference is to deal with real people rather vast, faceless corporations. And believe me, mega-publishing corporations are more than capable of making the dumbest publishing mistakes—size is no guarantee of quality or professionalism. However, it's no fun for an author to be published by a small publisher who is unresponsive, over-committed, and under-resourced. My ideal publisher would have the resources of a big company behind them, but be run as a small team.

Do agents submit to publishers who accept unagented work? If so, then can't the author do this for themselves just as easily? What are the advantages to looking for an agent in this respect?

The truth is that most publishers who say they don't accept unagented work will, eventually, get round to looking at it—even if it's the office dogsbody. So yes, I do deal with publishers like that. The advantage of going through an agent, though, is that we should have the right contacts and the right track record to command a publisher's attention. We can get you noticed right away. Before that stage, I will work on the proposal with the author to make it as good as it can be. And afterwards, I'll manage many aspects of the continuing relationship with the publisher. If I was still an author, I'd be very happy to part with some commission for all that.

Nearly every author wonders if they are "Big Publisher" material. Do agents immediately know where a manuscript fits in the publishing food chain?

Yes. But the author ought to know, too, even before they submit. On Litopia, I encourage writers to think about this aspect from the very start of their writing.

What do you look for in an author?

A grown-up attitude. The relationship I have with my authors is "equal but different." They're good at what they do, and I'm good at what I do. Together, we make a great team. I avoid relationships that are one-sided or manipulative—life is too short. And publishers appreciate this, too—all my clients are fantastic for publishers to work with.

How long after querying an agent should an author wait for a reply from you?

I'm different in this respect to other agents. Unpublished authors need to access me through Litopia Writers' Colony, a place where they can develop their work and finally pitch it to me. Authors who have already been significantly published (i.e. not POD or vanity) can access me through the Redhammer website, and I'll usually respond to their enquiry within a day or so.

What input do you need from an author when preparing to submit their work to publishers? Does the author write the synopsis and promotion packet?

They obviously need to do a synopsis—this will have been done a long time before the final proposal is assembled. I will then usually take over the preparation of the proposal itself. My background is advertising, and I can bring an objective view to things like the strap line and blurb, things that authors often find very difficult to do.

Does the author's work have to be completed before querying you? Is this common?

No, my basic position is that I need to understand (a) the concept and (b) the execution. I certainly don't need to see the whole manuscript to evaluate those criteria. However, this is unusual—most agents still ask to see the whole thing, which I think is very wasteful is so many ways.

How long should authors stay with an agent?

My own clients should obviously stay with me forever! From my own experience of being agented (when I was an author some years ago) I never found an agent who delivered what I wanted, so I had three separate agents. Which is perhaps as well, or I wouldn't have become one myself. Authors do have a remarkable ability to stick with an agent even if they're getting lousy service—and that's frustrating from my own new business point of view, because by providing a better service, I hope to attract the best clients. I'd say—if the relationship is terrific, then be loyal to your existing agent. If not, then tell your agent and see if you can improve it. And if none of the above, then speak to me!

How many publishers will you query before you feel the work isn't going to sell?

I never give up. Never.

Do authors need to provide a promotion plan? Will it help convince you to accept their work if they do?

It's not essential at the pitch stage, but it will help establish their professionalism, certainly.

Do agents sell foreign rights as well, or is that a separate agent?

Agents do sell foreign rights, either directly or through sub-agents. And publishers almost always like to acquire foreign rights, too, so they can sell them themselves.

Every author is dreaming of an auction. In reality, how often does this happen?

It happens when you succeed in getting two or more publishers wanting the same project. But I caution against auctions—that's very old-fashioned thinking, actually. You should aim to be wonderfully published, and not just go for a big advance from the wrong publisher.

Do you have personal relationships with editors from all sorts and sizes of publishing houses? Is that how you sell manuscripts, or do you still make "cold calls"?

The danger is that you simply deal with a small band of publishers who you know. I'm always trying to find new people and develop my contacts base, so yes, I'm always making cold calls.

My agent subbed my manuscript to everyone with no bites. I've decided to go with a Print-on-Demand publisher. Will you help with contract negotiations? If not, why?

Print-on-Demand is a very poor substitute for being "properly" published. A lot of publishers have been overly influenced by the "Long Tail" theory and believe that POD will be their savior. It won't, although it may at some point develop into a useful adjunct to mainstream publishing. You should ask yourself what a Print-on-Demand "Publisher" is really doing for you—how much risk are they taking? How will they promote your title? What is the opportunity cost of going with them? I think you may be disappointed in all these areas. The alternative is to use Print-on-Demand to publish yourself—in which case, I'd again advise you to consider whether you've developed a marketing plan? Have you understood the major investment of time and money? Have you addressed the challenging issue of distribution?

What kind of an advance can I expect? After all, that's why I got an agent.

Well, how good is your manuscript? But seriously, I do usually have a good idea about the sort of advance an author can expect. Having said that, it all comes down to what publishers believe is going to be economic. Today, the pressure on advances is certainly downwards for all apart from the very safest of bets. We're seeing the slow death of decades of unearned advances—money is tight, and publishers are looking to trim their sails. But there are still opportunities for talented new authors to earn good money—but I stress the word, "earn."

My agent told me I needed to edit my manuscript. Won't my publisher do this?

Your agent should have given you a lot more painstaking and specific advice than simply that. If you're an unpublished author, you need to show at least 100 pages of your manuscript—maybe more—that are perfect. I'm talking unreasonably good. Yes, a publisher will of course provide editing, but initially, to attract a publisher you must produce something that's extraordinary in every respect. Your agent should guide you on this.

Do you help with promotion plans once the book is published?

Yes, I get very deeply involved in this area, sometimes even writing the publicity brief and advising the publisher on the choice of an external PR agency. It's a big part of my time.

For example, with Michelle Paver (the *Chronicles of Ancient Darkness* series which has sold into 40 countries and multi-million dollar earners) we set up a fan site for her readers even before the first book was published five years ago, and that has become increasingly important in the overall marketing mix. We also were instrumental in getting Sir Ian McKellen to narrate the audiobooks of the series, and then sold film rights to Sir Ridley Scott. All these things start to build a virtuous circle of promotion. For MG Harris, we've set up a huge Internet game for readers with the aim of using their existing fan base to draw more and more readers into the game as it progresses.

I would never go out to publishers with a major proposal without at least having thought through this aspect of the book's promotion. And I think that's one of the differences between Redhammer and other agencies—we get deeply involved here, and the rewards certainly show.

What are your biggest frustrations when working with a client?

I love what I do more than anything! There are no major frustrations. I suppose the only thing that's an issue sometimes is the sheer time it takes to work on a client's manuscript—each iteration can take days, and there can be many iterations before we go out with something.

What steps should authors take to insure their work will be read by an editor? What elements do you look for in a query letter?

A good hook. Sell me the idea. Most query letters are very poor, and talk about everything that's irrelevant. Make it clear, simple and focused - pitch it to me!

What changes have you seen in the publishing industry, and do those changes affect how and where you submit your client's work?

The industry is today looking for reasons to reject projects. Anything that's not quite right is wrong. Safe bets are favored. Retro is in demand. If a project can't get an internal consensus around it, it won't fly. I don't like this direction the industry's taking, but it's the reality.

Corporate publishing is all about risk reduction, which is paradoxical, because the publishing business has always essentially been a casino— with talented publishers being able to call the shots better than the less talented. We're now seeing an extreme aversion to risk, so part of my job involves creating a lower-risk package that still allows a highly talented yet unproven first-time writer to be well published.

What kind of groundwork would you like the writer to do before querying you?

Read the Redhammer website at **www.redhammer.info**

Is it harder to sell an author who has no platform?

Yes, unless the concept of the book is a no-brainer that will sell itself.

It's important for the agent and author to have a good working relationship, e.g. finding the "right agent." How can authors prepare for this?

Authors looking to change agents often make a stupid mistake; they ask the potential agent to read and comment on a work in progress. They may end up meeting half a dozen agents, all of whom have been asked to read the same work. In the advertising game, we used to call this a beauty contest. Almost invariably, the agent with the finest silver tongue gets the client. Now, do you really want an agent who strokes your ego? Wouldn't it be better to find someone who appreciates you as a writer but who can take you to the next stage—which invariably involves criticism? So when looking for agents, the first rule is—leave your ego at home!

What is the most important thing for writers to know about agents?

The range of agents is truly vast. There are many whom I deeply respect, and just as many who make me wonder how they ever got into the business. In other words, there are lots of highly professional people in the business, but to be devastatingly frank, there are also lots of pretty unprofessional people, too. Remember, there is no professional training for agents, and no qualification scheme. Most agents fall into the business having formerly been publishers, and with a few shining exceptions, I don't consider that to be an effective background. The agent's skill set is quite different to the publisher's.

How can an author spot the difference? Well, you should certainly spend some time with the agent concerned, either face-to-face, on the phone, or on Skype, which is a good compromise if you live on separate continents, because it allows good quality video-conferencing. You should ask the agent to walk you through, step-by-step, every stage in the development, selling and publication processes—and explain what they do, and what you should do. If this takes less than half an hour, I'd say they're either skimping or don't know their stuff!

You also need to ask them about wider issues—such as how to start planning to develop your career. Most agents only think as far ahead as the next book deal, which in these challenging times simply isn't far enough. You don't want to have half a dozen books published over the next five years or so and then realize—I've done all this work, but really I'm no further forward in my career than when I started! A good agent will look at the big picture.

Final Thoughts from my side of the Pond

One of the essential tools in your tackle box is homework. Agents do not come with those neat little rating labels that tell us how fresh and snappy they are. We have to dig in and look for the expiration date—and dig, I do. I want to know with whom I'm working because the reputation of my publishing house rides on it. And so does yours.

I never take anyone for granted, and I research the agents who submit to me. "Cool," you say, "but how does this affect me?" Well, it affects you because your work may be in the hands of one of those agents I'm researching. Again, you say, "Whoopie doo, knock your bad self out." Now wait, don't grab another handful of beer nuts, and quit sucking down that mai tai . . . this impacts you, the author, so wipe your fingers and get comfortable.

What are the things I look for in an agent?

* First, I read the submission to see if the story scratches my literary itch.

* I go to the agent's website (if I don't know them) and look over every page of their site. I do this because I want to get a feel for the person I'm dealing with. I would expect that they would do no less of me.

* Lastly, I ask around. We're a gossipy lot in this business, and word spreads like a squashed Twinkie.

AAR Member: Case in point; a couple months ago I inspected an agent's site and found some inconsistencies that raised a couple flags. Their FAQ had a question regarding whether they a member of AAR (Association of Authors' Representatives). This is a yes or no answer, folks. You're either a member or you're not. The agent's dodgy reply was that he *abides* by all AAR standards. So he gives the impression he's a member, but is he? It's purposefully evasive when it shouldn't be. I really hate evasive. And so should you.

Publisher relationships: Continuing through the site, I noticed a long list of impressive publishers they've worked with. Read my lips—*worked with*. He wants everyone to think he's *sold* to these publishers, but, in reality, he's only *worked with them*. What does that mean? It could mean anything from thinking about these publishers while nicking his face with a rusty razor or sending them a submission. It takes consistently solid manuscript submissions and sales to establish relationships with that many editors, so how has he accomplished this in the course of the year that he's been in business with no verifiable sales? A submission does not mean "working with" someone, and the two should never be confused.

Bio: So maybe the guy has a publishing background and has a lot of friends. If this was the case, I'd be willing to bet my daughter's iPod that he'd mention it in his bio. But there is no bio! In place of his experience, he talks about how nice he is and that his client list is comprised of new and experienced authors. Who cares? I want to know if he's the next Super Agent with oodles of credentials or a bug exterminator who smelled one too many batches of Rodent Be Gone. Reputation goes a long way.

Sales: Nowhere on his site does he mention actual sales, so I question whether he has any. Sales are an agent's business card, and I have never known the good ones to be secretive for the simple reason that it enhances that ever-lovin' reputation. This agent had one sale listed, but I couldn't verify it anywhere. Others I've investigated have sold their clients to less than appealing publishers—those who have been sued for financial mismanagement or publishers who have no visible means of distribution.

Author Risk: Someone who is economical with the truth in order to inflate their reputation puts their clients at risk because I suspect everything they put in their query. Is that story really "explosive," or is this just more unsubstantiated hype?" Who loses in this scenario? The author.

Vibes: How does all this affect the author? Well, I passed on the project due to the overall vibe I received from his agent. Given the ambiguity of the agent's website and lack of sales history, I didn't trust anything he had to say, and that black mark leeched over to the author. Will other editors feel the same way? Maybe. I've considered that I am paranoid because they really are out to get me. Regardless of my character flaws, I do believe that a dodgy agent is worse than no agent at all. The sad part is that I'm sure the author has no clue of the slippery impression his agent projects.

Stupid or cunning? This agent's heart was probably in the right place and had no ill intent other than being dumb. On the other hand, he's purposely vague about his origins and business practices. Again, why should I care? Because I work very closely with agents and authors, and it does me no good if I have to sleep with one eye open. I can't be constantly worried whether I'm being lied to about those promised promo plans or guaranteed cover blurbs/reviews. And who loses? Again, the author. It's always the author. Always, always, always.

When you're looking for an agent:

Be sure to check their site with a fine-tooth comb. I've given you the tools in which to check for dodgy wording. You know what I mean by dodgy—it's like politicians who never answer a direct question. They dance around the facts like my dog does when I put peanut butter on the roof of her mouth.

Check their sales, check their bio. I can't say this enough. Their site has to have substance, which is a list of their clients and sales, not feel-good tripe. Who are the publishers they've sold to? Your agent MUST have a solid reputation. We don't want to work with an idiot, and neither do you. Take the steps to ensure you look like the consummate professional and work with nothing but the best.

Check Publisher's Marketplace. Every author should be a member. (**http://www.publishersmarketplace.com/**) You can check to see if the agent is a member and verify their sales. Not only can you find a huge list of agents, you can list your manuscript on there. I have a friend who struck a three-book deal by simply listing her work there. Agent extraordinaire Claire Gerus came along, snarfed her up faster than greased lightning and sold her works to Dorchester, Prometheus, and Kaplan before she could remember where she parked her car.

Email Address. Oh yes, check the email address. Come on ... a Yahoo email account? Real agents have real email accounts. Now, pass the beer nuts, willya?

2:   The Book Review

The idea of having your work reviewed is second only to the thrill of seeing your work in print. There isn't an author alive who doesn't have a dream of being reviewed in *The Los Angeles Times* or *The New York Times*. But the dreams are quickly overshadowed by the sheer numbers of books vying for their headlines across the sky.

So what does it take to be one of the fortunate authors whose book is plucked out of a cast of thousands? Is there some magic bullet shooting that lucky title to the front of the line, or is it luck?

We all wonder what goes on in the offices of *Library Journal*, or *Publisher's Weekly*, or even the smaller reviewers like *Midwest Book Review* or BiblioBuffet. What process of divination allows some titles to be reviewed while others are passed over? Are the criteria for the smaller review sites the same as a large trade publication reviewer?

Why do reviewers review? How do they see reviews? What do they like and dislike about their profession? What types of books do they look for? What are some of the good things and bad behaviors reviewers see? And lastly, what do those reviews accomplish? Bigger sales? Fame? Oprah?

"Lauren Roberts loves me!""Library Journal thinks I'm brilliant!" They are the validation that we've either done an admirable job or missed the mark. When it's good, we blast their blurbs across our cover art and make them the lead header on our promotion packages. That's a lot of power. So who are these folks whom we live in fear of and hope to please and thrill?

Come to find out. You'll see that they're lovely people who eat their Cheerios one spoonful at a time. Just like us.

Wilda Williams - Library Journal

Wilda Williams first became interested in publishing as a career when she attended the University of Denver Publishing Institute the summer after her graduation from the University of South Carolina with a degree in English. Since jobs were few for new college graduates, she postponed the inevitable and went to graduate school instead and obtained a Master's in Library Science at the University of Alabama.

Her first library job was at the American Museum of Natural History, handling interlibrary loan requests from around the world. Her first publishing job was as editor and indexer of the *The Wall Street Journal Index*, a monthly and annual reference book published by Dow Jones, which also indexed and abstracted the *WSJ/Europe* and *Barron's*.

Since 1990, Wilda has been a book review editor at *Library Journal*, the oldest professional library publication. She is currently Fiction Editor, assigning popular and commercial fiction and (with the exception of Romance) editing the genre and Reader's Advisory columns: Mystery, SF/Fantasy, Christian Fiction, and Reader's Shelf. She also writes the annual Mystery Preview in *LJ*'s April 15 issue, and blogs about books, publishing, and other bibliomatters on the book review editors' collaborative blog, In the Bookroom (www.libraryjournal.com.) In addition, she edits *LJ*'s monthly collection development series, which helps libraries build their collection of books, videos, and web resources in various subjects, and interviews authors, editors, and publishers for *LJ Talks To*, an occasional print and online interview series.

Wilda is a member of the National Books Critics Circle, a national association of review critics, and the Women's Media Group.

What does a reviewer do? What is the decision process that determines what titles to review?

Library Journal's primary audiences are public and academic librarians who use our reviews to make their purchasing selections of books and nonprint materials like audiobooks and DVDs. The purpose of our reviews is to evaluate and recommend titles for possible acquisition by libraries. My job as a book review editor is to select titles to be reviewed and to assign the appropriate book to the appropriate reviewer.

When I look at titles for possible review, I consider the authors. Is this title a first novel or the umpteenth pot boiler from Jackie Collins that most public libraries are going to order anyway without a review? If the writer is a debut novelist, has he or she won any literary prizes? This tells me something about the potential quality of the work under consideration. Of course, there are the big literary names you always have to review: Salman Rushdie, Richard Price, Philip Roth, Margaret Atwood, etc. In the area of nonfiction, I look at the author's credentials and subject expertise.

I also include the publisher's identity in my decision on whether or not to review a book. For example, certain houses like Algonquin and Knopf are known for high-quality literary fiction. Houghton Mifflin excels in outstanding natural history writing. Poisoned Pen specializes in mysteries. So when I receive galleys from those publishers, I always pay special attention. With a new, unfamiliar press, especially one that looks like a self-publisher (we do not review self-published titles), I am apt to be a bit wary until that press establishes a track record with me.

With the large, commercial houses, I also pay attention to their marketing plans for a book: the size of the print runs, author tour, sales to book clubs, foreign rights, online marketing to book-related blogs, planned author appearances at various library conferences, and more. All of this information tells me if the book I'm considering for review has generated enough in-house buzz to get an aggressive marketing plan. Is this a big book I should pay attention to?

A book's format (hardcover, trade paperback, and mass market) will also influence my decision. *Library Journal* does review trade paperback originals, but due to lack of editorial space skips mass-market originals unless it's genre fiction like romance and science fiction.

And, finally, especially in the area of nonfiction, I look at the book's topic. Does this book offer a fresh look at an old subject? Is it tackling a subject that has never been covered before, or is the publisher jumping on the trends bandwagon: the 100th study of the Iraq war, the latest celebrity handbook on how to go green, or yet another parenting handbook on how to raise girls as strong, confident women. The same rules stand in fiction as well. There are only so many pink-covered chick lit novels my reviewers can read before they burn out. And right now, I am inundated with vampire and werewolf novels.

Everyone has the same ideas, so if a publisher has a fresh idea, they better be the first sprinter out of the starting blocks to get any kind of review attention. And remember, the book review editors quickly weary of these trends and long for the fresh, original titles that stand out from the hordes.

How do you go about deciding which reviewer takes a particular title? Does everyone sit around and grab whatever looks interesting?

At *Library Journal*, the book review department consists of five editors, each of whom assigns titles for review in their specific subject areas. As fiction editor, I specialize in commercial, or popular fiction (thrillers, suspense, women's fiction, chick lit) and genre fiction: mysteries, romances, Christian fiction, and science fiction/fantasy. Another editor handles literary fiction. On the nonfiction side, I also assign science and natural history titles, as well as books in agriculture and technology.

When I speak to librarians about the book review department and how it works, I often compare it to a dating service: we editors must pair up the right reviewer with the right book. If we don't make the right match, the result (date or review) can be a disaster.

Once I have sorted through the galleys and picked out the titles I am going to assign, I look at my stable of reviewers, who are mostly public and academic librarians. Assigning genre fiction is fairly easy, as I have columnists dedicated to each genre who choose from the titles I send them each month, although I will request that they cover first novels or titles that the publisher is especially excited about.

Assigning other types of fiction is trickier, and I consider the reviewer's reading interests and previous track record. For example, I wouldn't assign a Tom Clancy techno-thriller or an Anne Rice vampire gothic to a reviewer who prefers Maeve Binchy or Jodi Picoult. Has a reviewer read previous novels by an author under consideration for review? That tells me that reviewer has knowledge of the author's work and can judge whether the new book under review is as good as or even better than previous novels, or note that the author has failed to maintain his or her previous high standards. On the other hand, if a reviewer has consistently negatively reviewed a certain writer, I would probably assign that author's new book to another reviewer for a fresh opinion. Over the years through trial and error, I have become thoroughly familiar with my reviewers' likes and dislikes.

With science books and other more technical nonfiction, I look at not only the reviewer's interests but also at his or her educational background and expertise in the subject. I will more likely send an academic physics title to a librarian who has a degree in that subject or who works in the field as a science librarian than to a reviewer who has no knowledge of the subject.

Do reviewers only review the large NY publishers' books, or will they review smaller independent press titles as well?

Library Journal reviews books from both the large houses and the small independent presses. In fact, we would love to review more independent presses, as they are the ones discovering the new voices later snatched up by the big publishers. We are trying to expand our coverage of regional publishers since libraries are very much interested in acquiring local authors and titles from local presses.

But keep in mind that this is a small but competitive market, and the numbers are stacked up against small presses. Over 300,000 books are published every year in the United States, and of these, *Library Journal* only reviews about 6,000 titles a year. So the competition to get a book reviewed in *LJ* is pretty stiff. It is important, therefore, before small publishers submit materials for consideration, that they read and follow our submission guidelines (**http://www.libraryjournal.com/info/CA6415258.html**). They can help make our jobs easier by being as professional as possible when sending us galleys, ARCs, and manuscripts for review.

And a little personal contact never hurts. If a small press is going to be exhibiting at BookExpo, the national trade show for the publishing industry, or at the American Library Association's summer convention, that publisher should make an appointment with the appropriate book review editors to introduce its list. That helps that publisher's titles stand out in the flood of books we get every week.

Do publishers have to advertise with the magazine in order to get their book reviewed?

No, at *Library Journal*, the separation between church and state remains strong. The book review editors are fierce about maintaining their editorial independence. Advertising in the magazine does not guarantee special review treatment. If a publisher's book is worth consideration of a review, we will review it whether or not that publisher advertises with us. If the book is unworthy of a review, we will reject that title no matter how many advertising dollars the publisher spends with us.

How do publishers submit to a reviewer? What materials do they require? Can anyone submit to a reviewer? Self-published authors?

We have submission guidelines posted on our website that detail the requirements. We need advanced reading copies, or galleys, submitted to us three to six months in advance of a book's publication. If a publisher is unable to submit a galley, we do accept bound manuscripts and finished review copies that have a sticker that states: "Submitted in lieu of galleys." The ARCs should include price, ISBN, page count, index, bibliography info (if it is nonfiction), and a brief author biography (is this a first novel or that author's twentieth) and a statement about the book. For submissions from the large houses, I also like information about print runs and marketing plans, as it tells me how much support and push that publisher is giving a book. For small presses, is this a lead title for the season? Has this book won any awards? Any information that can help the submitted title stand out from the flood of books we receive every week is very helpful.

Unfortunately we do not accept self-published books, including those published by the bigger concerns like iUniverse and AuthorHouse. There are just too many of these kinds of books, and we don't have the staff to sort through the flood of manuscripts. I know there are some jewels out there waiting to be discovered, but it's like looking for a needle in a haystack. In addition, these books have not been vetted, have not gone through the editing and copyediting process found in a standard publishing house.

We also don't accept unsolicited reviews. What I mean by this, a publisher will somehow track down one of my reviewers and ask that person to review its title. That's a big no-no. We prefer that the publisher sends the book directly to *Library Journal*.

Can publishers send in a printed out manuscript or does it have to be bound?

LJ editors prefer bound manuscripts and galleys, or advanced reading copies, but we understand how difficult it can be for small presses to get us galleys early enough to be reviewed so we will accept manuscripts. However with large bulky works such as multivolume reference sets or illustrated books, we would prefer finished copies. It is just too difficult to review those titles from unbound manuscripts. In those cases, we advise publishers to place a sticker on the book reading "In lieu of galleys."

Do reviews impact sales? How?

Both distributors like Baker & Taylor and publishers have told me they have seen a noticeable spike in library sales when a book is reviewed in *Library Journal*. Libraries do order titles based on our reviews. Even a negative review is better than no review, because it tells our readers that a book exists and maybe a particular library needs that book for its collection, even if the review wasn't great.

My publisher sent my book in to a reviewer three months ago. How can we find out if they're going to review it?

Probably the easiest way is to sign up on our new free email review alert service. **(Check www.libraryjournal.com for further details**.) Every two weeks after we close an issue, we send an email to subscribers listing all the titles that will be reviewed in that particular issue. Your publisher can also email our book room assistant editor to follow up, and in certain cases, contact the assigning editor. But please remember that book review editors are overworked with little staff support. They cannot remember every book with a pale blue cover that comes into the office. Make sure your publisher gives the exact information (author, title publication date). Also, and this advice goes to publishers and authors, don't make a pest of yourself. Don't call or email every week. It becomes very annoying, and review editors will resent you.

How far in advance of the book's release date should it be sent in for review?

At least three to four months before the book's publication date.

My publisher sent an Advanced Reader Copy to all the trade magazine reviewers, and no one reviewed it. Now that they have the final print run, should they send it in again? Or is a no a no no forever?

No is pretty much the final word. By the time a book is printed and shipped out to bookstores and libraries, it is too late for such pre-publication review journals like *Library Journal, Kirkus, Booklist,* and *Publishers'*

Weekly to consider. There are a few exceptions. At *Library Journal*, we will review finished copies of heavily illustrated art titles and reference books after the publication date; indeed, with art books and multi-volume encyclopedias, we prefer the finished copies so the reviewer can examine the binding, quality of the illustrations, index, bibliography, etc.

Choice magazine, which serves academic libraries, will review a book up to a year after its publication. However, many titles go out of print within a few months of their publication, so a very late review has little value to our readers. Thanks to the Internet, we can now post timely online reviews of late-released and embargoed titles.

Do reviewers ever change their mind about reviewing a book? What are those circumstances?

Yes, the two most common reasons why a reviewer will return a book to me is 1) they know the author, and 2) they already reviewed the same book for another publication.

A third reason is the reviewer feels so negatively about a book that he or she feels they cannot give that title a fair review. This is not to say that *Library Journal* doesn't review books negatively—we do—and our readers find negative reviews useful for their purchasing decisions. But there are certain cases where the reviewer's negative reactions can impede his or her impartial critical judgment.

Are reviewers more likely to review a book that came from the publisher or an author's publicist?

I have received galleys from both sources, so it doesn't really matter as long as they both follow our submission guidelines.

Are there circumstances that prevent you from reviewing a book? Missing information, type of publisher, etc.? Do you contact the publisher if they didn't include something?

Yes, lateness is a primary reason why I don't review certain titles. Because librarians want to order and have the books on their shelves at the same time as the bookstores, it is essential we have early reviews. We must have galleys three to four months in advance of the publication date. I also will reject a book if the publisher fails to include the essential information I need (price, ISBN, page count, a brief summary of what the book is about, and author bio). No, I don't contact the publisher. With a thousand galleys coming into the office every month, I just don't have the time. I have become pretty ruthless in my sorting. If any of the essential information is missing, I immediately toss the galley.

What are your biggest frustrations when receiving books for review?

That there are just too many books being published, more than *Library Journal* can review in a lifetime. I get frustrated because I know there are many titles worthy of a review, but we either don't have the space in the print magazine, I don't have a reviewer who could do the book justice, or the book arrived too late for consideration. And the irony, in this day of email and the Internet, is that I have less and less time to sort through galleys and make selections. When I first started at *Library Journal*, eighty percent of my job was dedicated to assigning books. Now with my increased online duties (author interviews, roundups, blogging, etc.), I devote only forty percent of my time to assigning, while the number of books published increases year after year.

Does cover art play a role in catching a reviewer's eye?

Sadly, with so many titles calling for attention, book review editors do judge a book by its cover. I tell small presses to spend a little more money and pay more attention to the artwork. If the art looks cheesy, self-published, and Photoshopped, I, more than likely, will skip that title.

Jim Cox - Midwest Book Review

In 1976, James A. Cox began reviewing books for a small community-sponsored public radio station show called *The Madison Review of Books* in Madison, Wisconsin. In 1978, Jim began doing book reviews and author interviews for a weekly half-hour television show in Madison aptly named *Bookwatch*. It ran for twenty-one years, with the final program airing in the December 2001. In 1980, Jim renamed his book review operation to *Midwest Book Review* because of the geographical expansion of the volunteer and freelance reviewers and the generated diversity and scope of the outlets for the reviews. At this same time, the first of what are now nine monthly book review newsletters and magazines was also launched.

Along the way additional platforms and forums for his *Midwest Book Review* organization were added, including a short-wave radio broadcast that beamed reviews to all of the countries of the world. The *Midwest Book Review* became a resource offering reviews to such online book review databases as alt.book.reviews, Amazon.com, Lexus-Nexus, Goliath, and the Book Review Index. The *Midwest Book Review* website was created for authors, publishers, librarians, booksellers, and the general reading public—becoming one of the largest and most respected of such sites in the publishing industry.

In addition to his editor-in-chief duties, Mr. Cox pens *The Jim Cox Report*, a monthly column of commentary and advice for writers and publishers. Over the past thirty-two years, Mr. Cox has acquired an extensive expertise in the art and craft of reviewing books and frequently gives workshops and seminars on book reviewing and the setting up of book review organizations.

How do you determine what titles to review?

Each month we receive more than 2,000 titles submitted by authors, publishers, and publicists for review. The books are removed from their mailing packages each day by our mail room staff member who places them, along with their accompanying paperwork, on my desk in one huge pile. I then go through them (an average of about seventy-five books a day) one at a time and segregate them into three specific stacks:

Stack #1: Automatic rejection. These are books that did not adhere to our submission guidelines. They were galleys or uncorrected proofs instead of finished copies. There was no accompanying paperwork (a cover letter plus some form or publicity release). The cover art is not commercially viable. Defects in binding. Problems with font size or selection.

Stack #2: Automatic acceptance. The book adheres to our submission guidelines and is thematically appropriate with respect to one or more of our reviewers in terms of its subject matter and their field of interest.

This means that I know of the particular preferences and areas of expertise of my reviewers, and I tell them about particular titles I've set aside with them in mind. They are still at liberty to accept or reject the assignment, but that only happens when they already have more books to review than they can dependably schedule, given their available time and the deadlines.

Stack #3: Provisional acceptance. While the book adheres to our submission guidelines and has no obvious problems with commercial viability in its physical appearance, we either have no prospective reviewer specifically interested in its genre or topic, or we have a great many other books within the same genre or topic already seeking review. It will then be necessary (but a practical possibility and a realistic expectation) that a reviewer is recruited to accept the book for review within a fourteen to sixteen week window of opportunity for such a review assignment.

How do you go about deciding which reviewer takes a particular title? Does everyone sit around and grab whatever looks interesting?

I select and try to pair a specific reviewer with a particular title according to the reviewer's tastes, preferences, skill level, and area(s) of expertise. When a book is accepted for review by an assigned reviewer, he or she has thirty days in which to read the book, write the review, and submit the review back to me. It my task as the editor to keep track of the assignment with respect to deadlines and to do any editing the review might need with respect to its appearing in one or more of our nine monthly book review publications.

Do critics only review the large NY publishers' books, or will they review smaller independent press titles as well?

While we review books from all of the major New York publishing houses, we give priority wherever possible to small presses, independent publishers, self-published authors, academic presses, and niche publishers. Of the roughly six to seven hundred reviews we publish each month, about one-third to one-half are titles published by these smaller presses, including the POD publishers.

Do publishers have to advertise in order to get their book reviewed?

We do not permit advertising in any of our publications. We have a bylaw prohibiting authors, publishers, or publicists from contributing financially to the *Midwest Book Review* in order to avoid any conflict of interest issues. All of our services to authors and publishers are free of charge.

Can authors submit to a reviewer or do submissions have to come from the publisher?

Authors and freelance publicists, as well as publishers, may submit books for review.

What materials do reviewers need?

In addition to two copies of the book itself (one as a control, the other for assignment), a cover letter and some form of publicity release are required.

Can a publisher or author send in a printed out manuscript or does it have to be bound?

The *Midwest Book Review* does not consider galleys, uncorrected proofs, pre-publication manuscripts or Advanced Reading Copies for review. We require two copies of the published book.

Can anyone submit to a reviewer?

Yes. Anyone seeking to have a book reviewed can do so at any time, providing they adhere to our submission guidelines. Those guidelines are available upon request.

Do reviews impact sales? How?

Reviews impact on book sales the same way that any advertisement does for any other product. It makes the prospective reader (consumer) aware of the book (product), and (in the case of a positive review) interested in acquiring the book, or (in the case of a negative review) avoiding the book.

My publisher sent my book in to a reviewer three months ago. How can we find out if they're going to review it?

When submitting a book for review, there should be an automatic follow-up about ten working days after putting the book in the mails to the reviewer. This follow-up can be by telephone or email and should consist of the following three questions:

* Did (name of the book) arrive safely?

* What is its status with respect to the review process?

* Is there any further assistance or information I can provide you with?

This inquiry does not impose an excessive burden upon the reviewer and will provide you with the assurance that the book was received, where the book is with respect to its being reviewed, and provide the reviewer an opportunity should he or she feel the need of any additional information than that which accompanied the book review submission. It will also inform you if the book failed to pass an initial screening.

In the case of the *Midwest Book Review*, for those titles that make the final cut and are reviewed, we automatically send a copy of the review accompanied by a notification letter to the publisher when a book has been reviewed in one or more of our nine monthly book review publications. It is then the publisher's responsibility to notify their authors, editors, illustrators, publicists, and anyone else they deem appropriate.

Publishers have full and automatic permission to utilize our reviews in any manner they deem useful in promoting, publicizing, and marketing their books.

How far in advance of the book's release date should it be sent in for review?

There are two categories of book reviews: Pre-publication and Post-publication.

Pre-publication reviews like *Publishers Weekly* or the *Library Journal* require galleys or proofs three to four months in advance of an announced publishing date. They will reject published copies of the book, and books submitted after a confirmed publication date.

Post-publication reviews like the *Midwest Book Review*, television or radio reviewers, and trade magazines (for example, *Home & Garden Magazine* for a book about gardening) require the published book and will reject a galley or proof from consideration. Some book reviews like the *Midwest Book Review* only require that the book be in print and available to the reading public and pay no attention to publication dates. Other post-publication reviews require the book within a specified time oriented around an announced publication date.

Before submitting a book to any reviewer, review organization, or review publication, contact them and request their particular submission guidelines—then adhere to them!

Do reviewers ever change their mind about reviewing a book? What are those circumstances?

Most reviewers don't change their minds once a book has been passed over. There are some infrequent circumstances where a previously rejected title will be reconsidered for review. Among them: arm twisting by an editor, an author wages a successful publicity campaign igniting interest in the reviewer to take another look at the book, or something happens in the world that makes the subject matter of the book especially timely or relevant.

Are reviewers more likely to review a book that came from the publisher or an author's publicist?

There is virtually no difference. What matters is how professional the submission is and how well it adheres to submission guidelines. Some publishers (and especially some freelance publicists) have established particularly excellent relationships with some reviewers. A publicist who has demonstrated their submissions to be of consistent good quality will have an easier time interesting a reviewer than a submission from a publisher or publicist that the reviewer is not already familiar with and does not come with a demonstrated track record of dependability with respect to the appropriateness of their book submissions.

Are there circumstances that prevent you from reviewing a book? Missing information, type of publisher, etc.? Do you contact the publisher if they did not include something?

The only circumstances that prevent me from reviewing a book that has passed successfully through the initial screening process is a lack of time to accommodate all the other such titles that also succeed in the screening process.

When publishers send a galley, a proof, or an ARC instead of a published copy, I have an email form letter that informs them of the ARC's safe arrival, our policy of not accepting them for review, and a request for the published title when it becomes available to the reading public.

For those books that fail the initial screening for any other reason, their publishers are not automatically notified. But if they make an inquiry, in a timely follow-up, they are informed as to what the difficulty was that precluded their submission from acceptance.

What are you biggest frustrations when receiving books for review?

Our simple submission guidelines have not been followed. The next most commonly encountered frustration is that the publisher (most often a self-published author) has no practical knowledge of the book review process because he or she hasn't done any homework on publishing and, therefore, suffers from unrealistic expectations as to the commercial viability of their work. Some examples of those unrealistic expectations are:

Publish it and they will read: This is when the author or publisher hasn't examined or researched a particular area to determine if there is a demand for the particular book. How badly does the reading public really need for that self-help book, that poetry volume, that personal memoir of Aunt Sally growing up in rural North Dakota, or that "Great American Novel" that was so great it couldn't find a commercial trade publisher and had to be self-published.

It's hard to deal with people who believe the reviewer is somehow morally obligated to review a book (and review it positively) just because they invested in its publication and assume that what they wrote is brilliant and inherently interesting. *Midwest Book Review* receives more than two thousand titles a month for review, and we have just seventy-six reviewers. Competition is fierce, and it's the savvy author or publisher who understands the volume.

Guilt: When a book is unsuccessful in making the final cut, the author and/or publisher thinks they can argue, guilt me, or bully me into granting a review. Not a wise decision.

Instant Success: The most common unrealistic expectation is assuming a good review will guarantee the book's commercial success with little or no follow-up exploitation by the author and/or publisher. These are the folks who believe that reviews will somehow take the place of sound marketing strategies and elbow grease to create demand for their book.

Does cover art play a role in catching a reviewer's eye?

In terms of commercial viability, acceptance for review, and inclusion upon the shelf of a bookstore or a library, the quality and importance of its cover cannot be over-emphasized. This overwhelming importance of quality cover art is true for book reviewers, booksellers, librarians, and most especially the general reading public.

All too often authors and publishers fail to understand that their book is in fierce competition with others of its genre or category. For example, we review novels every month in a column called "The Fiction Shelf." Each month we receive roughly two to three hundred novels from major publishers, small presses, PODs, and self-published authors. We are able, with our available reviewer resources, to review about thirty of them. If the cover art is substandard, amateurish, or otherwise flawed, no matter how gripping the storytelling inside, reviewers will pass it over and reach for a novel that they find attractive and interesting at first glance—and that first-glance experience is with the cover.

A good cover cannot rescue a badly written book. But a bad cover can most assuredly condemn a well written book to failure.

It's that important.

Lauren Roberts – BiblioBuffet

BiblioBuffet is an online literary publication designed for readers and book lovers. We specialize in writing about books, reading and related issues through reviews, personal essays, editorials, commentary, humor, interviews, profiles of people, places or things literary, and excerpts from upcoming or recently published books or original short stories with a bookish theme. BiblioBuffet is for readers with independent minds who want to use their reading time well, who are not averse to trying something new, and who demand quality regardless of genre. Specifically, we review for those readers who want to learn about first-rate books, especially from small and medium-size publishers and university presses. We also talk about our lives as readers, sharing thoughts, opinions, ideas and feelings about all things literary. In brief, we offer "Writing Worth Reading, Reading Worth Writing About®."

What are the elements of a book review?

Book reviewing is a literary form that melds the analytical insights of formal literary criticism to the emotional pull of the op-ed piece or personal essay. A professional review carries an expectation of professionalism: that the reviewer read the entire book; that the review is written with integrity and candor; that the reviewer has no hidden agendas such as undisclosed relationships (friendly or otherwise) with the author or publisher. There must be respect for the reader's intelligence, for the book's purpose, and for the standards of professional reviewing.

What do you feel makes an effective review?

First and foremost, honesty. Reviews are for the reader. Unless a review is specifically intended to provide a brief synopsis of the book for the trade (such as is found in *Publishers Weekly* and *Library Journal,* among others) a review should do two things: 1) be sufficiently well-written to hold the attention of the reader, and 2) provide professional analysis and insight (as well as an overview) so as to enable readers to determine if the book would be of interest.

What does a reviewer do, and why do you review?

A reviewer determines the intent of the book and the author and evaluates the success (or failure) of the attempt. Ultimately, each book must be judged on its own merits, on what it is trying to achieve and how well it manages. No one would say, for example, that *Finnegan's Wake* "reads well" or draws in the reader. It's a damn difficult book. But a savvy reviewer would weigh that difficulty against Joyce's rather joyful experiment in literary form, and find the book to be rather awe-inspiring in its success.

What a reviewer should never do is judge a book by some standard the book itself is not attempting to meet. You wouldn't complain of a mystery novel that the language is lacking in poetry. You wouldn't complain of a novel based on quiet introspection and internal monologue that the book was lacking in plot.

And as for why, that's easy. We at BiblioBuffet review because we are passionate readers who enjoy sharing our discoveries.

What background should a professional reviewer have?

Ideally, reviewers should be thoroughly grounded in the garden of fine writing. Regardless of their reading preferences, they should be familiar with a little bit of everything; classics, fiction, nonfiction, and the work of other respected reviewers or today's literary critics such as Michael Dirda. If they specialize in a particular genre such as science fiction or twentieth-century American history, they should have a working knowledge of other books in the same area as well as the relevant culture and history. The reviewer's reputation as an authority is at stake with each review published. A professional reviewer (even unpaid) is for better or worse a member of the media and has an obligation to be accurate, honest and knowledgeable.

How do you determine what titles to review?

For our reviewers, it comes down to personal interest. What appeals to us as readers is going to pass the initial round. That still leaves too many books so the next step in narrowing review possibilities is to consider the quality of the book—its cover art, the jacket copy, most of all, the writing. If the writing is good, and the approach fresh and intriguing it goes in the review pile.

Unfortunately, it may not stay there. Due to the number of books we receive, a third, less consistent, winnowing process may occur where a newer book takes priority over a previously chosen one. Since we cannot review all the books we would like, the pile is regularly re-shuffled and volumes jettisoned to accommodate limited time and space.

Do you only review the large NY publishers' books, or will you review smaller independent press titles as well?

We specialize in books from small and medium-size publishers and university presses though we will review books from any commercial publisher. Self-published books and vanity-published books are not considered. New houses must have been in business for a minimum of one year, have published a minimum of two books (by authors un-invested in the house), and have a legitimate submissions/editorial process and a commercial distribution channel.

Do publishers have to advertise with the magazine/newspaper in order to get their book reviewed?

BiblioBuffet does not as of now take advertising though we plan to do so in the future. But at no time will publishers need to advertise with us to get their books reviewed. The two sides—editorial and advertising—will always remain separate entities with no influence upon each other.

What do you look for when reviewing a book? Do you have a list of criteria, or do you just sit back and (hopefully) enjoy the ride?

I enjoy the ride, yes, but knowing I will be writing about the book means that I have to maintain a certain conscious awareness that doesn't exist when I read for personal pleasure. And it's this consciousness that defines the difference between the two.

The actual reading process involves handwritten notes—I keep a notepad next to me when reading for review in order to jot reminders to myself that I may want to highlight in the review. And as I read I keep the following questions in the back of my mind (since I focus primarily on nonfiction):

Is it enjoyable?

Is it well written?

Is it worth a reader's time?

Is it worth a reader's money?

Do I want to know more?

Does the writer offer new insights or information?

Is the subject as presented by the author as involving as a novel?

Are there info dumps or unexplained or excessive specialty language inappropriate to the general reader?

If it deals with a specialty subject (but is for the general reader) is everything explained clearly and in an interesting manner?

How does this book compare to others by the same author and to others on the same subject by different authors?

Are there any factual errors?

If it is fiction, is the story compelling? Does it fulfill the genre's expectations?

These are things to which I *must* pay conscious attention. Our readers have a right to know whether they are or are not part of the book and how they do or do not impact the reading experience.

How do I submit to a reviewer? What materials do they need from me? Can I send in a printed out manuscript or does it have to be bound?

Each publication has its own guidelines that should be followed. BiblioBuffet strongly prefers published books because we often quote from them, and ARCs (Advanced Reader Copy) are not only still in the editing process but may have a release date farther down the road than we like. However, we will accept them. Manuscripts, bound or not, are out of the question.

My book is geared more to a niche market, but it has a large potential audience. Would you consider reviewing it?

BiblioBuffet prefers to focus on general interest books, but it depends on the niche. Is the audience large (Civil War buffs or vegetarian cooks, for example) or smaller (knitters)? The former would likely interest us, but the latter is better suited to specialized blogs and websites even if they don't write formal book reviews. We make it easy for publishers, publicists, and authors with our "Submit Books for Review" page, which lists our reviewers' names, their contact information, and their reviewing interests.

I sent my book in to a reviewer three months ago. How can I find out if they're going to review it?

You likely can't. BiblioBuffet doesn't even come close to the number of submissions that places like *Publishers Weekly*, *Booklist*, the *New York Times* and the *Los Angeles Times* are sent, though we receive far more than we can review. While we will answer any inquiries, we request that you do not contact us to ask if we are going to review your book. We always notify publishers when a review of one of their books has been posted.

How far in advance of the book's release date should it be sent in for review?

Because we publish for readers who expect to be able to go into their local store or online and immediately purchase the book, BiblioBuffet prefers to receive new books no more than two or three months in advance of the release date, preferably closer. There is no limit after the publication date since we also review backlist and even out-of-print books.

Do reviewers ever change their minds about reviewing a book they previously turned down? If so, under what circumstances?

Not at BiblioBuffet. I cannot imagine any circumstances, including breaking events, that would change our minds once we've already turned a book down. Besides, a rejected book is likely to have been jettisoned. Like most review sites, we need to make room for new arrivals.

Are there circumstances that prevent you from reviewing a book? Missing information, type of publisher, etc.? Do you contact the publisher if they didn't include something?

Books should always come with a press release, though some come with a folder full of information. I've never had a problem with missing information, but if I did I'd simply find it online. The only reason I can think of to contact a publisher is if I cannot locate a sufficiently large image of the cover because we always include that with a review.

What are some of the biggest myths authors hold dear about reviews and reviewers?

I suspect that many authors think reviews will sell books. From the occasional letters we receive I know that sometimes happens, but I believe that reviews, for the most part, simply alert readers to a book of potential interest. Whether they buy the book immediately or put it on their wish list is another question. Another, less common myth is that reviews should be directed toward pleasing the author. This is incorrect. Excluding those for the trade, reviews, as I have noted above, are for readers. Ethical reviewers never forget this.

What are some of the ABMs (Author's Big Mistakes) that authors commit with regard to reviewers?

Oh, this is a hot topic. Probably the number one mistake an author—and invariably it's the author, never the publicist—can make is to contact the reviewer after the review is published to complain. (Remember, the review is for readers.) It is a terrible idea, and can often backfire down the road. Reviewers tend to be both underpaid and underappreciated. Blasting away at the reviewer will make the author memorable—not in a good way.

The second mistake, at least for us at BiblioBuffet, is authors who whine about our submission policies. We are open to most subjects. The few genres we do not review are clearly noted on our "Submit Books for Review" page, and each has a specific reason for being on the list. But our biggest problem is the complaints we receive about our refusal to consider reviews of self-published or vanity-published books. No amount of arguing will cause us to change our long-standing policy, and this type of behavior shows a lack of respect for our work and our values.

What are some of the best things that an author can do in regards to a review and/or the reviewer?

Gracious acknowledgements are as wonderful as they are rare. One of my fondest memories is of the time an author sent me a lovely handwritten thank-you note on a beautiful note card after I reviewed his book. I still have the card in the book. Another great experience happened to Managing Editor Nicki Leone who reviewed a Nicholas Basbanes book. He not only sent a courteous thank you email, but posted a link to the review on his website where he wrote a complimentary passage about her. These two people took a few minutes out of their day to let us know they appreciated our work.

How do you go about deciding which reviewer takes a particular title? Does everyone sit around and grab whatever looks interesting?

Our reviewers are scattered around the country. When books come in to our office, I send out an email to the reviewers with the titles, author names and a link to the book on the publisher's page. The first interested reviewer to get back to me gets the book. Occasionally, I know a particular book would suit a specific reviewer. In that case, I email that reviewer first. Of course some books interest no one. In those cases, the books are donated to literacy programs, schools, or other appropriate nonprofit organizations because we have a strict policy against selling them.

We have a policy that BiblioBuffet's reviewers don't review books of authors they know because it wouldn't be ethical.

Does cover art play a role in catching a reviewer's eye?

Definitely. It's an essential part of the book, and both reviewers and readers are inclined to interpret cover art as an extension of the text inside. It tends to be a subconscious or even unconscious influence in most cases but it is an important factor when deciding to pick up a book or pass it over with no more than a glance.

Book covers are communication tools which have the potential to communicate artfully. A great cover should always illuminate something about the book, however abstractly. It should suggest the tone and possibly the subject matter and/or setting. At the very least, it should convey whether the book is fiction or nonfiction. Bad or even just ineffective cover art hurts a book because we are unlikely to get past it to even consider the book for review. Great cover art may get us to pick up the book, but it is the writing that determines whether we will review it.

Final Thoughts From My Side of the Pond

You know that old adage that says you can tell the quality of a person if he cheats at golf? Well, I've learned a lot about people by the way they react to a bad book review. Case in point; one of my editor friends had a well-known author who wrote an epistle that called a reviewer a clod-hopping bovine who wouldn't recognize talent if it stung them on their backsides. Or words to that effect. The editor was aghast and fired off a hasty letter of apology to the reviewer. The author was placed squarely within my friend's gun sights.

No doubt about it, a bad review hurts, but sharpening your saber for battle is a literary duel that has no winner. Reviews are subjective, and they aren't personal. It's far more important to retain a professional demeanor at all times because your "enemy" today could write you a glowing review tomorrow on your next book. But once an author takes his revenge by hurling invectives, that bridge is beyond burned. It's scorched earth. The ability to smile through pain shows character and style. As Wilda Williams from *Library Journal* said in her interview, most books are never reviewed, so whether the assessment is good or bad, at least the author got a review.

If faced with this dilemma, grit your teeth, bite your tongue, and say, "Thank you." It's the classy thing to do.

3: Marketing and sales

Big Publisher, Little Publisher

I'm fond of saying that the only difference between small publishers and Random House is the decimal point. But it goes a lot deeper than this in terms of how manuscripts are bought, edited, distributed, and sold. Of course, nearly every author has visions of one of the Big Guys or their imprints nibbling at their fishing line. While this is certainly a validation that you've "arrived," it's also vital that you are aware of what this means for you and your book.

Big and small publishers work differently by the merits of their size and respective department layering. Small publishers have fewer operating costs and, therefore, have a lower threshold of what constitutes a successful sell-through. This means they aren't beholden to buying only the commercial blockbusters, but perhaps buying the "quieter" work that grows into a classic. On the other hand, few can take a title on a meteoric rise with more élan than the big guys.

Small houses offer a different publishing experience than their large, corporate counterparts, and it's important to know both sides of the coin because it may impact your decision on what kind of publisher is right for you.

Jerry Simmons was the natural interview choice because of his illustrious tenure with two of the world's largest publishers and his current advocacy of the independent author. His perspective and knowledge of big publishing is unimpeachable, and he delves into concerns that plague most authors during their research phase of the industry.

Jerry D. Simmons

Jerry is a veteran of New York publishing, he worked for two of the world's largest publishers, having spent twenty-five years with Random House and the Time Warner Book Group. His sales group marketed and sold over fifteen hundred titles a years across the US and Canada. He worked with some of the largest independent booksellers and mass merchants in this country. He retired as Vice-President, Director of Field Sales in 2003.

Jerry was fortunate to have worked on books written by such New York Times bestselling authors as:

David Baldacci	Robert Kiyosaki	Nicholas Sparks
Sandra Brown	James Patterson	Scott Turow
Michael Connelly	Alice Seabold	Robert James Waller
Nelson DeMille	Anita Shreve	Jack Welch

He was also fortunate to have worked on such multi-million copy bestselling titles as:

The Bridges of Madison County	Rich Dad, Poor Dad
Simple Abundance	Scarlett
Lovely Bones	Megatrends
The Celestine Prophecy	Along Came a Spider
The Notebook	Kiss the Girls
The General's Daughter	The Lion King
Presumed Innocent	Absolute Power
Catcher in the Rye	To Kill A Mockingbird

Jerry is the author of *What Writers Need to Know About Publishing*. He is the founder of the insider's guide to publishing website, **WritersReaders. com** and the internationally acclaimed newsletter **TIPS for WRITERS**.

He is also the founder of **NothingBinding.com,** the premier global stage and leading social networking website for publishers, writers and authors to promote their books, attract new readers and connect with fellow writers. He spends his time writing, consulting, and speaking with writers about the importance of understanding the business of publishing and the marketplace for selling books.

About Jerry's Book: *What Writers Need to Know About Publishing*

"The good, the bad, and the ugly aspects of book publishing, told in a straight-from-the hip manner. New writers take note. Simmons speaks from years of experience, as well as with a genuine caring for the would-be-published writer."

~Sandra Brown, #1 *New York Times* bestselling author

"The information was absolutely incredible! I would recommend to all aspiring and new authors."

Allison Brennan, *New York Times* bestselling author

~~~

My publisher told me they're printing fifty thousand copies of my book. I'm thrilled! Are those going to be in every store across the country?

While fifty thousand copies is a reasonable number to provide coverage to every store across the country, it depends on how many copies are being placed in each store and which stores. Store coverage is more than a number; it is based on the distribution for the book.

Distribution: This is the process of shipping books to accounts, which include bookstores, distributors, wholesalers, and mass merchants. Distributors are the big companies that re-supply titles to retailers. Some of the most notable would be Ingram Books and Baker & Taylor.

Wholesalers: These are companies that supply magazines and books to retail accounts such as supermarkets and drug stores, and mass merchants such as Target and Wal-Mart. The most notable would be the Charles Levy Company. Each account is pre-sold a list of titles, typically three times per calendar year. Once the account places their order and the book is released, publishers ship accordingly. This is called "distribution," and it's different for each book.

For example, a fifty-thousand copy distribution for one book could result in a completely different distribution than for another title because one book might get distribution to all mass merchants, wholesalers, and all retail bookstores, while another book might receive distribution to a few mass merchants, no wholesalers, a few distributors and a handful of retail bookstores.

All distribution is not profitable. A trade paperback with a cover price of $15 does not belong in certain accounts without something specific to support the title such as a movie tie-in or heavy advertising and promotion. For example, very few trade paperbacks with a cover price of more than $12 would belong in a supermarket or drug store account. This of course is a broad generalization, but if you are the author of a trade paperback non-fiction title and your publisher informs you that the majority of your fifty-thousand copy distribution is going to wholesalers, you know that was done for the billing potential of that book and not the sell-through.

Unfortunately in the illogical world of big publishing it's about how many copies can be shipped, not just how many can be sold. Let's take the $12 trade paperback non-fiction title example. If you are the author of that book, your future as a writer and author depends on your book's ability to achieve a high sell-through. If your publisher has pre-sold fifty thousand copies of that book and your distribution is to the wrong mixture of accounts, your sell-through will be below what it takes to maintain a career as an author. Such a book distributed to wholesalers, and eventually supermarkets and drug stores, would spell disaster.

Your publisher obviously would have sacrificed your future for their short term gain in gross revenue. It happens every day to thousands of unsuspecting authors. Unless you have some notion of how distribution works and what is involved, you take your chances. As an author you must protect yourself from these kinds of problems by understanding the process of getting your book published, sold, marketed and distributed as well as how to ask the right questions. So when your publisher calls and tells you they're printing fifty-thousand copies of your book, you can ask the question: what is the distribution for my book?

I don't like my editor. She wants me to make rewrites that I don't agree with. Do I have to make the changes? Can I change editors?

You can ask about changing editors, but if you do, you are likely to be labeled a difficult author and that could mean your book is doomed to failure. Keep in mind that when you sign a contract you no longer own the rights to that manuscript. You are obligated to make changes to your writing. It is highly unlikely your publisher will allow you to disagree with recommendations your editor makes. You can discuss the rewrites, but it's in your best interest to do as you are asked and make all recommended changes to your manuscript.

Besides, do you really think a new editor will disagree with another one working in the same house? Not a chance. Your publisher now has the right to do what they want with your book and when they want, including asking you, the author, to complete rewrites. Their goal is to ship as many copies as possible. It's not uncommon that they had one idea in mind when they purchased your manuscript and now after some editorial work, they decided to go another direction with your book. This is their right.

If you decide, as an author, that your editor made so many changes that you are not happy with the results, you certainly have the right to voice your opinion, but you do so at your own peril. They wouldn't be making editorial changes unless they felt it gave the book more legs, meaning a better chance of selling more copies. If you protest the edits and refuse to promote the book, they will allow you that privilege, but they will never publish you again and more than likely will do whatever they can to generate as much billing as possible without regard to your sell-through. And of course, that typically spells doom for the author.

As a final point, let me just say that today, the big publishers do not want, nor do they expect to spend a tremendous amount of time editing a manuscript. They simply don't have the time to invest. It would be in your best interest to seek a professional freelance editor to help you with content and copy. Unfortunately that is the way the business works today.

How are my books sold to the bookstores? Am I going to be on one of those end caps? Are they going to advertise my book?

The retail business today is such that only those titles with huge marketing budgets or titles of a proven bestselling author occupy the space in an end cap. That is very expensive retail space to get book placement. Questions such as these signals "amateur," and that is not the message you want to start off with at your new publisher.

There is a time to ask questions about marketing and retail space, but asking that to an editor would be like asking your new employer, "when do I get my corner office?" End caps are very expensive. For a large New York publisher who has a multitude of advertising and promotional contracts going at the same time, that end space could cost tens of thousands of dollars.

Whether or not your publisher advertises your book is dependent on a number of factors, the most important being your position on the list of titles being sold. Each season prior to the list being sold, the sales and marketing departments sit down and decide where books are positioned on the list by month. The key to positioning is how much the company has invested in the book, and how many copies and dollars in billing can they generate based on a title's position on the seasonal list.

Books in low positions on a list get little if any advertising, the company has little invested, and the resulting sales are largely based on positioning and season. Books are sold to bookstores in two ways: the small independent bookstores around the country buy their books from field representatives who visit three times a year and sell their seasonal list of titles to book buyers. The large chain or regional bookstores buy from account representatives who sell on a seasonal basis to company headquarters, and their visits are more often than three times per year. It could be as often as every other week, but most assuredly monthly.

The best way to have any influence on the position of your book on a publisher's list is to develop a relationship with everyone in-house who has a hand in publishing your book. Through the relationship, you send signals that you have a basic understanding of the marketplace; you are not simply out for favors but want to work with each of them to help sell your book, achieve as high a sell-through as possible, and maintain a career as an author. These are important facts if you hope to influence the way your book is positioned on a list and presented to book buyers by either the field or account representative, marketed, distributed and eventually merchandised on store shelves.

Is my publisher going to send me on a big book tour and media campaign?

This is not something you would pose to your editor or anyone you meet in-house. After you sign that contract, it will become apparent fairly quickly whether you are in line for a big book tour and media campaign, so asking the question shows a lack of understanding about what goes on in big publishing houses.

The first indication about where you fit in the possibilities of a media campaign is the amount you were paid in advance for the rights to publish. If that amount is far short of what you can retire on, then my guess is you are not being sent on a large tour or campaign. In fact, most of the biggest publishing companies expect authors to not only participate in marketing their own book, but they expect your cooperation and initiation of certain promotions without their help or financial assistance.

Once you get a fix on the marketing plans for your book, then you need to provide assistance in the form of ideas, both locally and regionally on how your book can gain the attention of readers. Publicity is the key. If you decide to hire an outside publicist, make absolutely certain that person works closely with your in-house publicist. Combined, they can provide you with the exposure to mid-sized markets that could be ideal for selling books. The bottom line is that you will be expected to contribute ideas to the marketing of your book and in some cases you might have to dip into your own pocket to make that happen.

How long will my book be in the stores?

The time frame from the point you sign a contract to the day your published book appears in stores can be from eighteen to twenty four months. If a book arrives and starts to sell slowly it might last from between eight to twelve weeks. However, new books are arriving every day, when store personnel begin to stock shelves and see your title still sitting, there is a chance they will not check movement, they will remove the copies and return them to your publisher, never to be seen or heard from again.

If you are taking an active role in the promotion of your book and the retailer is aware of that fact, you might manage to extend the shelf life of your book. But timing also plays an important role. If the big publishers have key titles arriving in store shortly after your book arrives and it's not selling copies, the chances are slim that your book will remain on the shelves, regardless of your own personal promotional efforts.

Does my advance have any relation to how much my publisher will push my book?

Yes, there is a relationship between an advance and how much a publisher pushes a book. However, publishing is about shipping books. So the higher the advance the more copies they need to push out the door. When publishers purchase the rights to your writing they do it to make money. The only way to make money on books is to sell lots of copies at retail. In order to sell enough copies to earn back their investment, they have to distribute as many units to as many accounts to get the book in the hands of the consumer. The more a publisher pays up front in the form of an advance, the more copies they need to sell, which means the more they have to ship. In publishing, you have to ship lots of books to sell enough to earn back the investment. It's about shipping books more than selling books. It's like the old adage, if you throw enough against the wall something is bound to stick. If you ship enough books, you are bound to sell some.

However, the author isn't concerned how many copies are shipped, it's about how many they sell. It's a crazy upside down business, but keep in mind that publishing runs contrary to the laws of supply and demand.

Over the course of the past fifteen years the sales of individual books have been in steady decline. When this happens, supply and prices increase—exactly opposite to the basic laws of economics. The only books that get the full support and push from a publisher are those where the author received a noticeable advance. The rest of the books with little advance are simply titles that fill a list to be sold. There is no push for those titles.

Publishers need a variety of titles to ship to cover as many categories as possible. The more categories they publish into, the more opportunity to ship books. And the more they ship, the more they sell. It's also about market share or shelf space. If a publisher cuts back on the number of titles they publish, the competition will quickly fill that void. Once that retail space is lost, it's extremely difficult, if not impossible, to get back.

My publisher told me they are remaindering my book. Why? Do I get royalties for those?

Selling remaindered books is a normal part of the afterlife cycle of a published book. Chances are, your publisher probably oversold your book and, as a result, you have copies that were returned by their customers. In today's marketplace books are oversold and over-shipped on a regular basis. Publishers do this to:

* Maintain their market share on store shelves

* To generate as much gross revenue or billing as they possibly can

* Hopefully find that one title that ends up a home run. All publishers are looking for that title that projects itself beyond the stratosphere and sells lots and lots of copies with little or no upfront advance.

If your title is being remaindered, then at least your publisher feels your book has value rather than having it shredded and the paper resold. Remaindered books are typically sold for pennies on the dollar. Your royalties depend on your contract. If you hired a literary attorney to review any and all contracts you signed with your publisher, then you shouldn't have anything to worry about. If you did not, chances are you will not be receiving royalties for your remaindered book because this is a secondary sale, and authors typically only get paid on the initial sale.

Ever wonder why you see deeply discounted prices on a hardback when the paperback version is still being published? Those are examples of remaindered books. The margins are small but the demand is based on the success of the author, volume and price.

What is a bestseller?

Depends on who you ask! The most prestigious bestseller list is the *New York Times* and of course everyone in the publishing business follows this list. However, there are many ways to define "bestseller."

Next time you visit a bookstore note how many books are labeled "bestseller." In the world of big time publishing, any title on sale at retail that is placed on a list of "bestselling" titles on any recognizable print medium, such as your hometown newspaper can be considered a "bestseller." The reason is that the book was placed on a list with other bestselling titles by a recognizable, objective, nonbiased print medium.

Authors are often confused by the fact that "bestseller" is not used as a way of identifying the book that has sold the most number of copies. The *New York Times* Bestseller List does not list books that have sold the most number of copies, merely the books that are "perceived" to have sold the most number of copies. A #1 *New York Times* bestselling title does not equate to the single book that has sold the most number of copies across the US during a given week. Fact is, the industry has yet to figure out exactly how to identify such a book. So the next time you find a book in a store and the banner across the front cover proclaims, "national bestseller," take that with a grain of salt.

Since I'm with a big publisher, do I need to promote my book? How does my promoting help sales? Do I need a publicist?

Yes, you should promote your book, especially if you are under contract with a big publisher. The biggest mistake any author under contract can make is to rely on their publisher to do everything to market and sell their book. You need to coordinate your own promotion with that of your publisher and even ask for their help in the form of financial support.

If your publisher does not provide you with an in-house publicist, then hire one on your own. Publishers have limited marketing budgets for each book and when you are producing several hundred or even a thousand titles per year, publishers need all the promotion help they can get. The more proactive you can be, the better they like you, and the more they will help you promote your book.

Work with your publisher first, solicit all the support you can get. Support can come in the form of information about the timeline of your book's publication and when decisions are being made and by whom. Only after you know their plans for you, should you step forward and offer to promote yourself.

From a purely marketing standpoint, publicity is the single best way of getting exposure for you and your book, and this is the one area where you want the most help. If your publisher decides not to advertise, fine. If they decide not to promote, fine. However they must generate publicity! The key to selling books is publicity. Publicity is the art of getting your face and story into newspapers and on television, your voice on radio, and anything and everything about you as an author on the Internet.

I'm unhappy with my book sales. I don't think my publisher did enough to promote my book. Is it a bad idea to go with another big publisher for my next book? Will this increase my sales?

Once your book has been out into the marketplace, it has a sales history. If that sales history is bad, less than a 50% sell-through (meaning half the titles distributed sold and the rest were returned to your publisher) chances are there are few, if any, other publishers that will be interested in publishing your next book.

If you are unhappy with your publisher, and they want to publish your next book, then you need to be proactive and work with them in all aspects of the publishing process to prevent the same problems from happening again. As an author, if you were unhappy with the promotional efforts of your book before publication you should have told them. If you develop relationships with the in-house folks who are publishing your book, then you can make your opinions known, including your unhappiness with promotion.

The rule of thumb, however, is that criticism must be followed with ideas. If you merely criticize or complain without offering ideas for how to correct the problem, your opinion is not going to be given much weight. If you didn't know the promotional plans for your book before publication, then you have yourself as much as your publisher to blame.

The key to becoming a successful author is to work with your publisher every step of the way. You start by developing relationships in-house, to the point where you can get your emails and phone calls returned. As an author you do this by understanding how the marketplace works, knowing what questions to ask, being an observer of the retail component of bookselling. The more you can convince your publisher you know what you are talking about the better chance you have of them separating you and your book from the rest of the list and that is absolutely key to improving your chance at having a successfully published book.

What is sell-through?

The percentage of books sold to books distributed is what is called "sell-through." Also referred to as percentage of sale.

Let's say for example your publisher prints ten thousand copies of your book and distributes every copy to booksellers around the country. After a few months the unsold copies are returned to your publisher. Once all copies have filtered through the system, meaning all sold copies are gone from store shelves and all copies are returned to the publisher, a percent of sale is calculated for the book.

In today's marketplace, 60% sell-through is considered the point at which publishers and booksellers are happy with the sale of a book. Below 60% yet above 50% is on the bubble, and any sell-through less than 50% is considered less than successful. Of all the numbers that publishers generate, sell-through is the single most important. Everything else is irrelevant.

Take for example, a publisher is considering two books for publication. The first sold only 3,000 units but had a 60% sell-through. The second sold 45,000 units but had a 40% sell-through. The first book would draw the most attention because it's not about how many units were sold, it's all about the sell-through. The 45,000 copy seller has a bad sales history and the 3,000 copy a good sell-through. The 3000 unit book has the greater potential and offers the biggest opportunity to ship more copies. Now when the next book is published and sold to booksellers across the country the first thing the customer will consider is the sell-through, that makes all the difference.

I had a lot of returns on my book yet my publisher signed me for another two books. I'm thrilled, of course, but shocked, too. I thought returns were a bad thing.

In the large publisher way of thinking, returns are not always bad, all books have returns, the key is exactly how many books were returned. If your sell-through was 60% or greater, then your return level was manageable and the publication of your book would be considered a success. Less than 50% the book is not considered a success.

Returns could have been 40,000 units, yet you sold 60,000 units. These are certainly high returns but relative to the overall sell-through of the book. You cannot judge the success of an author by merely evaluating the return number on that book. Based on the information, my guess is that your publisher feels you have potential to reach a bigger audience, and a two-book deal is an indication of their interest in expanding your readership.

Do I have the right to participate in the decision making process with my publisher? What suggestions should I make to them?

Yes you have every right to participate in the decision making process with your publisher, within limits. If you are a first time author, you will never be allowed to have "right of first refusal." In other words, they are not going to create a cover, develop a marketing plan or anything else related to the publication of your book and give you the opportunity to make changes before they are set in stone.

You can make suggestions on anything and everything, if you do it in the proper way, through proper channels, and to the right people. That is the best way to have your suggestions heard and possibly acted upon. For example, cover designers are responsible for hundreds of new compelling, eye-catching designs for books. As a new author, your publisher is not going to let you tell them how to package your book. However, if you have an eye for covers and understand your genre, then you can make suggestions on how to package your book. If you ask the right questions and give your editor an indication you understand the marketplace, then your suggestions will likely be given credence. Now you can download covers from competitive titles that you like and offer them as suggestions to your cover designer. You have just made their job easier and you will be considered an author who is working with their publisher to sell books.

My publisher told me that they're going to wait until the "next season" to release my book. What does this mean?

Books are sold in seasons, typically three per calendar year. Moving a book from one season to another merely means they are delaying publication. This is nothing to worry about, your publisher is doing this in order to give your book a better chance to sell copies in the marketplace and give them a better chance of pushing more copies out the door to increase their gross revenue. This is all part of the publishing dance that is played each season.

The most important thing for you to do is find out exactly why they moved your book. If you don't have a good relationship with your editor, then develop one. If you haven't met with those in-house who are handling your book, then do so.

It is critically important for you to know the names and responsibilities of everyone who has a hand in the publication of your book. The only way to make that happen is to set up a meeting with your editor and ask that those people be present for an introduction. That is your starting point for developing relationships that will help separate you and your book from all the others on the list and vastly improve your chances of becoming a successful author.

What was the toughest part about selling books for you?

The absolute toughest part about selling books in my former career was meeting the corporate expectations of each book. In the mid 1970s, when I started in publishing, time and attention was given to every title. It was the responsibility of the field group to make certain that each title had the maximum amount of shelf life and every opportunity to sell the most copies possible. Certainly we had objectives for each book, but the fact was that the market handled the titles differently—they weren't just products, but were books and treated as such.

Once the big corporate media giants began taking over the business in the early 1990s everything changed. Now books were products and treated the same as toothpaste. The pressure to ship more and more individual units and increase gross billing became the key to success. The books and authors were no longer as important; it was all about growth and dollars. Consequently the marketplace reacted negatively, and book sales began to decline. Retailers, in a mad dash for improved profitability, demanded money in the form of advertising subsidies, promotional allowances, and placement fees—all designed to fill that sales gap of declining book sales. Publishers paid, and the endless cycle continues today.

Can you please explain why authors and books became less important and how growth and dollars caused the market to react negatively? Are you saying that publishers needed more product and began buying lower quality manuscripts—and this is why book sales declined? And how did this new paradigm give way to retailers suddenly demanding subsidies?

The climate for publishing changed when the media giants began merging and buying up the publishing houses. As an example, Time Inc. merged with Warner Communications in 1990. This meant that the emphasis for us shifted away from books and authors, to dollars and market share. We began the move toward more titles—not necessarily poorer quality manuscripts—just more. The size of the list grew. The belief was that more titles meant more money and larger market share. So we tried launching new imprints with complete lists of books.

This began the slide away from making certain every book had an opportunity to sell for as long as possible. With more books flooding the market, the retailers could not help but start to return books more often, thus reducing the exposure every title had on store shelves. This resulted in increasing returns and creating a system that began to break down. New authors with great potential were not being brought along slowly. An author with 20,000 copies of sales suddenly went to the top of the list. Now we were asking for buys that quadrupled the last book while jumping over the notion of "growing" authors. It was a lot like going from first to home without stopping at second or third.

As one big company followed this path, so did all the rest. The business is a follow the leader mentality, and as everyone introduced more books and the list grew, the total number of titles began to rise sharply, and retailers had to create space for all these new books. The only solution was to return books faster and in larger quantities. Book buyers were buying more, everyone was happy, except for the fact that sales started a gradual decline that still exists to this day.

Sales on individual units. As sales continued to decline, the big mass merchants, who at this time were the dominant retailers in the business, would travel to New York and explain that the space in-store for books was being threatened by declining sales. If something didn't happen then corporate would take away space. It's all about turns per square foot. This dilemma created the subsidy issue, where publishers were doing everything to avoid losing retail space, so they began to subsidize the lack of sales by paying for placement, promotions, advertising, all centered around bolstering lagging unit sales.

This is what is meant by the business changing away from books and authors to dollars and market shares.

What advantages and disadvantages do you see between publishing with the large and small publishers?

One of the biggest advantages of publishing with a small press is the experience you will receive as an author. You will get more attention to your book and should never have to feel like you are a number on a list. Some additional advantages:

* A commercial small trade press provides authors with the platform of "legitimacy" from which they can promote themselves and their books without having to hide behind the vanity press issue, which in the marketplace is labeled "poor quality."

* Small presses do not require agents, and you have the freedom to submit your own manuscript to whomever you want without being

under the control of an agent who will take a minimum of 15% of your royalties FOREVER.

* Small presses typically provide better distribution for their books than other publishing options, and distribution is what makes for sales.

* Marketing is helped by the fact you are published by a "traditional publisher" and not a vanity press or POD model; it's much easier to generate publicity with a small press.

The disadvantages are all based around your goals as an author. Anyone who wants to get their work published must realize that the potential for success if not so much based on who publishes your writing, but how, as an author, you can market yourself and your book. Here are some of the disadvantages:

* Smaller advances with a small press, although the biggest New York publishers are paying less than $2,000 in many cases.

* Since small presses operate on a much tighter budget they offer less marketing. But keep in mind that, depending on where your book is published on a big company's list, your marketing budget will be small, and they still expect you to market yourself.

* Probably the biggest disadvantage is that a small press has limited options if your book should break out in a big way.

When Oprah started her book club, we, at Time Warner, were fortunate to have several titles selected. A couple of times, we had books that were initially distributed in the 15 to 20,000 range and when Oprah called to inform us that a book had been selected, orders would invariably jump to over 800,000 copies. Early on in her book club program, Oprah selected a couple of small press books and learned quickly that the small companies had an extremely difficult time of printing and shipping 800,000 copies of a book. Eventually, she was savvy enough to realize if her viewers could not go into a bookstore and find one of her selections quickly and easily, she would continue to field thousands of phone calls from angry viewers. Her solution; never again select a small press title for her book club.

The advantages of publishing with a big New York company:

* There is certain prestige and cachet with publishing under the imprint of a big New York publisher; certain doors will be open to you that would otherwise be closed.

* The distribution network is global. Being successful with a New York based publisher will get the rights to your book sold worldwide.

* They can react to a news report or major newspaper or magazine article, television or talk show appearance in an instant and air freight books to remote retailers overnight; their reaction time to events is unprecedented.

* The big six publishing companies in many ways control the marketplace, they set many of the rules and make it difficult for a small press to compete on an even playing field.

* They have the marketing muscle and can use it if necessary, plus they have the relationships with the major booksellers that cannot be matched.

The disadvantages of publishing with a big New York publisher:

* You must get used to the fact that you are a number on a list, you can be 1 of 1500 authors, all vying for the attention of editors and publishers.

* If you are fortunate to be successful with your first book, your publisher will quickly usher you to the front of the list where you will get much more attention, but the demands on you to perform as a writer is much greater. Here, one misstep, and your career can be over, leaving you no time to develop your skills. The risks are much greater.

* Publishing with a big company means you lose all control over your writing; they own it. They can change the title, content, decide to change the category, ending, and you have nothing to say about it. In fact, if you are under contract and they want you to change anything in your manuscript, then you are obligated to do so.

* I would not recommend any author sign a contract with a major New York publisher unless they had a basic understanding of the business. That is why I wrote my book, to give you that basic insight into what goes on behind the scenes. This is critical to your success as an author.

I'm intrigued by the difficult author you discuss in your book *What Writers Need to Know About Publishing*. **On page 195— "What Not to Do"—you talk about an author's outburst about the horrible sales job you and your sales teams had done on his book. You said: "He got zero action," and I'd like to hear more about what you mean by that statement.**

What I meant by "he got zero action" was the fact that the sales team has a tremendous influence of the success or failure of some books. James Patterson is going to sell, Sandra Brown is going to sell, and it's difficult, as a sales team, to negatively impact these kind of authors.

However, if you are an unknown or someone like the person I wrote about, who is still on the bubble with regard to success, a sales team can have a huge impact. I'm not talking about sabotage because we don't intentionally go out and tell our customers to start returning books. That won't work. But we can go back to our key accounts and describe the situation to our buyers, express our frustration and humiliation over this author. That word will get around because the sales team will tell everyone with whom they come into contact. What do you think happens? Word of mouth can hurt this author. If the book takes off, then fine. But if he continues to sit on that bubble, then this kind of incident and the word that a sales team can spread about an author, can have a dramatically negative impact.

Turn that around. Brad Meltzer was as nice a gentleman as you can imagine. He would come to our sales conference, not as a speaker, but as an interested author. At this point in time, his success was also on the bubble. He had yet to have a major *New York Times* bestseller. But he would meet everyone, drink a beer with us, play some pool, talk sports, basically get across that he wasn't looking for favors but simply wanted everyone to know him and convey that he would do anything anyone asked to help sell his books. Now look at him, he has had a #1 bestselling title.

How much impact did the sales team have on that? A lot. Keep in mind that there are many Brad Meltzers out there, but the relationship a sales team has with major booksellers and the genuineness of a Brad Meltzer makes for a great combination. Brad leveraged that without currying favor or being seen as a "typical author" whose only concern is often "what are YOU going to do for ME!" The sales team wanted him to succeed and went that extra mile just so the next time he showed up at sales conference they could feel pride in helping out one of the good guys.

Final Thoughts From My Side of the Pond

I'd like to echo what Jerry said about author attitude. From my perspective, the author who comes in with an eager attitude of "I can do that!" and "What can I do to help?" is someone who will always get our attention and undying gratitude.

We're human, at least that's the rumor going around, and we naturally gravitate toward the go get 'em author who checks their ego at the door and works *with* us to produce a great book. I know it seems like a natural extension of the publishing process—to work with us—but you'd be amazed how many authors believe their words come directly from the hands of The Great Cosmic Muffin, and it's our duty to stop everything in order to attend to their every need. The author who treats their publisher like the hired help never lasts long.

Whether you're with a large NY publisher or a small press, we're in this effort together, and the savvy, helpful author always has a leg up on the author whose ego requires retro-fitting the doorways.

4: Book Shepherd

There are times when an author wants total control of their book. Maybe he's a motivational speaker who talks to corporate crowds of thousands, and the corporate organizers want to pass out the speaker's book at the end—sporting their corporate logo, of course—all bought and paid for by the corporations. Or maybe she's a computer geek who travels all over giving seminars to fellow geeks on all the latest computer geek stuff, and she wants to supplement her information by having a book to sell at the back of the room. Or maybe he's a novelist who wants to parlay his talents into a contract with a large publisher. These are people with a marketable product, want total control over their content, and want to take home the lion's share.

This is a job for a book shepherd.

Why not go to a vanity press and let them take care of everything? Some take this option and, while it's not a bad idea in theory, authors have to seriously consider the quality of editing, cover design, and lack of distribution to the bookstores. Book shepherds, on the other hand, play the creative director to your personal symphony. They coordinate every aspect of production while keeping the author safe from the first-timer errors that plague most newbie publishers. They help the new self-publisher define their marketing and promotion strengths while helping them obtain distribution by insuring they have a quality product.

So why isn't everybody self-publishing? Well, it ain't free. And it's hideously time consuming. Most authors/self-publishers have day jobs, and they're competing against people like me for whom this *is* my day job. They have to learn the publishing lingo—sell-through, discounts, ARCs, binding, digital printing vs. offset (web based), backlist, returns, etc. This venture takes money, organization and commitment.

Whatever the reasons for going this route, there is satisfaction (and terror) at being at the helm and, should this look like a viable option to you, make sure that you don't go it alone. Get help. Get a good book shepherd.

Amy Collins

Amy Collins is the owner of The Cadence Group. TCG helps small publishers develop more cost-effective business strategies while improving their packaging, editing, marketing and sales efforts.

You may visit her page at www.thecadencegrp.com

What does a book shepherd do? Do they edit and design book covers, or is there more?

A book shepherd is a professional publishing consultant with the background, experience and current market knowledge to help an author or small press create their books. A book shepherd knows the book industry and works to help a new publisher improve and develop their entire publishing program.

A good book shepherd will not depend upon the past when shaping and formatting a publishing past; they will look to the current and future market place to help create the most marketable book possible. They will also give you access to designers, editors and industry service providers that you could not usually reach otherwise. They work with designers and editors to make sure that the book looks and reads like any other professionally published book by a larger, more experienced house.

What circumstances bring authors to your company rather than self-publishing their books on their own or submitting to a publisher/agent?

Most of the time, my clients are professionals with a large client base who want a book to sell to or expand their client base. Also, I have clients who want to get published by a larger house and decide to self-publish as a means to showing potential publishers the demand for the book. Finally, I have clients whose dearest wish is to start a publishing company and they need help getting started and learning the ropes.

Are you considered the publisher, or is the author the publisher?

The author is the publisher. Unlike many packaging companies, the author creates a publishing imprint, the ISBNs belong to them, and they make all the final publishing decisions.

Do you walk authors through every phase of publication? What are those steps?

For the beginning author or small publisher, the "to do" list for properly putting out a book can be quite daunting. It is my hope that by the time we are done working together they can duplicate the process on their next book. A sample list of items we do for clients who hire us to help them publish their books:

Create a Publisher name

Register Publisher with Bowker

Get ISBNs and Barcodes

Review manuscript for marketability

Get manuscript edited for content

Get manuscript copy edited

Research and develop book specifications. (A great deal of time goes into deciding whether or not a book should be hardcover vs. soft cover, what price, page count. . . etc)

Design and create cover

Design and layout book

Create marketing plan

Find and hire distributor

Find and hire publicist

Get several printing quotes

Work with printer to make sure files are to their specifications

Manage delivery and fulfillment contracts for first shipments.

Can you get an author's books on the store shelves?

It depends upon the book. I will only take on a client who I believe has the capacity to produce a book I could sell to the major book retailers. My current rate of success for books that make it into national bookstores like B&N and Borders is over 70%.

Do you work with publishers? If so, what do you do for them, and how do you make them better? What kinds of publishers hire your services? Small? Large?

I have a large publisher who would like help getting into new markets where I may have contacts. Mid-sized publishers often want to launch an aggressive Internet marketing campaign and don't know how to get started. Small publishers may be paying too much for printing. If I can be of service, I try to help.

How does a book shepherd differ from a vanity press?

A vanity press uses their ISBNs and imprint to "publish" the book. They own the source files and all the results thereafter. While you may own the copyright, it is the vanity press that holds the files and the ISBN on your book. You are stuck with them and their prices. If you use a book shepherd, you own all your files, your name, your image. You are beholden to no one. If your book shepherd is not living up to your expectations, you can take what you have learned, and the files that have been created and take them to another vendor. You are in control.

At what point would an author hire your services? Before the manuscript is written or after?

I only sign clients once I have read their writing and see the manuscript they are working on. If I took a client before I saw their work, I could not guarantee the results. Again, I only take clients with books I feel have a chance in the national arena.

Are there cases when a client comes to you with an idea that has little market potential? If so, how do you handle this?

I turn down more clients than I take for precisely this reason. All books have a potential audience, and I would never say a book should not be published. It is just HOW they are published that I feel should be addressed. If a potential client comes to me with a book idea that I believe will not be a good fit with the national marketplace's current needs, I say so. There is no need to spend $20,000 or more publishing a book if I KNOW the author will never make their money back. There are better ways and venues for the author who is most likely going to get a smaller return on their investment.

What should an author look for when looking for a book shepherd? Is it possible to know the difference an ineffective and effective one? What questions should an author ask?

The easiest way to judge whether or not a book shepherd is for you is to ask for a list of books that they have shepherded and the contact information of those clients as a reference. Once you have a list of books to research, you can go online to see the reviews and check out the book's design. If you go to B&N.com or Bordersstores.com, you can type in the ISBN and see if those chains carry the book.

Asking a book shepherd what timeline and budget guarantees they offer is also a good idea. A good shepherd will guarantee their prices and timeline.

What are some of the frustrations you encounter with your clients?

Clients with unrealistic expectations are the most frustrating part of the job. Many clients want to find a book shepherd who "believes" in their project. Yes, I need to believe in the potential, but I cannot go past my training and experience to encourage an author with unrealistic expectations.

I try very hard to weed out the potential clients who are self-publishing because they were unable to get a publishing deal and believe that they will sell "a million copies and go on Oprah." They won't. No matter how good the book is, the chances of that happening are SO small, that the "million-copies-and-go-on-Oprah" clients would be better served by another book shepherd. It is my job to be realistic and keep their costs and efforts in line with the current market. I would not be doing them any favors by "supporting" their unrealistic expectations.

What kind of rates can authors expect to pay for a book shepherd's services?

A good book shepherd charges from $5,000 - $20,000 for their time and expertise. On top of that will be the costs of design, editing and printing. A recent business book client of mine paid $12,000 for the development, production, and printing of the book and an additional $6,000 for the four months of training, guidance and research I gave to help publish the book.

Competition for shelf space is tough. Will you help with marketing and promotion? What tips do you have to share with authors to help them stand out from the pack?

Competition is a killer these days. There are so many wonderful companies that help with marketing and sales, but it is easy to get taken in by smooth talkers just out for your money. I recommend working with your book shepherd to create a regional thematic and national sales and marketing plan before your book is even copy edited. You need to know where your book is going to sell. Might as well know before you get started! For instance, a children's book author who has written and illustrated a new kid's cookbook should create a plan for her hometown, the regional cooking and kitchen stores, the national cooking and kitchen catalogs, the children's library market, and the national children's book departments at the bookstores chains.

This list is just a start, but each of those venues will demand a different set of tools and maybe even a different package. How do you decide which one to publish to? You pick the one with the most chance of taking your book to their clients and getting your book out in front of readers.

To stand out in today's market, you need to find your core readership and design your book to please THEM. You cannot be all things to all people. Just focus on your core readers and the rest will follow.

What kind of importance do you place on cover design? Interior design? Do buyers and readers really notice this?

What your book looks like is more important than how well written it is. Yup, I actually mean that. I will say it again . . . . It is more important to have a great cover than a great book. I am not saying that a great cover will make a terrible book a success, but I do know that a terrible cover will condemn a great book to the bargain bin.

We, as a buying culture, have been trained to look for a certain "look" in our packaging . . . dishwasher detergent, clothes, book covers . . . we are a slave to what is hot now . . . even if we deny it. If the average reader sees a cover that looks an awful lot like a best selling cover of a book they just finished and liked, they will pick it up.

Never copy, but emulate. If you can make your cover design "fit in" and use truly compelling images and art to make it also "stand out", you will have created a great cover.

Will you recommend how many books an author should get printed up? How do you determine this number?

I always recommend that an author/publisher do a realistic 180 day sales projection based on initial orders and reviews. I usually suggest that they print 50% above the estimated sales projection for those 180 days. If the print run at that point is less than 1,500, I suggest that they print digitally until they have built up more momentum.

Sharon Goldinger

Sharon Goldinger, owner of PeopleSpeak, is a book shepherd and editor specializing in the nonfiction book industry. Her business, marketing, and editorial experience ranges from small publishers to Fortune 500 companies and from national organizations to Capitol Hill. Under her guidance, Sharon's clients have published and authored award-winning books.

What do book shepherds do, and what kinds of clients do they work with?

Book shepherds are full-service contractors for book publishers. A book shepherd takes a book through all the necessary steps—writing, editing, design, printing, marketing, distribution—in the most time- and cost-effective manner possible. Some of the steps that a book shepherd leads a client through—in terms of setting up a book publishing company and publishing a book—include creating a name for the publishing company; finding, engaging, and coordinating the interior and cover designers; managing the crafting of the book; completing all the necessary paperwork (such as copyright forms and Bowker paperwork); obtaining a distributor and a marketing firm; creating a marketing campaign; and arranging print reorders.

Book shepherds usually work with small and new publishers and then help them grow. Most publishers I work with are authors who have ideas for more than one book. Having more than one book greatly increases an author's credibility. Also, national distributors usually do not accept one-book publishers. They want to see that publishing is a full-time venture (not just a hobby), and that includes a full publishing program— usually at least one book every twelve to eighteen months. This is a business, and everyone in it needs to earn a living. It is much easier for the author, publisher, and distributor to do that if a publisher has more than one book. Several of my client publishers plan to publish other people's works in addition to their own.

So much information about publishing is available in print, online, and via consultants that it's hard to know what's true, what's false, and what's applicable to a specific book. Some of the advice you find can be really good—but not for your book. A strategy that works for one book may not be appropriate for another (for example, nonfiction versus fiction, business versus self-help). A book shepherd brings his or her list of contacts, experiences, and war stories to each project. That's why it's important to find the right book shepherd for your particular book.

Changes in book publishing used to occur about every five to ten years; then the widespread use of computers made changes happen faster, but it was still possible for authors to keep up with what was going on and make the necessary adaptations. Now those changes have accelerated to warp speed—sometimes occurring from week to week. How can any one person, especially someone just entering the arena, keep up with all of that information, as well as the subject of the book he or she has written? It's almost impossible. That's where a book shepherd can be of most help: keeping up with the industry, what's new, what's being phased out, what's working, what's not working, which vendors are doing a good job, and which ones are not.

In short, a book shepherd helps prevent the "I don't know what I don't know" syndrome and associated costly mistakes and time wasters.

Are book shepherds similar to book packagers?

Historically, book packagers have brought a "package" to a publisher. For example, let's consider a book on arthritis. The packager would put together the book idea (proposal), which would include finding the author (most likely a medical doctor), hiring the designers, and developing the marketing ideas for the book. The publisher would buy the whole package, and the packager would produce the book (sometimes including printing).

Book packagers were the contractors for a book—hiring and paying for the book editor, proofreader, and indexer and overseeing the production process, up to and sometimes including printing.

What kinds of publishing options are available in the industry today?

Three basic choices are available for publishing a book today:

* **"Traditional" publishing**: This choice involves finding an agent or a publisher; that is, an agent who will find you a publisher, or a publisher that does not require an agent.

* **Independent publishing:** This usually applies to small publishers and can include self-publishers.

* **Subsidy publishing:** This involves working with a company that provides some publishing-related services (for example, editing, design, and printing); however, all costs are paid for by the author. With subsidy publishing, the author is not the publisher—the subsidy press is. An author using the subsidy publishing route cannot contract with any entities as the publisher. (For example, only a publisher can have a contractual relationship with a distributor. If an author wants to expand the distribution of his or her book, the subsidy publisher would have to enter into the contract.) Many authors think that since they are paying for everything, they are the de facto publisher and can enter into contracts, but that's not the case. The most important lesson here is be sure to read every contract, ask every possible question, and understand every provision before signing.

In the past, the term "self-publisher" had a negative connotation. It often meant poor-quality editing, design, production, and printing. In other words, if you placed a self-published book next to a book from a big publishing house, you could see the difference in a second.

With the advancement of computer technology and desktop publishing, the only reasons why small presses could not compete with the big houses were lower production quality and poor distribution into the marketplace. Today, a knowledgeable and experienced person can create and produce a quality product. (Modern technology has allowed this capability in terms of the actual production mechanism as well as the lower cost.) Distribution is still difficult but not impossible with the assistance of one of the national distributors that will work with small presses.

How does a book shepherd differ from a vanity press?

A book shepherd is a consultant. A vanity press is a subsidy press.

Originally, vanity presses were created so that anyone who had the money could have a book published. It didn't matter if it was edited or what it looked like. The point was, no editorial staff screened the book to make sure that it met industry standards (in terms of writing and editing) or that an audience for it existed in the marketplace. Years ago, many of these companies charged an exorbitant amount of money because there was always someone who wanted to have a book published no matter the cost (because of the cachet of being a published author). These companies often promised that they would produce the book to industry standards (and did not), market the book (and did not), and get the book into bookstores (and did not). So vanity presses got a well-deserved reputation for being scams or rip-offs.

Since desktop publishing software has made it easier to produce a high-quality product, more vanity presses have been created than ever before. This avenue is the ideal one for some people, depending on their goals. For example, if an author just wants to have a few copies of his or her book available for family and friends, a vanity press might be the most appropriate option.

What circumstances bring authors to your company rather than self-publishing their books on their own or submitting them to a publisher or agent?

Books still hold a sacred place in the marketplace, so it's not unusual for someone to approach me and say, "I have this book I want to publish. I don't care if it makes money; I don't even need to break even. But I feel this book will help people" (or "I want to create a historical record of this information"). This is a realistic goal, so we can reach a clear understanding of the costs and potential results. (However, when clients say this, I do challenge them by responding back, "There is nothing wrong with producing this book and making money. It's not against the law; it's not even immoral.")

The author's goals are very important. For example, if an author wants to write a history of his small town with the understanding that it will not be picked up by a national distributor and will be sold only in his local bookstore, that's realistic (if the person wants to spend the money). But if an author comes to me with a manuscript that could not be a viable book (which could mean the writing is too weak or the marketplace is not broad enough to sell through, based on the author's goals), I won't take the project at all. If the book needs writing help, a ghostwriter can be brought in or the author can hire a "book doctor" to rewrite the book.

Most often, people call me to discuss their options for having a book published. I ask a series of questions to reveal whether or not they have a national platform (required for nonfiction by most agents and publishers today). If they don't, then the conversation steers to whether they have the time, budget, and inclination to independently publish.

At what point would an author hire you? Before the manuscript is written or after?

A book shepherd can be engaged at almost any time in the process—while the manuscript is being written or when it has been completed. Some authors approach me even before the manuscript is written to evaluate whether the premise of the book is viable. I've helped create and shape books, starting with marketing research into what's in the marketplace already and what's missing from or needed in the marketplace. I've also guided authors through all editorial phases, including developmental, content, and copyediting.

What sorts of questions should someone be prepared to answer when contacting a book shepherd?

People who contact a book shepherd to have their manuscript reviewed and assessed should be prepared to answer these questions:

* Who is the audience for your book?

Answer: Every woman in the world.

Better answer: Women ages 20 to 50 in the United States.

Best answer:

— Career women ages 35 to 45 in the United States who read *Ladies Home Journal.*

— Married women ages 30 to 50 in the United States who want to improve their relationships with family members.

* What is the goal of your publishing plan?

Answer: To have a book.

Better answer: To have a book available for my clients and potential clients.

Best answer: To publish a book that will offer answers to a specific problem.

* What is your time availability?

Answer: I have some time. How much time will this take?

Better answer: I know this will take time. I'm ready to start now, and I hope to be able to have some time available each week.

Best answer: I know this is a long-term time commitment. I've read several books about the publishing industry and how to market a book.

I've started researching where and to whom I can sell my book in addition to bookstores and have already started my two-year marketing plan.

* What is your budget?

Answer: I have some money put aside.

Better answer: I have researched what this will cost. Please confirm the numbers with me.

Best answer: I have researched what this will cost. Please confirm the numbers with me. I have also set up a line of credit that I can tap so that when the book is ready for reprint, I will have funds available to pay for the reprinting while waiting for the money from the distributor to come in.

What should an author consider when looking for a book shepherd? Is it possible to know the difference between an ineffective one and an effective one? What questions should an author ask?

Whether you're building a house and need a contractor or have written a book and need a book shepherd, conducting your due diligence is vital. Here are some good initial questions:

* What types of books do you work with (nonfiction, fiction, categories)?

* How do you work with your clients (meet with them in person or by phone, have weekly meetings, delegate the project to a staff member, provide guidelines and lay out steps to take)?

* How long does the process take?

* How much or how little can you help me?

* How much do your services cost?

* What kinds of projects have you worked on? Can you tell me some of your clients' successes and failures and why you think they occurred?

* Do you charge for an estimate or assessment of my project?

If you like the answers to these questions, you should check the person's references and ask those publishers and authors the same kinds of questions that you asked the book shepherd.

What rates can authors expect to pay for a book shepherd's services?

Rates can be by the hour or the project. Much of this decision depends on how many tasks the book shepherd is going to do versus the publisher (or his or her staff). Every consultant is different and provides different services (sometimes directly contracted). You should ask what the book shepherd's typical project fee is. The needs of a project can vary so much that it is hard to say what fee is and isn't appropriate. However, the amount should be examined in light of how many books need to be sold to break even. Developing a cost analysis or creating a P&L (profit and loss) statement for each book is a good step.

Do you walk authors through every phase of publication? What are those steps?

Book shepherds can do as little or as much as the author or publisher needs. Some clients have more time than money; some, the opposite. A book shepherd can assist with any or all of the following:

* Creating the publishing company and obtaining all necessary legal, business, and publishing paperwork and forms, including resale permits, ISBNs, copyright, cataloging in publication data, and more

* Coming up with a book's title and checking to see what other books already are using it

* Determining if permissions are needed

* Setting a publication date

* Recommending and/or checking out interior and cover designers and indexer

* Assessing comps for the book (price, size, features, etc.) and determining the price

* Setting up or updating the author's or book's Website

* Making decisions about fulfillment and storage

* Developing an "elevator speech" (brief description of the book)

* Determining the audience (specific statistics: gender, age, generation, buying habits)

* Establishing the benefits the book brings to readers

* Obtaining endorsements and testimonials (whom and how many to include)

* Developing a marketing strategy

* Budget

* Author's participation—speaking, writing, Website, book tours, blogging

* Branding

* Other public appearances (libraries, colleges, book fairs)

* Media training

* Networking opportunities (for example, via groups the author belongs to)

* Email and direct marketing

* Partnering with an organization

* Number of galleys to be sent out

* Length of the publicity campaign (e-blasts, galleys)

* Collateral materials (postcards, bookmarks, flyers)

* Bookstore promotions (co-op and advertising dollars)

* Internet publicity (which websites to target, time, method and length)

* Special sales opportunities (via trainings, workshops, conferences, reading groups)

* Foreign language translations and serial rights

The book shepherd ensures that all the tasks get done, whether by the author, the publisher, the book shepherd, or a virtual assistant. What's important is not who does the tasks, it's that the tasks—all the right steps in the process—are done when they need to be done.

Can you get an author's books on the bookstore shelves?

With more than 200,000 books in print each year and the average superstore carrying 100,000 books, it is impossible to get every book on a bookstore shelf. The question a publisher should ask a book shepherd is, "Can you get my book into the bookstore system?"

Getting into the bookstore system generally means having a book listed with the nation's wholesalers (for example, Ingram and Baker & Taylor). While there are exceptions to every rule, most of the time a publisher needs to be represented by an exclusive national distributor. Having a national distributor (which does all the warehousing, invoicing, billing, collections, etc.) has many benefits, but the bottom line is that a publisher needs a distributor more than a distributor needs a publisher.

Remember that publishing is a business: everyone has to make some money in the publishing process. How does a distributor make money? By selling books. How does the consumer know that a book is available for sale? Through marketing. Who's responsible for that marketing? The author and the publisher. Once those responsibilities and relationships are understood, it will be easier to partner with a distributor.

A distributor wants to know what a publisher's marketing budget will be—in detail. What's the total budget? Who is the publicist? How long is the publicity campaign? How big are the author's and publisher's mailing lists, and how often will the people on the lists be notified? How, when, and where will the consumer be pushed into bookstores to buy the book? And, since there are so few "one-hit wonders," what are the next books that the author will be writing, and when will they be published?

Competition for shelf space is tough. Do book shepherds help with marketing and promotion? What tips do you have to share with authors to help them stand out from the pack?

Book shepherds often help with marketing and promotion. Services can range from providing a referral to a competent and experienced marketing company and publicist or doing the work themselves. The decision depends on the project, the genre, and the budget. When it comes to marketing, specialists are important. A book can be viable, but it may not be the best fit for certain experts. I always check to make sure I create win-win situations with my clients, projects, and vendors. While every book goes through similar marketing and publishing steps (for example, reviews need to be sent out four months in advance to *Publishers Weekly*), every marketing plan needs to be tailored to the audience. Should direct-mail pieces be created and sent out? Where can the author write and speak to gain attention (local and national networking groups, local and national publications)? What should the book's Internet marketing campaign look like, and how should it be built?

Fiction is tough to sell these days. How do you help authors get their novels noticed?

I specialize in nonfiction—although I'm pleased to say that when I did make an exception for *Rashi's Daughters*, it was a great success story. The key to my accepting this project was how it was referred to me (by an experienced colleague who is a fabulous fiction editor) and the amount of homework that the author had done. She was an exceptional client in terms of producing an exemplary product and following directions.

The author's primary goal was to create buzz about the book. Her first step was to research her audience. She knew that her historical fiction book would appeal to a niche audience of Jewish women—a group that reads and buys a lot of books. She then had to find where they were and how to reach them. An Internet search of Jewish women's organizations revealed a number of national associations, all of which she joined a year before her book came out.

She wrote articles for and bought ads in their newsletters. And she contacted them to speak at their local and national conventions. She spoke for free—all she asked was permission to sign and sell her books at their events. A critical element was her relentlessness. She sent emails, made phone calls, and followed up, followed up, and followed up some more. She also created a Website for the book where she could direct people if they wanted to learn more. She spoke at libraries and bookstores. One final note: she made sure to get the names and addresses of everyone who attended her speaking engagements so when her second book was released, she already had a mailing list of thousands of interested readers.

How much importance do you place on cover design? Interior design? Do buyers and readers really notice these elements?

I think all the elements of a book (editing, cover design, interior design, back cover copy, marketing and publicity) are important. I believe that buyers and readers notice them, especially if they're done poorly, and we work with our clients' distributors in these areas as well.

Book shepherds ensure that every book they work on meets industry standards, which means that the interior and cover designs are created by experienced book designers. It's important to note that there is a difference between a graphic designer—even an award-winning graphic designer—and an experienced book designer. Creating a Clio-winning advertisement is not the same as knowing which fonts to use in a book and what colors to use on a cover. Just as you would not ask a dermatologist to treat your broken leg (dermatologists and orthopedic surgeons are both doctors, but their experience and knowledge are obviously quite different), a publisher needs to use an experienced book designer—not just a designer.

Will you recommend how many books an author should get printed? How do you determine this number?

A book shepherd should be willing to make recommendations on every aspect of a book's life (font, cover design, marketing, printing, etc.). Depending on the market (Is the book a calling card? How many copies does the distributor want? How many presales have occurred?), I provide recommendations for that number as well as the appropriate printer type (digital for short runs, offset for longer runs).

The number of books that should be printed depends on how many the distributor wants and how many pre-orders have been received. Book shepherds help determine that number for the first run as well as re-printings.

I have found that many people don't plan for success. I ask my clients to consider this: What happens when you sell out your first print run? You won't see any money from your distributor for three or four months, but you need to print again now.

Do authors ever come to you with an idea that has little market potential? If so, how do you handle this?

I come from the land of straight shooters. If I don't think a project is marketable, I will tell the author and turn down the project.

What are some of the frustrations you encounter with your clients?

I'm pleased to say that I don't have any, and that's due to one simple reason: I gather good information up front. I know the client's goals, I feel that I can assist him or her in meeting them, the client has been truthful with me regarding the goals and budget—it's that straightforward.

In conclusion, I call publishing a game—but it's a winnable game. Like any game, you need to know the rules, have the proper equipment, know what players you need on your team, have a good coach, develop a winning strategy, and be willing to put in a lot of hard work and money.

My final advice: do your homework, check references, and read and understand every sentence in a contract before you sign it.

Final Thoughts From My Side of the Pond

Contrary to what people might think, I have a lot of respect for people who decide to self-publish PROVIDED they know exactly what they're getting into, they use a good book shepherd, and they have the money to burn. 'Cause burn it will. But it can have some very sweet benefits. I've seen some incredible works come out of the self-publishing arena – whether they used a book shepherd or not.

For example, we shared the same distributor with Brunonia Barry, author of the wildly successful *The Lace Reader*, a book she and her husband self-published with the shepherding help of Blu Sky Media Group—our distributor. We shared a display table with Brunonia and her husband at our distributor's booth at the Book Expo in New York. We were nonstop, mind-bending-busy talking about our upcoming lineup with librarians and indie store owners while Brunonia and her husband watched us in silence. At the end of the weekend, they told us they were in awe of our ability to patter off enticing nibblets of six brand new titles (librarians and store folks want it fast and mouth-watering) without batting an eye, while they had their one book. I felt badly for them because they seemed so overwhelmed by the whole ordeal.

Six months later I read about their two million dollar sale of *The Lace Reader* to William Morrow. They may have had only one book but my, oh my, did they ever know what to do with it. Who's in awe now? Rock on, Brunonia.

Obviously the Brunonias of the world are few and far between, but I do believe that any author who has the will, guts, determination, and a good book shepherd to see a project through while spending a minor fortune (which Brunonia did), then I do believe they will enjoy the fruits of that labor.

5: Bookstore events - Being prepared

This came to me the other day from Gayle Shanks, the lovely owner of Changing Hands Bookstore in Tempe, AZ and president of the American Booksellers Association. It was in response to my telling Gayle the promotional efforts I am undertaking for a writer's seminar I'm giving.

"I can't wait to meet you. You are the 'dream' author. You do your homework, encourage people to come to the seminar, contact resources, etc. How wonderful it would be if everyone who came to the store did the same."

What a heartwarming thing to say (thanks, Gayle!) — and what an alarming commentary regarding author preparation. Gayle's observations tell me one thing; many authors don't lift a finger for their own promotion. They schedule the book signing and foolishly expect the store to undertake all the publicity of their event. We all know what it is to assume, right?

The first thing to ask yourself is this: "What is the goal of my signing/reading/event?" The answer should be to have a successful event, of course. There's only one way that's going to happen; you need to tell people about your upcoming event, and this takes planning.

In my case, I contacted all of the surrounding writer's groups in the Phoenix, Tucson, Tempe, Scottsdale area. I have a good friend who's respected in the area, and he served as my "big mouth"—someone who graciously spread the word about my event.

What can you, Joe Author, do to take the necessary steps to a successful signing? Plan. Tell people about your signing. Analyze your book and approach those who would find your book interesting.

* **Send postcards that have your cover art on the front and event info on the back to the local book clubs.**

* **Advertise for your signing in your local newspaper by providing interview information.** Make sure the article is released the week before your signing. If it's released too soon, people will forget about it. Sometimes the store will submit the information, saving you the trouble. The store can either request information about you and your book for the newspaper directly from you, or go to your website to pull it.

* **Advertise on a local radio station, or do an interview.** The store may be able to give you contact information; other times you will have to hunt it down yourself.

* **Fliers.** If you are doing a signing at a local store, advertise it with fliers at the local library in the same town.

* **Provide fliers with your book signing information.** Have the store place them near the registers. Provide them at least two weeks in advance, and don't print more than a hundred. You usually can make two fliers out of an 8 1/2" by 11" piece of card stock paper. Don't print the fliers on colored paper; it makes it too hard to read. Instead, make your wording colorful. Make the time, date and place of your signing stand out. Sign the fliers to entice people to take it, or ask the clerks to stuff them in the customers' bags.

* **Set up your signing at least one month in advance.** **This** gives you enough time to prepare, and the store enough time to order your books. (side note: it's a good idea to check two weeks before your event to make sure they ordered the books—oh, the horror stories I could tell)

* **Poster display.** Not all stores will make a poster advertising your event, so be sure to ask. Obviously, window placement is ideal, but take whatever you can get. It's perfectly fine to ask if they have a poster holder they can put in a high traffic area.

Remember, having a crowd is far better than yawning into your coat pocket. And store managers ALWAYS remember the successful events. The important thing to remember is to do your part to make sure you have a fun, successful signing.

Gayle Shanks - Changing Hands Bookstore

Gayle Shanks is the owner of Changing Hands Bookstore, an amazing independent bookstore, located in Tempe, AZ. Gayle, along with Cindy Dach (GM and Marketing Director), and Pinna Joseph (Events coordinator) were kind enough to answer questions about the genesis of a successful book event.

Gayle has been a bookseller since 1974 when she and a friend opened a tiny, 500-square-foot used book store, Changing Hands, in Tempe, Arizona. The store moved twice and grew to 12,000 square feet and carries new and used books and lots of gift items. The store is a work of art with round edges, curving walkways and shelves stocked with the very best books.

She has a degree in English Literature from ASU and never imagined that she would have a career as a bookseller. But once the store opened she never wanted to do anything else. She spends her days ordering books, recommending books, creating a community gathering place where authors come nearly every day of the year to read from their work. The children's section, one of the largest in the state and includes books and educational toys for children and teens.

There are many civic activities Gayle has been involved in over the years, serving on social service agency boards, city planning committees, and has served on the board of the Mountains & Plains Booksellers Association and was president for two years. She is currently the President of the national Bookseller's Association board. Gayle's busy life includes being a community organizer and activist. She relaxes with one of her big loves; working in her garden.

What background preparation goes into a book signing event?

Once an author is scheduled to speak, the entire marketing department (PR person, graphic designer, and events coordinator) brainstorm to determine the best way to market the event. Not every store has the staff to do this brainstorming, promotion or planning. In smaller stores the author must do much of their own "homework" which might include working with friends and family to best determine avenues for promotion.

At our store, we discuss perfect partnerships with organizations that tie-in to the author or the book's theme. We identify those partners and find the connector. We write a press release and a fifty word "elevator pitch" about the book, author and event. This is created from the author's materials. We then use this material and send it to the press, our customer email list, community organizations, universities, etc. We follow up with the press.

Again, many smaller stores do not have staffing for these endeavors. Promotion is time-consuming and often has zero results. When it does produce results, it can make an event very successful. It often comes down to timing. If a book's theme is timely to the media at the time of the promotion, the media will pick up on it. For some events, we arrange with the local Trader Joe's, cookie store, etc., for co-sponsorship which translates to having refreshments donated.

What do you look for in an author when considering booking them for an event? Do they have to be well known? Provide a list of potential buyers? Do you automatically accept an author for events at your store?

The requests for author signings come into our store directly from publishers and also from authors who are promoting their books themselves. First, we determine if the book is a good fit for our store. We've been in business for over 34 years and host over 400 events a year. We've learned what events work and what events do not work. The authors who are supported by publishers in their marketing efforts start with a request from our buyer for that author to appear at our store, or there is a request from the marketing department via the sales rep. We write a proposal stating why we'd like the author, how many books we think we can sell, whether it will be an on-site reading or at a nearby venue, etc.

For a local or author without publisher support, the process begins with a written proposal from the author—we ask the author to pitch the book and event to us. How they do this helps us determine whether to host the event or not. We ask for a co-operative advertising fee, something that is standard with large publishers. This fee helps us support the event with payroll for the promotions that we do. This fee also forces the author to think about whether he or she wants us to host the event, as it is not a given nor is it a free promotion on our part. Sometimes we find that authors have paid large sums of money to print their books and have not allotted money to support the marketing. Mostly, we look for professionalism, courtesy, and well-written books. We expect the author to invite all their friends and family to attend the event and ask if the author has at least 20 guests/local contacts who will attend the book signing.

There are many authors who don't know the first thing about a book signing. What should authors do to ensure they have a successful signing? Provide food? Posters? Music? Flyers? Newspaper articles?

First, authors need to write good books. If they are non-fiction, they need to provide useful information. If they are fiction, they need to be well written. It's difficult to host a great event for a mediocre book. The audience at a bookstore is a highly intelligent discriminating crowd. Sometimes, self-published authors are much more successful hosting book parties at the homes of families and friends.

Authors should provide refreshments at their expense. This helps generate interest from those passing by. It also helps retain an audience for discussion.

Before providing any printed materials such as posters and bookmarks, the authors need to check with the store and see what can be accommodated. Posters backed on foam core or cardboard can be used above bookcases if the images are large enough and the space is available. There is limited space in a bookstore. However, it's a great idea for an author to take any materials they might have and post them in coffee shops and other community gathering places. Music can be included, if it ties in with the book. If the signing is co-sponsored by a charity or nonprofit that usually adds to the list of people who will be contacted to advertise the event.

Customers are sometimes shy about making eye contact with an author at a signing. What are some of the tricks of the trade that you've seen authors do to bring customers into their table and engage them in a conversation?

It's difficult because many people coming to a bookstore seek solace. They do not want to be approached. Chocolate is always a good idea. Saying, hello without acting like a salesman. Raffles are good draws. Small dogs. We have had authors dress in the costumes of their characters to let people know about their children's book during a local author signing.

Does the author have to supply their own books for their signing, or do you order them?

This depends on the source for the books. Self-published books need to be supplied by the author because author books need to be returnable.

Do you automatically put any unsold books on your store shelves, or do you send them back to the publisher?

We determine the book's "keep" based on the quantity of books that sold at the event. We also have an author consignment program for authors to use after or instead of an event.

Will you book an event for a Print-on-Demand author? Vanity press author?

Again, we determine whether we think any author and book will get an audience at our store. Events are high maintenance activities, and bookstores can only manage them if they generate an audience and book sales. By hosting an event at a bookstore, the author is requesting the endorsement of the bookstore and banking on that store's reputation in their community.

Print-on-Demand books are a way for an author to test the waters without the huge investment that most vanity presses require of authors. We have no problem having these books for a signing as the technology has improved so much that these POD titles often look and feel like most other books. On the other hand, we often tell new authors that self-published books need be thought of like business cards. They are investments. Authors should not expect to make their investment back, but think of their book as a way to launch themselves as authors.

What is your opinion of Print-on-Demand/vanity press books in terms of quality, pricing, and design? Do you feel they can compete?

Print-on-Demand/vanity in terms of quality has much improved over the past few years. The pricing is difficult for authors and the design is largely dependent upon the author. The biggest challenge is distribution for these books.

Many authors state that bookstores are hosting fewer and fewer signing events. Why is this?

Bookstores cannot afford to take on an event, manage the promotion and the inventory and then have no one show up for the event. Sadly, this happens too often. There are thousands upon thousands of books being published each year. Readers are making choices from a large pool of what books to read and what events to attend. For a new author who is relatively unknown, it's very difficult for a store to generate an audience. The audience wants to learn something or be completely entertained. We are hosting fewer signings with first-time novelists because we cannot generate an audience for their books unless they have gotten broad recognition first.

Do the sales from a signing event get logged into the Bookscan database?

Yes. To Bookscan, *NY Times* and Indiebound

Do you feel that book signing events impact sales?

Absolutely. When an author goes on tour, a community has an opportunity to get a signed book and have an experience with the author. A tour cannot only double or triple book sales, but it creates word of mouth buzz within a community. There are usually additional sales of the book after an author visit.

What are some of the best and worst you've seen with a book event?

Worst is more fun, so we'll start there.

Worst:

* Authors who show up to an event intoxicated.

* Authors who treat booksellers like menial labor.

* Arrogant authors.

* Authors who are terrible readers and/or don't know how to talk about their book.

* Authors who beg the audience to buy their book and act like victims of the publishing world.

* Authors who gossip about other bookstores.

* Authors who don't know when to stop talking and are not mindful of their audience.

Best:

* Authors who know how to read and talk about their books

* Authors who can talk about the writing process and can sell their books as well.

* The author who connects with an audience, speaking to a universal experience.

* Authors who hand out a gift that ties into the book—linen handkerchiefs for a book about aprons, Twinkies, if the main character loves Twinkies, etc.

* Food samplings for cookbooks.

* Illustrators who actually show kids/fans how they draw.

Final Thoughts From My Side of the Pond

I had the chance to attend one of my author's book signing events. The first things I noticed upon walking into the bookstore were his posters surrounding his table. I saw how their natural curiosity brought buyers into his territory.

Many people would rather eat a bullet than make eye contact with an author who's planted behind a table full of books. However, the posters offer a safe way of drawing the reader in. There's no eye contact, but it suddenly gives the author the chance to get up and talk to the customer about what's on the poster. Before anyone knows it, they're picking up the book and giving it a look-see.

Visual aids can help any kind of book of any genre. One visual aid should always be of you and your cover art, and the other is the hook. This could be photos of places where your book takes place along with synopsis bullet points that a buyer can easily read. Be creative and have fun with it. These are the face to you and your book.

6: Cover design

"I've got this neighbor. . ."

Yes, yes, we hear this all the time. Joe or Jane Author has a neighbor who is a "great graphic artist." Invariably, he's great at designing garage sales posters and bake sales flyers, maybe a church program or two. But there is a world of difference between fudgie brownies or scratched armoires and a winning cover design.

Covers are the author's calling card, and they set the tone for what's residing inside. As such, they should be reflective and complimentary of the content. Nothing bugs me more than to buy a book based on what I see on the cover (and no fair casting aspersions about my methodology) only to discover that what I saw on the cover had nothing to do with the story. Dang it, if I see a unicorn on the cover, there better be one in the book. And it better be a dominant feature of the book. I bought a book last year whose light shades of blue, green, and pink cover suggested light-hearted humor. Upon getting into the story, I discovered it was a morose journey about a suicidal stripper. Yikes. Talk about missing the cover-art mark. I felt like I'd been a victim of bait and switch.

Readers don't cotton to bait and switch tactics any more than they appreciate the used car salesman who fixes up a 1974 rust bucket with fresh paint and new tires while leaving ripped seats and missing steering wheel inside. Salesman Bob should fix the upholstery and get a new steering wheel, and the suicide stripper's cover should have had heavy fonts and dark colors. This is a "neighbor" mistake, and your neighbor should stick to his garage sales, and let the pros take over.

And don't be taken in by professional graphic designers either. I see many designers who create amazing artwork, but they don't necessarily make great covers. I had an instance where an author asked to use his designer. Sure, sez I. The graphics were fabulous. Problem was, they were so intricately detailed that they melted into a mish mash of white noise. The second problem was his use of colors. One color was dominant over everything else, and he used shades of it in all the characters. All those hues morphed into an indistinguishable globby mess. This was a design better suited for a giant poster or a puzzle, not a 6 x 9 trade paperback.

Put a sticky note on your forehead: a professional *graphic designer* does not indicate *book cover knowledge*.

For that reason, I had the pleasure of interviewing George Foster, a delightful man whose award-winning designs have helped shape and enhance author's books for twenty years. George has designed the covers for more than a thousand books and continues to design up to eighty book covers every year for small publishers and self-published authors. You can see examples of his work at **fostercovers.com**

George Foster ‑ Cover Design

"People judge a book by its cover. Here's how that can be good news for you and your book."

George Foster earned his BFA in 1978 and began working for himself in 1982. Soon after, he was creating covers for books by world-renowned book marketing expert John Kremer and designing covers for early books in the Chicken Soup for the Soul® series while it was still very small. He thoroughly enjoyed himself, and it wasn't long before he realized book cover design was his passion.

George has designed covers for other national and international bestselling books and lately has been appearing regularly as a finalist or winner of *ForeWord Magazine's* Book of the Year, the Ben Franklin Awards, the Indie Excellence National Book Awards, and others.

George has contributed to the Independent Book Publisher's Association's newsletter *The Independent* and taught classes at their annual Publishing University. He contributes a column to Brian Jud's e-newsletter *Book Marketing Matters*, and wrote the chapter on book cover design for John Kremer's legendary bestselling book, *1001 Ways to Market Your Books* (and designed the book's cover). Without further ado, here's George.

~~~

Let's look at the big picture. Why do you even need a book cover? Here's why. If you've glanced at a book and instantly thought, "This looks like a really good book," then that cover did a good job, didn't it? But if you actually pick the book up and turn it over to learn more, the cover did a *great* job. If your cover does not perform its job at this level, you and your book may be largely overlooked by the people who would make you money. That is, distributors, book reviewers, retailers and customers.

If the back cover is done right, it delivers an experience of a great product with the solid feeling of quality and overall value. You'll likely open that book to look inside. If the interior is expertly done, the content will really shine forth and the decision to buy is an easy one. But you wouldn't have arrived there if the cover didn't first draw you in.

You've heard that a book is judged by its cover. That's true. In fact it happens in roughly five seconds. Experts say it is the most important part of your marketing because every person involved must believe your book is worth their time. High-profile book reviewers routinely refuse books because of an awkward cover. Book distributors do the same. They bring so many books to the world that they only have time to work with winners, so they have to judge your book quickly. The cover can make or break the deal.

No doubt about it, the real value of your book is what's inside. It's the hard-won result of your commitment, talent and dedication. But now, what you have written is largely dependent upon its presentation in order to be an attractive and saleable product. This visual aspect of your book should be approached seriously. It is not self-indulgent decoration. It's marketing. Wise publishers use this wisdom to their advantage. Make sure you do, too.

Let's consider the techniques and some of the rules. Like anything else, rules can be broken, which is how innovative designers evolve this or any other art form. But to break the rules you need to first know them. It's like professional drivers taking new sports cars to their limits for television commercials. They are not reckless. You shouldn't be, either, so I'd like to show you some of the elements that make a winning book cover.

```
Tip: Show your cover to someone and ask
  them to tell you within five seconds what
    the book is about.  If their answer is
  wrong, they didn't fail.  Your cover did.
```

What are the most important elements of a winning cover?

There are three important elements for a book cover: dominance, contrast and balance.

Dominance: This means that something meaningful on your cover is bigger, brighter or somehow gets noticed first. Think of a rug merchant in the marketplace yelling "rugs!" If you stop he'll talk to you in a normal tone, but he got your attention by shouting one word. Does your book cover clearly shout something? You must get attention. It's the first job.

Contrast: The use of opposing elements, such as colors, forms, or lines, in proximity to produce an intensified effect in a work of art. Bright colors, for example, may or may not be appropriate for your cover but at least have good contrast. Test this by squinting at your cover design. This simplifies it to basic light and dark. Can you read it? If so, you have good contrast. This is obviously important. Your book has a great title. Show it clearly.

```
Tip: Don't put a dark blue title over a
bright red back-ground or a white title
      over a very light background.
```

Balance: This pertains to all the parts of the cover working together as a whole. You might think your cover is done when you've put in the title, your name and a picture of something, but if they look like separate items that do not relate as a whole, it's simply awkward and your book gets thrown away by the reviewers.

Every item on your cover must connect to the other. How? Not by pushing them all together. Instead, the space between them holds them together in harmony. The space is called "negative space," and this really matters. Think of a staircase. What makes it useful is the space between the steps. Think of a nice melody. If you take away the space between the notes, it isn't so nice anymore. You need space. Negative space. It makes your book cover sing and helps get you those book reviews.

Test this by looking at your cover's negative space, the space between the items. Does it push them away from each other? Does the book cover feel alive and breathing, or just sit there dead? This is not easy at first, but with practice you'll never see a book cover, or any artwork, the same again. You'll know the inside secret of balance.

Use these three principles together for a more attractive cover. Please bear in mind that rules are to the designer what the rules of writing are to the author. Rules do not create art. People do, with talent and practice.

```
Tip: Don't let the distance from your title
  to the edge of the cover be less than the
  title's line spacing.  The same applies to
               the subtitle.
```

Don't let your cover blend into a mess of too many photos, subtitles, claims, shapes and colors. They cancel each other out. It may be an effort to grab attention but, instead, you force the eye to glance right past it. Sure, everything you choose to show is relevant to the book, even important, but too much becomes cluttered. Test this by placing your cover among some books and see if your eyes can too easily drift away to what's beside it. If so, simplify.

Whether fiction or non-fiction, the sales maxim of "keep it simple" applies. Using less items gives each item more power. A strong first impression of high quality just always works. For example, a popular author's name might fill most of the cover. Why? It easily attracts the author's fans and the job is done. If your book cover can put forward just one thing that really does this job, do it very strongly. However, if you have a really compelling endorsement from somebody who matters, it can be useful on the front cover if it is not too long. There are other things you can put on a front cover such as "A million weeks on the New York Times Bestseller List!" which adds value. The trick is to add value, not just more information.

Should an author's photo be on the cover?

Some say "only if they're famous." The familiar face gets attention. However, any face looking at you has the power to attract. If the author's face adds great energy or conveys meaning then it will be hard to ignore. Please be sure it is a high-quality, high-resolution, professional photo, not an obvious point-and-shoot snap shot at a birthday party. The face has to convey quality. Otherwise, don't use it.

How do you make a cover stand out from the rest of the pack, especially in cases of a crowded genre?

As a writer you know the power of the simile and metaphor to magnify meaning. This can apply to your book cover, too. I recently designed a cover for a book about methods for curing back pain. It needed to really stand out from (and be perceived as better than) the rest of the books of the same genre. All the books showed a picture of someone's back, so we instead used a floating feather. The visual connection to lightness, comfort, naturalness, flexibility and gentle strength is instant and sets this book apart. A visual metaphor like this can also give your book a special appearance because it is more conscious. It speaks between the lines and makes the viewer engage with it.

How do you decide what cover fits best on any particular book? Do you read the book?

Reading the fiction manuscript is important to find the emotion inside and bring that out in an appealing way. Non-fiction is less necessary to read every word but at least see every page. Before I start designing a cover I get a clear understanding of the book, who would buy it, and to which books it might be compared.

Fiction is entertainment, so I strive to create that right away on the front cover. Does the cover convey a thriller, romance, political drama? Does it look like a great read? When the cover does this job well, the customer will pick the book up to get a little deeper into it. The entertainment has begun!

Non-fiction covers must answer your customer's basic question, "what's in it for me?" If they believe they'll benefit from your book, you'll grab their attention. If it's self-help, the cover should look optimistic. If it's health, look vibrant. If history, look authentic. If finance, look smart. A cookbook should look appetizing. How to do this?

This brings us to the psychology of shapes and colors. Before we explore that, let's start with why we care. You are aiming your book at your target audience. Another term for this is demographics, the description of a particular population. It starts with defining whether your readers will be mostly male or female (since women buy more books than men).

Shapes: Men prefer solid and predictable squares and hard edges while women prefer tender and loving circles, curves and soft edges. The triangle shape is highly visible to both, carrying a feeling of mystery and power but women may also feel threatened by it. The oval (the primordial womb or egg) traditionally brings a positive response from both genders. It is an archetype that resonates deeply with everyone.

Colors: Bright colors are great and get attention, but are not necessarily better than muted ones. I might sparingly use red to quickly communicate a book's benefit (red is the color for action and always gets attention), but too much could look cheap, even comic. Muted colors can draw you with their quiet charm. They can convey beauty, drama, longing and hope. Movie directors know that black-and-white can be more dramatic than color and will sometimes choose it for this reason. So, use colors wisely. Don't abuse them and they'll help you.

The psychology of color is a prized and powerful tool of marketing. Generally speaking: pink is feminine, green is leisurely, orange is healthy or good-tasting, brown is rich, traditional and warm, yellow is hot, purple (violet) is spiritual, white is clean, clinical, credible and authoritative. Black is sensuous, powerful, expensive, mysterious or evil depending on your use.

For example, solid black and bright red together can evoke danger. Yellow type over a black background is shown by many studies to be the most legible at a distance. Black and gold together make effective magazine ads for luxury items, and also work well for the cover of a classic book. Frank Lloyd Wright said gold goes with everything. I say it adds prestige to your cover if it fits the book's content, and you can mimic it pretty well with normal printing inks (standard four-color process) or instead use real metallic gold ink or gold foil stamping if your budget allows. We'll look at that in a moment.

Generally, men respond positively to blue. The color has the association of reliability and intelligence. Women consider it professional but depressing. They prefer red which is warm and intimate. They also respond well to pink, black, teal and brown (men also like brown). You've seen books that are clearly aimed at women and they share certain styles of shape and color.

Some colors become associated with a topic, such as green with the environment. You can plug into these trends but the basic psychological associations with color and shape, used appropriately, can help create an emotionally positive response.

In printing, there are very bright versions of some colors. They are so bright they almost glow and are called fluorescent. You frequently see them on magazine covers, but they are used effectively on book covers as well. They cost extra and not all commercial printers use them.

Here are some other methods that cost extra at the printer.

Foil Stamping: Metallic gold and silver inks are shiny and rich looking but foil stamping is the shiniest possible and can reflect light very brightly. Foil is available in different shades of gold, silver, various colors, even multi-colored holographic effects. When appropriate for the book's content, and used tastefully, these effects add perceived value to your product. It looks lavish. Ask your book printer to send samples.

Die Cut: Your cover has a small area cut out of it like a hole, or the cover's edges are cut short or are shaped. This can be a great effect but must be planned with care because a book cover can be torn if something gets through that hole and rips it, and the book will appear damaged.

Emboss: Something on the cover is raised so it seems a little bigger and you can also feel it, like a bump, with your fingers. This tactile quality adds more to the positive first impression of the book. You'll find this effect used mostly for titles but it can be used in other ways. An emboss can also be "sculpted" which means the effect is more than just raising, but the shape of the raised image is also carved like a sculpture up to almost an eighth inch high. The opposite of embossing is called debossing which pushes in your type or image, rather than pushing it out.

Matte and gloss varnish: Books don't always have to have a glossy cover. There is an alternative called matte. It does not shine but, instead, has a velvet-smooth feel under your fingers. It softens the cover's color contrast a little bit, so be prepared for that. For a nice effect, you can use both matte and gloss on the same cover. For example, make the title shiny while the rest of the cover is matte. This makes the title stand out. You'll notice this popular effect used on many books in different ways. Unlike the other effects, varnish is a standard printing practice and does not cost extra unless you combine two varnishes on the same cover. A printer may tell you about laminating your cover. This is similar to varnish. Ask for samples and cost comparisons.

Do titles and subtitles play a key role in an effective cover? Does the designer ever suggest a title or subtitle change?

I offer title ideas to authors who request it, but every author should be open to this kind of input. You can get too close to a project and a fresh perspective might be just what you need.

Get the best title you can. It should be memorable. Otherwise, your fans can't remember it to tell their friends! Don't skimp time on your title. Give this a lot of thought. Your book can only have one title, so make it count. You've spent a lot of time writing the book, so give it the title it deserves. You could benefit greatly from the input of a writer who specializes in marketing. Specialists in book marketing can bring you new and unexpected ideas for a creative, descriptive and memorable title. Search your title online to be sure it is not already used by someone else. (Titles of books cannot be copyrighted, but can be applied for a trademark.) Obviously, you don't want your target audience to confuse your book with another one.

What about a subtitle? If the title is memorable but its meaning is not obvious, add a subtitle for clarity. A title that needs no help is *How to Win Friends and Influence People* by Dale Carnegie. *The Power of Now* by Eckhart Tolle was given a clarifying subtitle. Both are huge bestsellers, so either way can work for you.

Are there colors and fonts that you avoid using? Why?

Colors, fonts and shapes are akin to words in a story, or maybe letters in the alphabet. When you put them together the right way, you create the desired response. So there are really no wrong letters, fonts or colors. It's how they're used.

On the other hand, maybe there is something you can avoid. You've seen the ice cooler at the supermarket with the word "ice" displayed largely. The font looks like it has ice all over it, right? This is fine for selling ice, but this font would cheapen the perceived value of your book unless you're being ironic, or your book is about an ice cooler. If not, you're asking to be judged unfairly because a cliché can instantly give a cheap, half-baked appearance to your cover and, by implication, your book. Avoid looking unoriginal and small-time. Avoid the cliché unless you are reinventing it somehow or bending its meaning to something new.

Another thing to avoid is too much cleverness. An inside joke. It may be fun to show someone the book (or tell them the title) and wait for them to get it. Maybe they don't get it, but that doesn't matter because you enjoy the idea so much. It may be precious to you, but it doesn't sell. Imagine someone seeing your book without you there to explain it to them. They don't get it. They walk away. Confuse, and you lose. Remember, you only have five seconds to create a positive and meaningful first impression.

What should an author look for when choosing a cover designer?

If the goal is to have a cover that will help sell many thousands of books, find a cover designer with experience doing that. The cover designer is a specialist and should be seriously dedicated, indeed passionate about their work. When you communicate, do they listen to you? Do you believe they can create the best cover for your book? Do you like their past work? It's a good sign if the covers they've designed make you feel an interest in the books themselves.

Reputation is also important. What do others say about them? Like choosing a contractor to build your house, you must be confident they know what they're doing. You'll be living with the results for a long time.

How does one tell a "designed" cover?

A well-designed cover makes the book appear well-written, current, even great. You sense the presence of quality. You want to own it right now, even before opening it. The secret behind this is the fusion of the title and its graphic treatment into one powerful, compelling moment of perception. It's like a bell that rings beautifully, and you can hear it. Many admit they sometimes buy a book solely because of its cover.

Genre plays a part in cover design, so how does one fit into their book category yet stand out?

When I start a new book cover design I must review what is already out there so I can position your book as superior. Sometimes that is easy because the other books look pretty lame, but it is wise to study the commonalities of the other books in your category so you'll fit in. You don't want your self-help book to be mistaken for fiction!

One basic way to fit into a category is with color. White is a common background for business or finance books. White is the clean, pressed shirt, right? Maybe it's even a laboratory coat which works well for other genres such as medical, health, even cooking. Bright pink is popular for "chick lit" and has been for years, but to say book categories will always look a certain way would be misguided because trends change. Sometimes the big publishers give an older book a new cover to keep it looking current. I visit amazon.com to research a category. You can, too. I love that website because it is a veritable sea of book covers.

How does the title play into cover design?

The title is fundamentally important (and the best one is memorable as I mentioned earlier). In graphic terms, the designer works with the title to make it convey its meaning instantly, fused with emotional power. For example, if the story is about hidden meanings it might be right to blur the type or otherwise slightly obscure it. If a non-fiction book is hard-hitting in style, the title will work very well in a simple, bold typeface. If the topic is history, use a typeface from that time period. If a title is especially long, vary the sizes (and you can also vary typefaces, but don't use more than two) of words and enlarge the important ones. If someone must look too long to understand your title you'll lose them fast unless you have something else on the cover that is very attractive.

The title typeface does not have to be special in itself. There are many bestselling books with covers that use ordinary type, and by ordinary I do not mean ugly or dull. Type design is a beautiful craft and type can convey meaning very well with dignity and emotion without visual gimmicks. In fact, it can be annoying if a typeface calls too much attention to itself with an awkward style. Some huge bestsellers use just ordinary type alone. In every case, it's the treatment of the entire cover that matters.

How important is the spine and back of the book design? After all, isn't the customer only looking at the front cover?

The back cover is certainly not a throw-away! It's the second of three short and fundamentally important steps of deciding to buy a book.

The first step is the front cover. The back cover is the next step. You'll pick up the book and turn it over to find out more—how great the book is, what you'll get from it, how it's better than the rest, how others have praised it, and a word about the author's special merits. All of this allows your customer's mind to justify the emotional decision that was already made with the front cover. Step three is to look inside the book, so be sure the interior is also well-designed.

A headline at the top of the back cover can help get attention and convey meaning quickly, as does a strong closing phrase at the bottom if there is room. You'll see books that do one or both of these, but only if they offer a benefit, ask a question, or create anticipation. Just plain information is not worth the space. You only have a few inches of space to sell, so do only that.

When editing back cover text, I'll use the words "you" and "your" as much as possible. You'd be amazed at how a dull paragraph of information can come alive with personal relevance when you use those magic words.

Your customer will read every sentence and even want more—when they believe it's about them.

When writing your back cover text, think of the radio interviews you'll be doing. How would you answer the question, "what's your book about" in a brief, compelling way? Use this framework to create a short paragraph or two. Write it like you would speak it. Talk to your reader. Empathize. Don't brag. It may feel like you're addressing the whole nation at once, but what you write will connect to people one at a time so when you write, aim your attention to one person.

Try to get some endorsements and testimonials. The more heartfelt they are—the more your book changed their life—the better. Use the endorser's entire name. Don't identify them as V.R. or Peggy H. or some other abbreviation or worse, their city. Anonymity throws doubt on their authenticity and hence your book's value. If you get great endorsements that are very long, edit them.

You can also make a summarized list of benefits, often called bullets. These are not necessarily complete sentences and you'll often see them on non-fiction back covers because they give an easy-to-read overview of "what's in it for me." Bullet points allow to you:

* Grab your reader's attention fast

* Save space

* Point out your book's strongest benefits

* Create a desire for your book

* Impress your friends!

Did you notice each bullet starts with a verb? It is more active and engaging that way. Notice also that the sentence introducing the bullets ended with a colon. "You'll discover how to:" is another way to introduce your bullets. Discover is a good word. In advertising, it's a much better word than learn. We don't really want to learn (too much work!) but we love to discover, and so do your readers.

The ISBN barcode goes in the lower right corner with a human-readable price nearby. Add U.S. after your price so buyers in other countries will know to convert it to their own currency. You may add a converted Canadian price (indicated CDN or CAN) near the U.S. price if you want to make it simpler for your Canadian neighbors. You'll see this on many books.

Include the book's category (genre) in the upper left corner or near the price. Don't invent a new category and don't combine categories or the bookstore chains will ignore you.

Visit www.bisg.org/standards/bisac_subject/index.html to find the latest trends in bookstore categories.

Your publishing company name or logo (or both) placed in the lower left corner adds credibility. You may put your website address near the logo. Study the back covers from major publishers and you'll find all these things. You don't have to invent a new way to do it.

Be sure to keep all your text, the logo and barcode at least a quarter inch away from the book's edge so it will not be trimmed off at the printing press (and remember this applies to the front cover, too).

The spine is the smallest part of a book, but plays a big part on a bookstore shelf. Actually, the spine might be seen before any other part of a book because when browsing, it's all you see on the shelf. A wider spine lets you show your title at a larger size. To thicken your book, an interior designer can help by increasing the line space, margins and type size to increase the page count. This also gives your book a bigger presence overall, more weight and a higher perceived value. Another method is to print on thicker paper. 50# is the standard paper choice, but 60# gives you more heft and many books use this. Ask your printer about a comparison of costs.

Graphically speaking, keep the spine simple and legible. The title and your name are obviously important, but the author's last name will suffice if room is tight. The subtitle also might not fit. Cramming too much in with small type sizes will make your spine hard to read and rather worthless. Make something big enough to see clearly and if you must choose one thing, make it the title. Add your company logo near the bottom. If you have no logo or it looks terrible at such a reduced size, just print the company name.

If you have enough room on the spine to include a picture, a face looking at you has real stopping power. Other images or strong variations of color can certainly get attention, too.

Another aspect of a book cover is flaps. A dust jacket naturally includes them. They tuck in to hold the jacket onto a hardcover book. Study the flaps of dust jackets and you'll typically find sales text. I like to also carry the color scheme or images from the cover into the flaps for added excitement. A softcover book can also have flaps, called french flaps. They fold into the book just like dust jacket flaps do. They add perceived value by evoking the more prestigious feel of a hardcover book.

What are the joys you've experienced in your profession?

There are many joys of being a full-time artist but as a book cover designer I've most appreciated the aesthetic partnership with authors and the lasting nature of books. In my experience, most self-publishing authors and small publishers are great people for whom this business is a labor of love. They make the world better, and make my world better. I always look forward to the next assignment.

Final Thoughts From My Side of the Pond

Every author gets emotionally wrapped up in their cover designs, and it's only natural to conjure up what you believe to be the perfect cover—and to be shocked when the real cover is a departure from your imagination. I've had authors call me up in tears, begging me to reconsider our stylistic choice. To date, we haven't honored those wishes. It's not because we enjoy sticking forks into our authors' eyes, but rather that we have a better idea as to what will attract John and Jane Buyer.

In reading George Foster's informative interview, you now realize there are a thousand tiny elements that go into a winning cover, and this is why we don't go about making changes to appease the author. This really is a case where Mom knows best.

Regardless of your publisher, be it Random House, a smaller independent commercial publisher, or if you are self-published, it's essential to understand the elements that go in to creating an effective and eye-catching cover, and I'm grateful to George for laying it out in such an eloquent manner.

In order to have a great cover, you need to have an experienced cover designer who understands packaging, color, font use, font choice and size, graphics, what's hot, what's dated, and, most importantly, does it meet the ten-foot test. The ten-foot test is, simply put, whether the customer can see the cover and title clearly from ten feet away. Most authors never take that into consideration until they're at a book event and see a cadre of squinting customers pass by. If the customers can't see it, they'll keep walking. And you know what? So will reviewers.

I'll never forget our meeting with the editors at *Publisher's Weekly*, and how they pawed through our books, oo'ing and ahh'ing over our covers.

The fiction editor picked up one of our books and waved it in the air. "I really love this cover," she cooed. My marketing director nearly passed out on the floor. The following month, that book received a glowing review.

I'm not saying that a great cover will guarantee a good review, or even a review at all. But I am saying that a lousy cover with muddy colors, hard-to-read fonts, and sophomoric graphics will be easily pushed aside.

In closing, I'm happy to report that every one of my crying authors called back to say how much they loved their covers and that, gee, maybe we were right all along. I'd love to bottle that kind of praise.

7: Distributors

Sam Speigel - Partners Publishers Group

You've taken great care to write a great book, but it doesn't end there. You have to make sure that your book is in the best possible hands in order to ensure that it sits on the store bookshelves. And this is what distribution is all about. Your publisher should have a knowledgeable sales team who has good relationships with the buyers. Many small presses sign with an independent distributor who has contracted sales forces meet with genre buyers to pitch their lineup. If your publisher doesn't have a distributor, then your chances of being in the bookstores and libraries are next to impossible.

To give some further clarification, Sam Speigel of Partners Publishers Group was gracious enough to answer some questions. Sam Speigel is the co-owner of Partners Book Dist., Partners/West Book Dist., Partners Publishers Group and Thunder Bay Press. He has worked in the book industry since 1980 and co-owned the various 'Partners' entities since 1984. Partners Book Dist., a wholesaler, opened in 1984; Thunder Bay Press followed in 1990; Partners Publishers Group, a distributor, opened in 1995 and Partners/West Book Dist., opened in 1997. Sam has had extensive experience with many aspects of the book business from wholesale to distribution to publishing but doesn't consider himself a book 'guru' and dislikes the term intensely.

What is a distributor, why are they important, who do they sell to, and how do they go about doing that?

A distributor in the book business is a step up from a wholesaler. In return for discount considerations (and please remember, you can't get something for nothing), a distributor will provide the following services that a wholesaler usually does not:

Selling to wholesalers: This would include Ingram and Baker & Taylor. Ingram and B&T are wholesalers, although Ingram now has its own distribution division, Ingram Publisher Services (IPS). The only remaining national wholesalers are Ingram, B&T, Partners, and Bookazine. (see FAQs: Bowkerlink for an independent comment on this).

Sales representation: Distributors will directly (either through regular catalogs and/or sales representatives) present publishers' titles to the major book retailers and wholesalers. Often distributors hire outside sales groups known as commission representatives who typically represent many different publishers, although usually only one distribution group. IPS has its own in house representatives, and so does Partners Publishers Group (PPG). Since most commission reps want a piece of the "big pie," one usually needs to give them a major account, which adds yet another cut into the book sales value. PPG does not hire outside reps and deals with the major accounts in house.

Time management: Distributors enable publishers to devote their time to marketing and developing new titles. Since distributors sell to both retail outlets and wholesalers, they generally assume the storage, shipping, and accounting costs. The publisher fills one PO at a time for their distributor, and they receive one consolidated statement from their distributor. The time/money savings more than make up for the extra discount given to the distributor.

Penetrating markets: Distributors may also help penetrate other markets, like big box stores such as Costco and Walmart, gift markets, and corporate sales. Not all do this and various additional costs may be involved.

Marketing: Distributors often provide help with marketing publishers' titles including directing them to co-operative advertising programs with the major book retailers and with wholesalers.

National Presence: Having a distributor rather than a wholesaler gives publishers a more "national" presence.

Distribution channels are particularly important to publishers with national titles that need maximum penetration into the marketplace. In the case of regional titles, the major book companies rely more on electronic access to titles in their database rather than physically placing—for example, a California title in a New York store.

Who qualifies for independent distribution, and what elements do you look for when considering a company/book for distribution? What are you looking for in a client?

Most distributors have different criteria for the publishers they accept. Most prefer larger publishers with many titles. Self publishers with just one or two titles are generally rejected by the larger distributors. PPG will still take on single title publishers as long as there seems to be a national market for the title and the publisher presents a national media-oriented marketing plan. In-store signings do not count.

When looking for new distribution clients, I look at several main items:

General "presentability": Does the layout and the overall graphic design make it pleasing to the end consumer, and does the book meet industry standards for barcodes.

Future Plans: The publisher has a direction/ plan for future titles, and is not just a one-time (maybe) wonder.

Marketing: The publisher has a marketing plan that will meet the standards of buyers. In-store signings may mean something to the individual store but they do not to a national buyer unless the author is nationally well-known. There is no point in touting a "national" tour if the buying public doesn't know who you are. A successful marketing plan needs to address media marketing, such as talk show appearances, whether on radio and TV, and possibly paid media promotional ads. Publisher/authors who do not orient promotion to the bookstores are not going to be very pleased with the sales results. I've had too many publishers, particularly those that have inspirational/self help titles, only promote their titles to "staged" groups and neglect the bookstores.

Realistic: The publisher is realistic about sales, and his EGO hasn't overtaken common sense. Whenever I hear an author/publisher say, "I'm the next Grisham/Clancy/Rowling, it immediately turns me off.

Marketability: PPG's approach is to tend to stay away from "national" fiction written by unknown authors because there is too much competition and marketing from major publishers. We also avoid memoirs. Most memoirs—WWII, Korean War, Vietnam Police Action, Panama Police Action or "growing up down on the farm" memoirs should be POD books destined for their relatives bookshelves.

Demand: Has some major company requested that I stock this title for them? This is a good start because it gives me a base retail client from which to work. And if one major retail client wants a title, there is a good chance I'll be able to sell the book to others.

With respect to vanity books, there are cases where considerations are made in relation to the book market and viability of the title. Those considerations are where the author retains the rights and can reprint himself. If it's a decent title, and the author has the rights, PPG will help arrange a reprint as long as the author obtains a new ISBN.

In one instance, Partners publishing division took over a title that was originally published by a Canadian Vanity Press, and now our press has published three titles for this author. I must reiterate that in the case of my companies, the decision about a title is based on the potential of the title itself.

Are there fees associated with book distribution? What happens if the publisher can't sell their books?

Most distributors charge a sliding scale of fees and you have to read the fine print in often long and boring contracts. Distributors don't want to wait to make their money from the profits of a sold title. As soon as a distributor touches a book, warehousing and handling fees come into play. When a distributor says the basic charge for services is 50% of net, this means that the net to a distributor on a $10.00 book is $5.00. And this is only the beginning.

There are fees for in and out charges, storage charges, returns charges, catalog charges, and a whole laundry list of charges. The publisher expects to net $3.00 on a $10.00 book and will have to pay prepress and printing costs out of that $3.00. A distributor is also not generally going to act as a prepress consultant without charging fees, since that is not the role of the distributor, unless they see some advantage in doing so.

Even with these fees, distributors will drop a title/publisher if there are insignificant sales, or if the sale of a significant quantity of books ends up generating an equally significant number of returns because a) the publishers has not effectively marketed the book, or b) the marketplace did not respond to the title (and this even happens to titles that make it to the zenith of book promotion—Oprah).

Most distributors will, or should, give their publishers some advice and suggestions over the telephone (layout/cover art for examples), particularly when it makes the end product more marketable.

As a distributor's client, what are the publisher responsibilities?

There are a number of responsibilities that must be assumed by the author/ publisher:

Marketing Plan: Buyers are not inclined to buy any quantity of an independently published title unless the distributor presents them with a marketing plan. It is the responsibility of the author/publisher to develop that marketing plan, and it is unlikely that most distributors will accept a title without at least a preliminary marketing plan.

Timing: Next is making sure the book(s) are printed and ready to go by or close to the announced release date. When buyers commit budget dollars to a title and usually these are allocated by a "season" (which may be 3-4 months in the case of chain buyers and correspond to the typical major publisher three seasons per publishing year), they become very upset if that title is not released within that buying season because the money allocated to that particular title could have gone to another title. Titles not on the shelf by the publication date cost the buyer budget and sales dollars. There can be occasional glitches, but a publisher who is consistently late with titles will find buyers less willing to buy those titles. If a title is going to be late, you have to let your distributor know and give them a new firm date. Excuses that sound like the old 'dog ate my homework' excuse are not acceptable when money is involved.

Marketing Implementation: While the distributor can help with marketing suggestions and opportunities, most of the legwork still has to be done by the publisher. Most major publishers only allow their publicity departments to work on a title during its publication "season," which is usually 3-4 months. Once that season is over, the publicist moves on to titles for the next season. If an author wants to have their title to maintain any shelf life or "legs," then they have to constantly work on marketing instead of just calling their publisher and whining about the lack of sales.

Shipping: Shipment of books to the distributor is essential. If the distributor is not warehousing the entire print run or is waiting on a reprint, the publisher needs to either ship the books asap when ordered, or arrange the reprint quickly. Distributors do not reorder just to fill space in warehouses: they order because they have orders for those titles.

What are a distributor's responsibilities?

* **Database Setup:** Once a title is accepted for distribution, the distributor needs to set this title up in various databases, typically Ingram, B&T, Amazon, B&N, Borders, and the other customer databases with which the distributor works. It is usually the responsibility of the publisher to make sure the Bowker database has accurate information.

* **Send Information:** Once the title(s) is in those data bases, the distributor has to send the buyers information about the title. Some only need a buy sheet, others want to see the actual book.

* **Follow Up:** Once the presentation is made to the buyer (and this doesn't necessarily have to be face to face since buyers will only see sales reps if they have five titles in a category for the CURRENT season), the distributor has to follow up to make sure the title is bought. Sometimes buyers will give the rep an approximate initial order quantity, and it is likely that the actual order will not come through for three or four months because that is the typical "season" with which the buyer works. Sometimes buyers will buy titles based on just a cover and marketing plan. It is more likely that these buyers will ask for a finished book particularly from independent publishers. Most major buyers will not buy a title based on seeing only an ARC (advanced reading copy).

* **Shipment:** Once the distributor has the order, then it is essential that the title(s) is shipped in a timely fashion.

How do clients get paid for sales? How often?

Typically, distributors pay for sales when there are confirmed sales to consumers at the bookstore level. Several years ago, Nielsen Bookscan began gathering sales figures from many booksellers, so now distributors can check the number of copies actually sold. Most distributors will pay in 90 EOM (end of month) based on sales date (for a book sold in

May, the publisher will be paid the end of August), but there are many variations on this.

With single titles publishers, PPG, for example, often starts at 180 day EOM payments because if a single title publisher is paid at 90 EOM and the books are returned 90 days later, the publisher will be in a negative cash flow with the distributor. Distributors are not banks so you can't expect the distributor to fund your publishing program. Once a book establishes a sales pattern, it is likely that the distributor will be willing to adjust the payment schedule. The sooner you ship your books to the distributor, the sooner the distributor can ship to stores, the sooner sales can start and the sooner you will be paid.

Some distributors have huge client lists, so how do they avoid competing against each other?

Often distributors have catalogs an inch or more thick and represent three to four hundred clients. While it may sound harsh, the truth is that publishers do not receive equal representation. In order to see a buyer directly, the publisher or distributor must have five titles in a season. To get around that, distributors will often pick up several cookbook publishers, for example, in order to directly present the one or two titles they really want to sell.

There is certainly competition for sales among similar titles in a category and the titles with the more effective marketing plans (and/or marketing dollars budgeted for co-op—meaning the amount of marketing dollars that go to a specific customer to display a title on a specific table or in a promotional feature) are the titles that are bought. Although most bookstores now inventory 125,000+ titles, far more titles are published annually than bookstores can effectively shelve.

My own experience is that if a distributor has a good relationship with a buyer, it is not necessary to add "cannon fodder" to the list. You can accomplish as much by e-mail and telephone as with a direct visit. Not that I'm disparaging direct visits entirely since one of their primary purposes is not simply to sell titles but to maintain the relationship with that buyer.

Do you go to the trade shows?

Keeping one's contacts is the main reason for going to trade shows. Fewer and fewer actual sales are made at trade shows (except perhaps at shows such as Frankfort, which are specifically geared toward language rights sales).   Most serious buying is done away from the trade show floors and in general, these trade shows are little better than dog and pony shows.

How does one determine a quality distributor? What should publishers look for in a distributor?

Deciding on a distributor is the most difficult initial decision a publisher has to make. Publishers can make their decisions based on:

* Distributor presentations

* Distributor websites

* References from other publishers

* A distributor's track record of sales

* Recommendations from a distributor's customers

* How long a distributor has been in business

* The range of a distributors accounts and how these relate to their title(s). Some titles do better in bookstores; others in the gift market. Keep in mind that not all distributors handle the gift market.

Distributors who charge upfront fees have already made a certain amount of money (they would say this is an insignificant amount) from their publishers, so do they have a real incentive to go out and sell their clients' titles? If they want to make money from the actual book sales as opposed to processing fees, the answer is yes.

My company, PPG charges a flat discount and does not have a fee scale based on title listings, in and out charges, returns processing charges and cataloging fees. We do charge if the publisher wishes to participate in advertising programs. For example, a full color page in an Ingram Targeted Advance is approximately $1800.00

There isn't an easy or simple formula for deciding on which distributor to use. I have had publisher clients come to PPG from other distributors, and I have had clients who have left PPG for supposedly greener pastures. I have had some who have left and returned. And some have switched from wholesale to distribution, and vice versa. Many distributors have a totally inflexible formula and agreements. Publishers need to do comparative homework to find a distributor who will make some accommodation to their needs.

Do you help with marketing plans?

PPG will help with marketing plans insofar as to generally review a publisher's marketing plan and make suggestions. We can also guide the publisher to certain marketing opportunities, either directly with stores, or online promotions with Shelf Awareness, Booksense, PW, and with wholesalers.

What is the biggest frustration you encounter with your business and your clients?

The biggest overall frustration I encounter is clients who have unreasonable expectations; from the ones who think they are the second coming of JK Rowling, to the ones who think theirs is the only book about a certain subject on the market. There are many others:

* Publishers who don't understand the complexities of the various data bases and the time frames under which particularly national buyers operate.

* Those publishers who do not publish their books on a timely schedule and then wonder why buyers won't buy them, or cut the buys.

* Publishers who tell us about new titles at the last minute and expect them to be in the stores by some process of osmosis.

* New publishers (and sometimes ones who should be more experienced) who think they are going to change the way the book industry operates (as flawed as it is, no single independent publisher is going to change it).

* Publishers who don't realize and accept the fact that RETURNS are a part of the business: some stores order and some return.

* The particular foibles of publishers, trucking companies and shippers who don't understand that books are fragile and, if they are going to arrive in stores in saleable condition, then they must be packed properly at all stages in the process.

* And last but not least, publishers who have attitude and their own agenda which may have nothing to do with the distributor's agenda or the workings of the book world.

The point is that there is still opportunity in the book business. You couldn't walk into a Toys 'R Us and expect anyone to pay attention to an independently produced toy. Yet, in the book business there is still this opportunity. Many bookstores may not want to buy a title(s) directly, but by working with a wholesaler or distributor that has the connections, that same title(s) have at least a fighting chance to be on bookstore shelves.

The principle task is that the publisher must do the necessary promotion to get customers into the stores and buy them.

If you think of the book industry as an hourglass, with 60,000+ titles per year in the upper half and bookstores with 125,000+ titles in the lower half, you will soon see that the bookjam is in the middle of that hourglass. By using a wholesaler or distributor, you can make the flow through that hourglass go much more smoothly and effectively.

8: Independent Editing

"My editor will clean it up"

I heard this comment while eavesdropping on a group of writers at a conference. They had just come out of a seminar that discussed the importance of editing a manuscript before it goes out for submission.

"Why should I worry about POV switches and dialog tags," one writer said. "My strength is in my story, and I don't have time to bother learning all the other stuff."

Ok, let's assume you believe your story is so great that it will transcend any niggly mistakes like POV switches or excessive dialog tags, and off you go into query-ville. This is often where a dose of reality is good for the soul.

Unfortunately, many authors experience this reality check backwards. They are rejected over and over again by large numbers of editors because their story has a serious case of editing dysentery. And if the author stops to fix the work, chances are pretty good that we'll remember the work should it land on our doorstep again. So the author is in a bind. Do they risk re-submitting to the same editors knowing they may have a black mark next to their name, or worse, do they decide not to resubmit and decrease their options?

My recommendation; don't do this backwards. If you are unsure about manuscript finesse, have an independent editor read and critique your work. Let them look for all the warts. Are there effective transitions between paragraphs? Are you working with one POV per scene? Are you "comma-tose" and need a lesson on how and where commas go in a sentence? This can be the difference between a rejection and a contract. Yep, it's that important.

Editors don't have to be happy with "it's good enough" because the competition is tough these days, and "great" lurks around every corner. Don't be the writer I overheard and assume we'll clean, powder, and press your Freddy Krueger literary nightmare into a work of art, no matter how great the story. Chances are very strong that we won't. Never forget that he who has the shiniest fishing pole gets the most fish.

Mike Sirota

Mike is an award-winning feature writer and editor for a Southern California newsmagazine, the *San Diego Jewish Times*. Honors include a Simon Rockower Prize (the "Jewish Pulitzer"). Mike facilitated many private read and critique workshops, and taught seminars and classes for various educational systems, including Palomar College, MiraCosta College, and the San Diego City Schools GATE (Gifted and Talented Education) Program. He served for many years as an instructor for the University of California, San Diego (UCSD) Extension and is currently a workshop leader for the two Southern California Writers Conferences, and the La Jolla Writers Conference. The latter conference honored Mike with its first "Person of Letters" award "for his ongoing and unselfish contributions to and support of the writing community." Many of his students and clients have found agency representation and publication with the help of Mike Sirota Writing Services (www.mikesirota.com).

Published Works

1977-1981, seven novels (*Prisoner of Reglathium, Conqueror of Reglathium, Caves of Reglathium, Dark Straits of Reglathium, Slaves of Reglathium, Berbora, Flight From Berbora*), Manor Books

1982-1989, six novels (*Master of Boranga, Shrouded Walls of Boranga, Journey to Mesharra, Demons of Zammar, Twentieth Son of Ornon, Golden Hawk of Zandraya*), Zebra Books (editor: Roberta Grossman)

1990-1992, two novels (*Demon Shadows, The Well*), Bantam Books (editors: Carolyn Nichols, Jana Silverstein)

1993-present, four novels (*Quantum Force [Young Adult], Bicycling Through Space and Time, The Ultimate Bike Path, The 22nd Gear*), Pocket Books and Berkley Publishing Company (Berkley editor, Ginjer Buchanan)

What is an independent editor, and why do writers need one?

Literary agents—the current accepted conduit between writers and publishing houses—state that they return (read: reject) 99 percent of all manuscripts that are submitted to them. A writer, especially an unpublished one, needs every conceivable edge to become part of the one percent who will find representation. It is not enough that a writer's spouse, her sister-in-law, or her nephew loved her manuscript. (It's true. I hear this from many writers: "My family and friends thought it was a great story.") This initial "fan base" only serves to stroke egos while offering little in the way of constructive critiquing—unless, of course, they are professionals in the field, which is seldom the case.

An experienced independent editor/writing coach can prove invaluable to a writer. For starters, he is not part of your "fan club" and will look at your project in an objective manner. Let's say, for example, that you want to have a fiction manuscript evaluated. A skilled editor will look for the following: Does the story immediately grab a reader's attention (the "hook")? Are the characters believable? Is the dialogue powerful, and have you balanced it well enough with your narrative? Have you chosen effective point-of-view characters to tell your story? Is your setting realistic? Have you framed your plot well? Is your pacing consistent?

But beyond all of the details involved in helping a writer develop a submission-ready manuscript, perhaps the single most important service that an independent editor can offer is to see that the new writer handles every aspect of this venture in a professional manner. The word "professional" cannot be emphasized enough. I have heard more than my share of literary agents complain about the lack of professionalism from so many of the writers who contact them. A professional approach to marketing your manuscript is often the edge you need for your manuscript to become part of the aforementioned one percent.

This true story illustrates the point about professionalism, or lack thereof. At a writers' conference, a significant literary agent who had been networked from the moment she set foot in the building needed a break. She went to the ladies' room, entered a stall and sat down to take care of business. Suddenly, a manuscript came sliding under the stall door. There followed the patter of little feet as the perpetrator hastily exited the ladies' room. (Had I been in the stall, my response would have likely been, "Thank you, I just ran out of paper in here.")

How did the idea of independent editors come about? Is this something publishing houses wanted to take the load off of them?

This might be a "chicken or egg" question. For starters, let's go back in time to when there were few literary agents and fewer, if any, independent editors. Writers mostly submitted their manuscripts right to publishing houses, and the editors there would review a considerable portion of the submission—unless it proved totally unreadable—before either rejecting the project or taking it on. The editor would then work closely with the writer through all of the stages of the revision process to elevate the manuscript to "publishing-ready" status.

For the most part, those days are long gone.

As publishing became more of a "bottom-line" business, smaller publishing houses began to merge under large corporate umbrellas. Harried editors found themselves reading submissions for two, three, or even more imprints. Attention spans grew shorter, tolerance levels lower. If every aspect of a submission was not top notch (read: professional), the manuscript went back in the SASE posthaste.

Enter, the literary agent. While they had been around for a while, their roles grew in importance as more and more people dreamt of becoming published authors (this is the entertainment business, after all) and editors at publishing houses became overwhelmed with submissions. Before long, literary agents evolved into the "screeners" for the publishers. With their reputations on the line, agents made sure they were submitting only the best of the best. Nowadays, the majority of the larger houses, and some smaller ones, state in their submission guidelines wording such as: "Agented submissions only," or "Does not accept unagented submissions."

So now, the literary agents were (and are) receiving hundreds of submissions a month. If anything, the independent editor evolved from literary agencies, not publishing houses, needing to take the load off of them. Agents will reject submissions for many different reasons, some of which are not even about the book itself. (Remember: professional.) Nor will they wait too long. We independent editors and writing coaches identified this need to impress an agent in every aspect of a submission, having experienced it ourselves as published authors, former literary agents or one-time publishing house editors. From this, I suppose, a new industry was born.

Publishers look for the story and don't pay that much attention to spelling and grammar, right?

I would hate to answer a blanket, "wrong," on this question. In all my years of experience, I have learned that nothing about the publishing business is carved in stone. One successful writer I know placed a manuscript full of typos and grammar problems with a literary agent, who then placed it with a major publisher. How? Because she was (and is) an exceptional storyteller. In this (rare) instance, the technical problems were overlooked.

That said, a significant literary agent speaking at a recent writers' conference told attendees, "If I find one typo in the first five pages of your manuscript, I stop reading and send it back." True, this may be the other extreme—but is it worth taking the chance? I would opt for the

"Mary Poppins" manuscript: practically perfect. This, again, is about being professional.

Won't my publisher's editing team take care of my manuscript? Is this true for large and small publishers?

To reiterate, you may not get this far if your manuscript is in bad shape. But if you do, don't count on the publisher's editing team to right all wrongs. A smaller publisher will be more involved in the editorial process, since they're only publishing a handful of books a year and want them to be their best. They may even offer suggestions for improving the narrative. A large publisher, which may release dozens of titles a month, will likely have a copyeditor do a quick cleanup on the manuscript, but not much beyond that. So okay, your book gets published, but who knows how much better it could have been if someone with a strong editorial eye had worked with you beforehand? This is the role of the independent editor/writing coach.

One of my writers placed a mystery novel with a small press publisher. I had guided him through the entire process, including a final line edit. The publisher took the novel on because she loved the story, but she told the writer that what cinched the deal was how "clean" the manuscript was, that they had so little to do to it, editorially.

At what point should I hire the services of an independent editor?

I prefer to work with writers who have completed a manuscript and have gone through at least one round of revisions. This is the point where many writers lose objectivity about their own work and need a good second eye. Having an overview of an entire project enables me to offer the most effective suggestions for improving it. Upon occasion I will look at the first fifty to one hundred pages of a work in progress, and if it shows considerable promise I may assist the writer throughout the process. The more a writer has completed, the more "bang for the buck" he/she will receive when working with an editor or coach.

There seem to be editing services advertising everywhere on the Internet and in magazines, and all of them charge varying fees. It can be an intimidating and daunting task choosing one. How does a writer go about finding a good editor? What qualities should writers look for?

Nothing is better than a personal referral. Network others who have used freelance editors and find out what their experience was like. Study editors' websites to learn the extent of their services, as well as their background in the publishing business, and, of course, their successes. Some publishers and literary agents keep lists of editors with whom they are familiar, and they will provide these to writers. Check the website called "Preditors & Editors" for any red flags that might have been raised about an editor's services.

As an independent editor I provide my writers with detailed written evaluations of their projects, though not until I have personally discussed all of my notes with them, either face to face or over the phone. Your editor should do this. Make sure their experience in the publishing world is extensive. Before working with writers I owned a bookstore, wrote over two dozen novels and published nineteen of them, taught classes on writing from middle grade through college, served on the faculty of a number of writers' conferences, and worked as a feature writer and editor of a newsmagazine.

An independent editor should be able to perform the work in a timely manner. My own lead time is normally six to eight weeks to begin the work. I often need to put in "overtime" to make sure no one has to wait much longer than that. I've known of independent editors giving writers lead times of four, five, even six months. This, I think, is unreasonable—unless you know that you won't be ready to have your manuscript looked at for at least that long a period of time. Then by all means get yourself scheduled, if you feel that the editor is the best one for you. On the other end of the spectrum, if a freelance editor can take your project on "next week," I would have serious issues with that. Those of us who are worth our salt are normally kept quite busy. As for fees, like all things in life, you get what you pay for.

Make sure your editor is well connected in the profession. I personally know many literary agents, and even some publishers. If I feel strongly that a writer's work is what I refer to as "professional grade," I will refer that writer to an agent. In nearly all cases I will initiate the contact.

How can a writer know they're getting what they paid for?

A writer once came to me with a 90,000-word manuscript, which I first evaluated, and then helped her with chapter-by-chapter revisions. Toward the end of the process she told me, "I had a large manuscript when I first came to you, but it was not the story I had envisioned. Now, it is." If your editor has done his/her job, you will see the difference in your work, and I think there is no better measure for getting your money's worth.

Do independent editors have connections to agents and publishers?

Not all of them do. But those of us with connections offer an invaluable extra service to writers, the chance to cut through the "slush pile" and have their work noticed. As I said before, I would make this a key part of the criteria for seeking out the best freelance editor for you.

Do publishers recommend independent editorial services to potential authors? Why would they if they have their own editors?

Publishers appreciate clean, well-written, "professional-grade" manuscripts, so it can benefit them to recommend a freelance editor to a writer whose project is "on the bubble." That is, they like the subject matter or storyline, but the project requires too much work for their own limited resources—including in-house editors—to take the project on.

Do agents contact independent editors to help make their clients' work more saleable?

My own experience has been that agents refer writers to me before they agree to representation, because they feel that the project has too many problems for them to take on. But they may also request a second look if the writer has significantly improved the project, and this second look is rare for most agents.

Along those lines, I have spoken with agents after they've indicated issues with projects that I referred to them. After finding out what they're specifically looking for, I've gone back to writers and assigned them the revisions. Some agents have taken on projects after the second, even third go-round.

How long does a normal/standard edit take? How many rewrites can authors expect to make?

There is no "one size fits all" answer to this question. Some manuscripts need extensive rethinking and revisions. After their initial evaluations I have worked with writers for six months, a year, and even longer to raise their projects to a "professional-grade" level. Other manuscripts are so well conceived and presented that a minimal round of revisions has taken a couple of months or less. Some writers "get it" quicker than others. Others have already begun to "get it" before even approaching me.

What are some of the frustrations you have when working with writers' manuscripts?

Wow, I could probably fill a book with answers to this question alone! Rather than get all nit-picky, I would say that my biggest frustration comes from recognizing (rather quickly, in most cases) that the writer who just sent me a 95,000-word fiction manuscript to evaluate had no clue what he was doing, either before he started writing the story, or all during the year or so it took him to write it. He had not taken any writing classes, or attended any writers' conferences, or participated in either a facilitated or peer read/critique group, or subscribed to writers' magazines, or for that matter read any how-to books on the craft of writing. Nor did it seem, inexplicably, that he was well read in his genre, or in any type of novel, for that matter. Okay, he managed to get all of these words down on paper, and for that he deserves some credit. Still, is this manuscript close to professional grade? Is it ready for prime time? No more than the piano that you just bought and put into your living room means that you're ready to perform at Carnegie Hall. A few years of PRACTICE are in order before that has a chance at becoming reality. It is no different with writing a book.

A writer that I meet at a conference, for example, will tell me that her manuscript starts off slow, but after ten pages it really gets good. I tell her that, before she sends it to me, she should move page eleven up to the front. Slow, expository pages will neither hook nor hold anyone. More important, let me paraphrase what nearly all agents are telling writers these days when asked how they go about judging whether a manuscript is worthy of representation: "I read the first sentence. If I like it, I read the first paragraph. If I like it, I read the first page. And if I like that, I turn the page." That's the HOOK, folks. Had you paid attention to the craft of writing, I would not have had to tell you about it."

I've told writers that their POV was ineffective, that they were mixing first and third, or bouncing omnisciently between numerous characters. Their response: "What's a POV?" I'm not making this up! You've spent a year writing a manuscript and you don't know what a POV is?

Serve your apprenticeship. Learn the craft of writing. Read a hell of a lot. Network with your peers and others in the business. Then, PRACTICE, PRACTICE, PRACTICE.

And when the student is ready, the teacher will appear.

Final Thoughts From My Side of the Pond

I have had the pleasure of hearing Mike speak several times at conferences, and he said something that impressed me so much because it is so true, and that is the idea of, "Yeah, I can do that."

"Can you flesh out the main character's motivations?"

"Yeah, I can do that."

"Can you move the story arc more toward the beginning?"

"Yeah, I can do that."

"Can you give your main character a better ending?"

"Yeah, I can do that."

"Can you get rid of all these dialog tags?"

"Yeah, I can do that."

Sigh. There are no sweeter words than an author who's willing to learn and work hard. I've worked with Mike several times, and I've always appreciated how he subliminally prepares authors for the editing process. By the time those authors have a contract in hand, they are able to deal with critiques in a professional manner and know to check their egos in at the door.

Mike is there to take care of the major editing meltdowns and get a manuscript submit-ready. But that doesn't mean authors won't be scrutinized by their publisher's editors. They will absolutely go through another round of edits, so authors are smart to be prepared. But by this time, the author understands the elements of writing and is mindful about keeping them very handy in their tackle box so they can always say with confidence, "Yeah, I can do that."

9: Warehouse Distribution

Playing Hopscotch

Publishing is a lot like hopscotch. You have to find a good rock to toss down on the little square before hopping your way down the grid on one foot. You only get two chances to put both feet down at the same time, so you have to maintain your balance most of the time. If you lose your balance and put your other foot down, you have to go to the back of the line and wait your turn. Hopscotch is frustratingly unforgiving—a lot like publishing. You have to stay balanced and have the right rock in order to get your books out to market. And one of those ways is establishing a relationship with Ingram—the Great Yoda of warehouse distribution.

So what is a warehouse distributor? It's simply a centralized location that bookstores and libraries can call to order books. Ingram warehouses books from thousands of publishers from all over the world, and is far more efficient than having bookstores call fifty billion individual publishers.

You, as the author, may not feel this information is important to the outcome of your success. But if author events and book signings are a part of your promotional strategy, then you need to be sure your publisher is making your book available to those stores that need to order and stock your book. And it has to be easy. For that reason, Ingram is the standard go-to warehouse distributor for those orders. If the book isn't available through Ingram, chances are the stores won't bother trying to order it from another source. Goodbye potential sales, hello frustrated author. Yep, Ingram is that important.

There is often a lot of confusion surrounding Ingram—what are they? What do they do? Do they have a sales force or just distribute books to bookstores? Can any publisher be a part of Ingram? I'm grateful for their participation.

Again, why is this important to you, the author? Availability is key in this business, and you need to understand how easy it is for a publisher to be a part of Ingram. It will help you make intelligent decisions if they aren't.

Ingram

What is Ingram, and who uses your services?

Publishers with titles that are trade ready, but have not chosen a print services provider should consider Lightning Source, an Ingram Company.

For publishers representing offset or post-print production titles, Ingram manages product as a wholesaler, Ingram Book Company, and as an exclusive distributor, Ingram Publisher Services.

What is Lightning Source?

New technology has fundamentally changed the way people access and read books. As the book industry continues to evolve in this fast-paced, demanding world, Lightning Source provides essential services for both print-on-demand and e-book fulfillment. We handle the technology so publishers, booksellers and libraries can concentrate on what they do best.

Lightning Source provides comprehensive end-to-end digital fulfillment services. These range from content management and storage, and digital rights management to secure e-book delivery, and distribution of printed "on demand" books. A title can be delivered any time, anywhere in any available format. This is made possible by the transparent infrastructure Lightning Source provides.

Titles represented by Lightning Source can be made available in Ingram Book Company inventory. More information on Lightning Source can be found on their website:

https://www.lightningsource.com/

"My publisher is small and publishes very few books. Can they still be a part of your database?"

Publishers not represented or publishers seeking to establish a direct purchasing relationship with Ingram Book Company must first meet our minimum of having ten or more titles actively in print. Our ten title policy is relative only to titles that a publisher will be selling to Ingram Book Company. Publishers not meeting our minimum are able to provide their titles to Ingram indirectly, through the services of companies managing small press. A list of these companies can be found on our website:

http://www.ingrambook.com/new/distributors.asp

If interested in establishing terms with Ingram Book Company, a qualifying publisher is required to submit materials for our review. Our guidelines for submission can be found on our website here:

http://www.ingrambook.com/new/publishers.asp

What do they need to provide?

For the purpose of our review, an interested publisher should submit a parcel containing our questionnaire, (found on our website), book samples, (one copy each of your ten best selling titles), and any current catalogs or marketing materials.

Publishers with questions can contact us at:

bookbuyer@ingrambook.com

Ingram is a wholesaler to the trade market. Do you have distribution services for commercial presses who are looking for sales teams to pitch their books to the market?

Launched only three years ago, Ingram Publisher Services has become a leader in the publishing industry. We have a very strong roster of 65+ client-publishers.

We are a full-service book distributor, providing publishers with a menu of services including sales representation, marketing programs, title marketing, physical distribution, inventory storage and management, and many other services. We sell to the widest possible range of retail stores and wholesale companies.

More information can be found on the Ingram Publisher Services website:

http://www.ingrampublisherservices.com/

Publishers with questions can contact us at:

acquisitions@ingrampublisherservices.com

Final Thoughts From My Side of the Pond

How many times have I heard heartbreaking tales from authors who arrived at their book event only to find that the store didn't have any books? How many times have I heard about an author trying to book an event with a store only to be told "sorry, no can do"? In both scenarios, the author lost out because their publisher didn't have a relationship with Ingram. If these marketplaces can't get their books from Ingram, they're usually not going to get them. And the author rarely knows about this until it's too late.

So why doesn't a publisher warehouse their titles with Ingram to make it easier for bookstores? In every case I've investigated, the publisher is looking to cut costs. There is a fee per title associated with Ingram's services—and it's worth it. Let me say right now that publishing is not a poor man's occupation, and you have to spend money to make money. Yet many publishers try, and it always, always, always works to the author's disadvantage.

I know what you're thinking; isn't the publisher also affected? In truth, they are. But this is offset by fact that these publishers aren't dependent upon outside sales to keep them afloat because their primary buyers are their own authors. If you're operating a company on a shoe-string budget, it's more economical to charge your authors whatever price you want rather than pay Ingram a per-title fee to warehouse books that may or may not sell. Is this right? I'll leave that up to you to decide after you've read Section 3—Fishing For a Publisher.

I know what your other question is, too. Aren't there other warehouse distributors who don't charge a per-title fee? Yes, there are, but they are far smaller and usually cater to niche markets, such as libraries or specialty stores. Ingram covers all the mainstream bookstore market, including online stores, and if your publisher doesn't have a relationship with them, you and your book will be at a disadvantage. Plain and simple.

10: Internet Resources

Help In Cyberworld

There is no lonelier place to be than residing in your own skin when you're scared and filled with questions.

Who are the good agents?

Is my query letter any good?

What do agented-only submissions mean?

How can I recognize a scam publisher?

What's Print-on-Demand?

What is a comma splice, and how do I check for POV switches?

How long do I wait for a reply from an editor before contacting them?

Where can you go to get trustworthy answers to a wide range of topics? Why, the Internet, of course! When going to a writer's site, consider the source. Who is the person writing the blog or hosting the message board? Are they a thinly-cloaked vanity press who discusses the evils of trade publishers? If so, you aren't going to get anything close to a balanced opinion. Are they an agent who justifies all sorts of reasons why paying reading fees is normal business? Or are they well-published authors who have an instinctual desire to uncover the seamy underbelly of the industry? Read sites and blogs with this in mind: do they have an agenda?

I've seen many sites who profess to be benevolent benefactors while spilling out all sorts of erroneous information that serves to confuse the new writer and service their agenda. On the flip side there are many wonderful Internet sites that are designed to help the author learn about all aspects of the industry, and I've been granted the good fortune to include three fine examples, Writer Beware, Litopia, and The Absolute Write Water Cooler. Their experience and good will have helped protect thousands of writers and even seen the launch of a number of successful careers.

Victoria Strauss - Absolute Write Water Cooler

Victoria Strauss is the author of seven fantasy novels for adults and young adults, including the Stone duology (*The Arm of the Stone* and *The Garden of the Stone*) and the Way of Arata duology (*The Burning Land* and *The Awakened City*). She has written hundreds of book reviews for magazines and ezines, including SF Site, and her articles on writing have appeared in *Writer's Digest* and elsewhere. In 2006, she served as a judge for the World Fantasy Awards.

An active member of the Science Fiction and Fantasy Writers of America, Victoria is Vice-Chair of the Committee on Writing Scams, and co-founder of Writer Beware, a publishing industry watchdog group that tracks and warns about literary schemes, scams, and pitfalls. She moderates the Bewares & Background Check forum at the Absolute Write Water Cooler, and maintains the popular Writer Beware website (www.writerbeware.org/) and blog (www.accrispin.blogspot.com/).

Learn more about Victoria at her own website:

www.victoriastrauss.com/.

What is the Absolute Write Water Cooler, and why is this site such a great resource?

The Absolute Write Water Cooler is an online writers' community attached to Absolute Write, a writers' resource site. The Cooler includes forums on a huge variety of subjects and issues of interest to writers—publishers, literary agents, self-publishing, freelancing, markets and genres, critiquing, job and networking opportunities, reading groups . . . the list goes on. There are also several Coffee Break forums for socializing and getting silly, a number of general discussion groups, and last but certainly not least, the Bewares & Background Check forum, moderated by me, which lets writers ask questions about, and discuss their experiences with, agents, publishers, editors, contests, and other writing-related professionals and organizations.

We're all familiar with Internet flame wars, and most people have had some experience with how nasty online forums can get. Of the many groups, forums, and message boards I've participated in over the years, the Cooler is one of the friendliest and most supportive. Alert moderators make sure that things stay civil, that discussion doesn't get out of hand, and that trolls don't sideline topics. The Cooler has sparked many friendships—and even one marriage!

What kind of people read and post to the Water Cooler? How informed are they? Can I trust the information?

Water Cooler members represent an extremely wide range of interests, skills, and expertise. Some are hobbyists; some seriously aspire to publication. Some have just sold their first work; some have decades-long careers. They are small press-published, large press-published, self-published, magazine- and e-zine-, and newspaper-published. They write in every genre and every market. They represent many writing-related careers—editors, agents, publishers, publicists, and others.

The participation of these publishing professionals is one of the Cooler's strengths. Since most post under their own names, or provide links in their signatures to their websites and blogs, it's easy to confirm that they really are experts. Of course, as in any writers' community, there are those who don't know as much as they think they do, or who are misinformed, or who have biases or agendas that make them less than objective. If you're new to the Cooler, you do need to take a bit of time to get to know who's who. Once you do, you'll have a better sense of whose advice it's safe to trust.

As wonderful a resource as the Cooler is, and as much solid information and advice as the knowledgeable people there provide, no writers' forum is a substitute for independent research. Even on a reliable forum like the Cooler, information is often given piecemeal or out of context, which can make it difficult to put the puzzle pieces together. Writers owe it to themselves to become as educated as possible about the publishing world before they start trying to sell their work. Knowledge is your greatest ally, and your best defense. This is true of any profession, and no less true for writing.

How did the Water Cooler get started, and why?

The Absolute Write website was founded by professional writer Jenna Glatzer, who wanted to create a comprehensive writers' resource. In addition to a newsletter, articles, interviews, and market listings, she included a writers' forum where writers could gather to discuss writing and publishing issues. The original Cooler was a fraction of the size it is today, with a fraction of the membership. I don't think even Jenna could have foreseen how much it would grow, or how popular a resource it would become.

If I have questions regarding a publisher, agent, or the publishing process can I ask my questions on this site?

Absolutely. For general questions, the Water Cooler includes Ask the Agent and Ask the Editor forums, as well as forums for different markets (fiction, nonfiction, children's writing, etc.) and genres (romance, mystery, literary, etc.)

For questions about specific agents, publishers, and others, the Bewares & Background Check forum is the place to go. It includes hundreds of threads about agents, publishers, editors, contests, writers' services, and more. As "Bewares" suggests, the forum is a resource for information on publishers, agents, and others with abusive or nonstandard business practices—but "Background Check" is also important, and there are at least as many threads that focus on reputable individuals and companies, where writers post helpful information on submission guidelines, response times, changes in personnel, etc.

Is there a place where I can get writing critiques?

The very active Share Your Work forum includes topics for just about every kind of writing—cookbooks, plays, screenplays, memoirs, nonfiction, various kinds of fiction, even query letters. Any Cooler member is welcome to post his or her work for comment and critique. Moderators keep an eye on things to be sure the discussion remains constructive. Criticism is honest, though, and sometimes blunt—so writers need to be sure they're ready for that.

Can the Water Cooler help me get an agent or publisher?

In the sense that the Cooler can help you research markets and improve your skills and knowledge, it can certainly be helpful in the search for an agent or publisher. But you'll still have to do the legwork yourself. The Cooler won't make connections for you, nor do agents and publishers cruise the site looking for clients. As for the agents and publishers who participate at the Cooler, they will gladly receive a submission from you (as long as you follow their guidelines)—but they won't give you special preference because you're a member.

As a moderator, what is the toughest part of your job?

Making sure that all sides are heard. The aim of the Bewares & Background Check forum is to provide as much information as possible, so writers can make up their own minds about agents, publishers, etc.

That means that all points of view need to be aired, no matter how divergent.

Most of the time, this isn't a problem. As I've noted, there's a much lower tendency toward flaming and trolling at the Cooler than at some other writers' forums, and people tend to be reasonably tolerant of disagreement. But things sometimes do get heated—for instance, when the subject of a "beware" shows up to angrily respond to complaints or questions, or when writers whose agents or publishers come in for criticism feel that they are being slighted too. Keeping the conversation on track and on topic, while allowing it to take its course, can be a real challenge. I abhor censorship, and delete posts or close threads only rarely and with the greatest reluctance.

What are some the hardest stories you hear about on the Water Cooler?

Writers who are scammed by a dishonest agent, or jerked around by an amateur publisher, yet instead of learning from the experience, get involved again with the same kind of person or company. I find these stories the saddest—and most frustrating—of all.

There are several Cooler members who've been serially taken advantage of in this way, in some cases despite several warnings. Hope and desperation are powerful emotions. It's far too easy for writers to allow them to overtake good sense.

Victoria Strauss - Writer Beware

No, this is not déjà vu all over again, and yes, Victoria is a busy woman who wears many hats. In fact, she was honored by the Science Fiction & Fantasy Writers of America (SFWA®) with a 2009 SFWA Service Award during the Nebula Awards® Weekend. Victoria received the award for work she had done with Writer Beware, a publishing industry watchdog group which "shines a light into the dark corners of the shadow-world of literary scams, schemes and pitfalls."

Since she one of the most hooked-in people in the industry, I asked her to discuss her other site, Writer Beware.

Why did you start Writer Beware?

People often ask me if I got involved with Writer Beware because I myself was scammed. The answer is no—my publishing experiences have mostly been positive. Naively, I thought I was typical. When I first went online in the mid-1990s and began checking out writers' forums and message boards, I was amazed to see how many writers had gotten mixed up with disreputable agents, publishers, and freelance editors. It was a whole slimy publishing underworld I'd never suspected existed. I began to follow the scam stories, and to take note of the names of agents and publishers that popped up over and over again.

I'm a member of the Science Fiction and Fantasy Writers of America (SFWA). Like many genre-focused professional writers' groups, SFWA is concerned not just with issues that affect professional authors, but with the problems that face aspiring writers. When I learned that SFWA was looking for a volunteer to create a page of warnings about literary scams for the SFWA website, I jumped at the chance. At around the same time, Ann Crispin, another SFWA member, was working on establishing a Writing Scams Committee. Neither of us had any idea what the other was doing until a mutual acquaintance put us in touch. Our activities dovetailed perfectly, and we decided to join forces.

The Writer Beware website and blog are the public face of the Writing Scams Committee. The website provides warnings about common schemes, scams, and pitfalls (there are sections on literary agents, vanity publishers, independent editors, contests, print-on-demand, electronic publishing, writers' services, and copyright, as well as a page of writers' alerts, a series of case studies of actual scams, and our famous Thumbs Down Agent and Publisher Lists), advice on how to avoid them, and links to helpful online resources. To complement the website's general warnings, the blog covers breaking news of interest to writers and warns about new scams and schemes. Its reports are often picked up by other bloggers or the media.

Behind the scenes, the Writing Scams Committee collects documentation on questionable agents and others (right now we have files on nearly 400 agencies, more than 250 publishers, and assorted editors, publicity services, contests, vanity anthologies, magazines, websites, and writers' services). We provide a free advice service to share this information with writers who contact us with questions about agents, publishers. We also assist law enforcement in civil and criminal investigations.

All members of the Writing Scams Committee (there are three of us at present) are volunteers. SFWA gives us space on its website, pays for our URL, and reimburses some of our expenses, but other than that we receive no funding. To avoid any appearance of conflict of interest, we do not accept donations.

What's a talented, well-published fantasy author doing in a place like writer's advocacy and publishing investigation?

Corny as it sounds, I like the idea of paying forward. As I said, I was never scammed—but I easily could have been. When I began trying to sell my first novel, there was very little information about writing scams and pitfalls (of course, back then, there weren't anywhere near as many as there are now). Writers need reliable information about what to watch out for—and that's what Writer Beware endeavors to provide. With Writer Beware, I feel that I am actually making a difference for people—and that's an incredibly good feeling.

I also have to admit that I'm fascinated by the psychology and methodology of scammers and schemers. The shadow-world of fraudulent and amateur agents and publishers and writers' "services"—whose only point of connection with the real publishing world is the authors it entraps—is an endlessly bizarre and wacky place. Every time I think I've seen it all, something new comes along. It certainly keeps things interesting!

Have you been sued by anyone for your troubles? Can you discuss the circumstances?

Writer Beware has been sued twice to date, in both cases by individuals or companies who consider our warnings defamatory. One of the cases is still ongoing, so I can't comment on it, but the other, brought by purported literary agent Robert Fletcher and his company, The Literary Agency Group, Inc., was dismissed in March 2009, with prejudice, due to the plaintiff's failure to respond to discovery or otherwise prosecute the lawsuit. Through counsel, we intend to file a motion against Fletcher and the Literary Agency Group, seeking recovery of our legal fees incurred in defending what we believe to be a frivolous lawsuit.

We are, and always have been, acutely conscious of the risks of what we do. We take care to keep our warnings and statements factual, or to clearly identify them as opinion. We make sure that our warnings are supported by documentation—correspondence, contracts, brochures, invoices, canceled checks, multiple similar advisories from writers. Our responses to the questions we receive are scrupulously researched. We also have strict criteria for what constitutes a complaint (there's a full discussion of these on the "About Writer Beware" page of the Writer Beware website).

Have you ever exposed a major scam?

Yes indeed!

George and Janet Titsworth of Helping Hand Literary Service in Texas charged hefty fees for providing writers with the names of (usually totally inappropriate) publishers, plus stick-on labels they could use to send out their own material. After many complaints, local law enforcement launched an investigation. Writer Beware helped find and contact victims (hundreds were ultimately identified) and was able to track down and expose the several new agencies started by the Titsworths after Helping Hand closed down. The Titsworths were arrested, tried, and sentenced to ten years' probation plus restitution payments.

Lisa Hackney, alias Melanie Mills, set up a fee-charging literary agency in North Carolina. After abruptly canceling a scheduled writers' conference, she faked her own death and absconded to Canada with the conference proceeds. There, under the alias Elisabeth von Hullessem, she set up another fake conference—and absconded again. When news of the second conference broke, Writer Beware spotted the similar M.O. When Hackney was found and arrested, we were able to confirm, with a photo in our possession, that "Elisabeth von Hullessem" and "Melanie Mills" were the same person. We were also able to put Canadian law enforcement in touch with the police officer who was investigating Hackney in North Carolina.

Hackney turned out to be a career criminal with a history of theft and check kiting, who was wanted in Arkansas for attempted murder for trying to run over her mother with a car. Eventually, Arkansas was able to extradite her from Canada. She pleaded guilty to all charges and was given a suspended sentence. She's currently living in California under yet another alias, and has self-published her memoirs (!).

Martha Ivery ran a vanity publisher. Under the alias Kelly O'Donnell, she also ran a fee-charging literary agency and editorial service (despite the fact that she was virtually illiterate). Once they'd been bled dry by the agency, clients got a publishing "offer" from the publisher—for just a small fee. There was no disclosure of the connection between the agency and the publisher, or of the fact that Martha and Kelly were the same person. As often as not, the books writers paid for were never produced.

Writer Beware got scores of complaints about Ivery. As a result of our lobbying efforts, an FBI investigation was opened. We extensively assisted the case officer in locating victims and gathering documentation. By the time Ivery was arrested and indicted, nearly 300 victims had been identified, for a total take of more than $728,000. Ivery is currently serving a 65-month sentence in Federal prison.

Much more detailed (and amusing) accounts of these scams and others can be found on the Case Studies page of the Writer Beware website.

What is the biggest problem you see in the publishing industry?

The problems are numerous and familiar: the acquisition and conglomeration of publishers by media companies that demand corporate-style profits from what has historically been a low-profit business, the downsizing that has transformed editors into administrators with little time to actually edit, bloated advances and the focus on blockbuster books, the decline of the midlist, the challenges of the digital world and how to market in the age of the Internet.

I don't see any one of these issues as taking precedence over another. They are all major problems, and they are in the process of utterly changing the face of publishing—though how exactly they are changing it, and what will result, is anyone's guess. I believe we're in the midst of a paradigm shift, and despite the prognostication of which the publishing industry is so fond, I don't believe it's possible to comprehend a new paradigm until it has actually replaced the old one. All we can know for sure right now is that things will be different. We need to be open to that, not terrified of it.

There is a lot of discussion about Print-on-Demand and vanity publishing. Do you feel these are viable publishing options for authors?

I don't believe that vanity publishers—which I define as publishers that require authors to pay in order to see their work in print, yet present themselves as "real" publishers rather than as book manufacturers or self-publishing services—are ever a good option for authors. They are expensive, rarely offer better marketing or distribution than the self-publishing services, and are often quite deceptive about the extent and value of what they provide.

A straightforward, reasonably-priced print-on-demand self-publishing service can be a viable option in specific circumstances—people who want to print a family memoir or recipe book for limited distribution, writers with niche nonfiction projects that target audiences they can reach directly, people who can exploit back-of-the-room situations, such as a chef who can sell her cookbook at her restaurant or a lecturer who can sell his self-help book at his speaking engagements. It's also a reasonable fallback option for authors who feel that they've exhausted the possibilities of the commercial marketplace, but still want to see their work in print.

But for more general nonfiction, for most fiction, and especially for authors who are interested in achieving volume sales and wide exposure, POD self-publishing is rarely a good alternative. POD services' policies on pricing, marketing, and distribution limit their books' availability, resulting in small sales and readership even for authors who diligently self-promote (average sales, according to statistics from the major POD services, are around 150-200 per book). Something else to consider: POD self-publishing is widely regarded as vanity publishing, with all the pejorative connotations that implies.

Unfortunately, myths and misconceptions are rife among aspiring writers—including the widespread notion that it's impossible for new writers to find commercial publication. Writer Beware regularly hears from aspiring writers who believe that POD self-publishing is their only alternative. What we tell them is this: instead of starting at the bottom in hopes of working your way up, start at the top and work your way down. Query agents. If that doesn't work out, look to reputable independent publishers. If that doesn't work out, you can always revisit self-publishing.

If an author can't find an agent to represent their work, do you advocate that they give up trying to be published?

Certainly not. There are plenty of other possibilities. Set aside the book that isn't selling, write another and try with that. Many authors never sell their first, or even their second or third books. You may have to try several times before you break in.

Investigate reputable independent publishers, many of which are willing to work with unagented writers. Such publishers don't have the marketing budgets or the distribution clout of the large houses, but they can do an excellent job of publishing your book, and will provide you with a solid writing credit.

If your work is romance or erotica, investigate some of the larger e-publishers. In these very popular genres, some e-publishers are racking up substantial sales. If you do well, they may even take your book to print.

You do have to be realistic, though. Consistent rejection by the commercial market may be shortsighted and unfair—or it may be justified. The main reason that manuscripts fail to find publication is that they aren't of publishable quality. A deep conviction of your own talent is important, but there may come a point at which you have to reassess.

What are five things you would tell a new author before they begin the query stage?

* **Make sure your manuscript (if it's a novel) or proposal (if it's a nonfiction book) is completely finished, and as polished as you can make it.** Many writers think it's the editor's job to clean up mistakes and sloppy writing. Wrong. It's your job, and if you don't do it, your chances of publication are slim.

* **Educate yourself.** With writing, as with any profession, you need a knowledge base to start. Find books about the publishing industry. Read industry journals like Publishers Weekly (much of its content is available online). Check websites like Writer Beware, Preditors & Editors, and Absolute Write. Read agents' blogs. The more you know, the more effectively you'll be able to submit your work, and the less likely you'll be to be taken in by dishonest or incompetent people.

(Unfortunately, this incredibly important step is one that many writers skip. Ignorance is a huge problem among aspiring writers; in my opinion, it's the thing that's most responsible for keeping scam and amateur publishers and agents in business. If all writers made the effort to learn about publishing before sending out their queries, rather than long after, Writer Beware's work would be cut in half.)

* **Do your research.** Make sure the agents and/or publishers you query are appropriate for your work. Never query an agent without first checking to be certain that s/he's reputable and has a track record. Never submit to a publisher without being sure it can actually market and distribute your books.

* **Avoid amateurs.** Amateurism is rampant in the writing world, from the well-intentioned but clueless people who think it's fine to start a publishing company or literary agency without knowing a thing about publishing or agenting, to the individuals who set themselves up as experts on the strength of one self- or micropress-published book, and dispense misinformation and bad advice with as much apparent authority as those who actually know what they're talking about. Don't take anyone or anything at face value. Make sure that the people you approach or listen to have the professional background and credentials to back up the services they promise and the information they provide.

* **Keep writing.** Many aspiring writers pin all their hopes on the book they've just completed, and put their writing life into stasis while they submit. But as noted above, many writers don't break in with their first book. If that happens, you'll want to try again with another—and you'll be able to do so much sooner if you don't wait to write it until after you've given up on Book 1. Plus, if you do sell your first book, the publisher may be interested in your second— so it'll be good to have it on hand.

Authors assume that if they've signed with a large NY publisher their troubles are over. Do you agree, or are there pitfalls/concerns they need to be aware of?

Selling your book isn't the end of the struggle; it's just the beginning of a different one. With so many books being published, it's hard for any individual writer to stand out in the crowd—even though, contrary to popular misconception, commercial publishers provide marketing for all their books. Publishers also are less willing than in previous decades to nurse writers' careers, or to stick with established writers whose sales are flat.

There's also the question of self-promotion—when, what, how much—and the myriad possibilities of bad covers, mis-marketing, being orphaned (when the editor who acquired your book leaves the company and you're passed on to someone else), getting bad reviews, and—possibly through no fault of you, your book, or your publisher—failing to sell in sufficient numbers. Poor sales of a debut book won't necessarily kill your career, as some pessimistic pundits like to opine, but it certainly won't help.

All of that said, the fact that these things happen to some or even many writers doesn't necessarily mean they'll happen to you. Everyone's story is different. You need to be aware of the circumstances you may encounter once you're published—but since there is no way to predict whether you will encounter them, or in what form, obsessing about them before a contract is even in the offing can be demoralizing and counterproductive. This is one reason I suggest that writers who are still in the submission phase avoid the "tough love" blogs and websites that offer up harsh (sometimes exaggeratedly harsh) truths about the perils of the commercially published author. There'll be plenty of time to worry about this new phase of your writing life once you've gotten a publishing offer.

May an author contact you if they are worried about their agent or publisher?

Writer Beware welcomes contact from writers with questions, concerns, complaints, or advisories about publishers, agents, editors, and others. We also welcome questions about publishing in general. We'll do our best to answer, and if it's relevant, we'll share documentation from Writer Beware's files. We'll also collect documentation of complaints, where the writer is willing to share it. This documentation is a very important part of what Writer Beware does, because it supports our warnings. We don't provide warnings, alerts, or advisories of any kind unless we can fully document them.

Writers can reach us at beware@sfwa.org.

Litopia – Peter Cox

No, you're not seeing double. You read Peter's interview in the Agent chapter on page 38. Peter Cox became a literary agent after a successful career as a writer. Working with his wife and writing partner, Peggy Brusseau, they collaborated on 27 books, mainly published by Bloomsbury and Random House in the UK. Many of them were UK bestsellers, and one—*Linda McCartney's Home Cooking*—became a major international bestseller.

Peter's background is in advertising and marketing. "I had three very traditional literary agencies representing me while writing", he says, "and I wasn't really happy with the degree of service and attention I received from any of them. Redhammer, my own agency, was created specifically to look after the unmet needs of authors—not the needs of the literary agent. I believe we are the prototype of the literary agency for the 21st century. We already do a lot more for our clients than most agencies, and as the publishing industry goes through today's seismic changes, I think our way of doing things will become more and more relevant and attractive to authors."

Peter's clients include the worldwide bestselling children's author Michelle Paver, US Senator Orrin Hatch, television journalist and former Member of Parliament Martin Bell, OBE, science writer Brian Clegg, children's author MG Harris and former deputy editor of the New York Post and Britain's *Sun* newspaper, David Yelland. Redhammer is recognized by the Association of Authors' Agents.

What is Litopia, and why is this site such a great writer's resource? How does it work?

It's a community for writers on the net—one of the first, actually. We're by no means the largest out there now, but I think we have the most positive and supportive feeling. It was intended to be a meeting place—somewhere for the seriously committed writer to come for community, help and support, information, criticism and all the other things that writers need. Writing is a pretty solitary lifestyle, and I wanted Litopia to be a place where writers could find both good company and practical resources.

What are Litopia's unique characteristics from other writer's sites?

We're very different to most of the other sites out there. One of the differences you'll notice immediately is that we're not backed by venture capital, or by a publisher hoping to cash in on the slush pile. Our first priority is to be a great place for writers to go—not to make money for some 24-year-old in a Maserati. This does, of course, mean that we don't have millions to spend on site frippery, but we more than make up for that in our sense of community.

We do have a good social side, of course, but beyond that, there are something like two dozen other areas, many of them to do with writers' own work-in-progress and critiquing. One of the successful offshoots of the Colony is our series of daily and weekly podcasts for writers. The daily is a brief ten minutes that you can listen to over your morning coffee or on your iPod going to work. The weekly—*Litopia After Dark* is a panel discussion on which we feature both members of the Colony together with interesting guests from the wider world of publishing. Our audience for this is really going through the roof—it grew by 300% last quarter alone.

Another thing you can do in the Colony is to get advice from both me and also from a hard-working publisher. Writers are usually so grateful to have this kind of access—the business can often feel more like a secret society to the unpublished author.

Can anyone join? What are the parameters?

Yes, anyone can join. We've experimented with this quite a lot and now have a system that works pretty well. Anyone can register themselves as a basic member. But to become a full member, and therefore to get access to our full range of facilities, you must have a piece of work accepted by our Assessments Officers. This ensures that we maintain some important standards, and frankly keeps the place manageable and personal. It also means we'll never have the sort of membership statistics that, say, a site like Triggerstreet has—but that's not the point of Litopia.

What kind of people read and post to Litopia? How informed are they? Can I trust the information?

People who are seriously committed to their writing read and post to Litopia. They are published and unpublished and usually quite well informed. But as I said, they love having direct contact with an agent, with a publisher, and indeed with other writers at various stages of their careers. Can you trust the information? Well most of the "information" is subjective, so it's hard to take a view on that.

I've found that the Colony will typically give you a range of points of view, and it's up to you to decide what seems appropriate. For example in my own "Ask The Agent" forum, other people regularly pop in and answer questions (sometimes better than I can!) and it's this diversity of opinion that I think helps give us a wonderful richness.

How did Litopia get started, and why?

I've been on the Internet for decades (yes, I'm very old) literally from the time before the worldwide web was created. I was one of the early members of The Well, a virtual community/offshoot of The Whole Earth Catalog, and that gave me some feeling for what communities on the net could be. Since most (but not all) writers use computers, it seemed to make sense to set up a virtual community for writers using the latest technology. It's been a labor of love since I do believe in supporting writers. They are, by definition, unusual people, and I had always sensed an unmet need for the kind of watering-hole experience that many more sociable occupations take for granted. So we sort of stumbled into existence. We are still evolving.

If I have questions regarding a publisher, agent, or the publishing process, may I ask my questions on this site?

Absolutely! That's one of our strengths. There are two forums just for this—"Ask the Agent" and "Ask the Editor." I will often take questions that arise in the "Ask the Agent" forum and answer them on the daily podcast ("Litopia Daily") because I like the chatty, informal way of answering this permits me. Also, I'm a lousy and slow typist.

Is there a place where I can get writing critiques?

Yes, there are two places. First, we have The Houses. This is an area that's sub-divided into various writing genres—the exact number of sub-divisions can vary, according to the interests of members at any particular time. But there is an area for children's writing, another for romance, one for mystery, an area for fantasy, and so on. Writers can join whichever House reflects the genre that they're interested in. We have very specific guidelines about critiquing, and we insist they are followed. When done properly, a writer can actually learn more from giving a critique on another's work than from passively submitting their own work and waiting for a report.

I'd say we encourage active critiquing; as with everything in Litopia, the more you put in, the more you'll get out. We aim to get the writer to freely move from author to reader in their head and back again. The easier this transition becomes, the more control you develop as an author. I often say that writing is not a monologue, it is a dialogue with the reader—giving a critique is an excellent way to develop an awareness of this dialogue and to understand how to direct it.

The other place where you can receive a critique is in the Pitch Room. This is an area where more senior members can submit their work directly to me and receive a critique –actually, they can watch me read their submission as I make comments about it live on video camera. We're proud to be the first website in the world to allow writer access to this part of the submission process. There is so much inaccuracy and mythology about submissions, so we thought it would be a great idea to make the whole process completely transparent. The videos are recorded and accessible for other senior members to watch.

Who does the critiques?

As I've mentioned above, I firmly believe that authors can benefit enormously from the process of mutual critiquing. The Litopia process of critiquing is very different to other "review" sites on the net. Quite frankly, some are little more than bitch-fests—where one or two people with over-sized egos throw their weight around. We won't tolerate that. Other sites use a points system or ratings system by which work is evaluated - some of these sites are either sponsored by a publisher or boast publishing connections. In reality, these sites are more about "monetizing the slush pile" than actually discovering brilliant new talent. You won't get much useful feedback from either of these approaches.

When you give a critique to someone else on Litopia, it forces you to consider the bigger picture. For a start, it provides you with an omniscient-like viewpoint from which to consider another person's work. As a writer, you will be very familiar with the "can't-see-the-wood-for-the-trees" syndrome. Writers almost inevitably (and perhaps necessarily) lose their objectivity when they write. As you become more and more engrossed in the world of your manuscript, it becomes progressively harder and harder for you to dispassionately view the fruits of your labor.

However, when you assess another person's work, you bring a pair of fresh eyes and an open mind to the task. To you, the faults are glaringly obvious. To the writer, they're painfully obscure.

As our members critique more and more manuscripts, they find that a handful of common mistakes comprise the vast majority of fatal flaws that are found in submissions. They also find themselves saying, "How could I have avoided this? How could I have written this more effectively?"

This kind of mental self-talk not only increases a writer's sharpness, it also develops their own sense of confidence. A confident writer is someone who is in control of their skills and who can strategically deploy them to maximum effect. Believe me, you will learn more from carefully critiquing other peoples' writing than you will from any amount of expensive writing classes.

Can Litopia help me get an agent or publisher?

We don't offer a matchmaking service, but we certainly help indirectly. One way we can help is to give members access to me (I'm a working agent) and to a working publisher, too. Most of the questions I'm asked in the Ask The Agent forum relate to the getting of an agent, and I'm very pleased to help here. Members do say some very nice things about this aspect of the Colony. We do have a commercial feel, in the best sense. We want our members to succeed, and we celebrate when they do.

Are you the moderator, or do you have a team of moderators?

I'm the administrator—meaning I do a lot of the behind the scenes work, especially the technical aspect. We do indeed have a valiant team of dedicated moderators, without whom the Colony would not exist. They are wonderful.

As a moderator/owner, what is the toughest part of your job?

Very occasionally, and this really is unusual, we have a problem that requires a member to be expelled—but before this happens, there is a whole lot of debate and discussion behind the scenes with the moderators. It's never nice to get rid of someone, but if they persistently threaten the ethos and spirit of the place, then there is sadly only one option.

What are future plans for Litopia?

Well, the podcasts are doing really well now, and I do want to see them continue their explosive growth. The Colony will continue to put on new members—there is no membership target we're chasing here, it's more important to preserve our ethos than to boast big numbers.

Publishers are casting their hungry eyes at writing communities at the moment, and I don't like a lot of what I see. Some of it seems to be simply motivated by the desire to "monetize the slushpile"—in other words, "join us today, and get published tomorrow!" That seems to be to be on par with vanity publishing—they're making unrealistic promises and are eventually bound to cause a lot of disillusionment. At Litopia, we don't pretend that writing is anything other than a hard discipline, learnt and honed over many years. It's less exciting, but it's the truth, and to pretend otherwise is dishonest. So we won't be going that route.

I am aware that we are in competition, to a limited extent, with the growing number of writers' sites out there. Not perhaps in terms of terms of profitability, but certainly in terms of quality of members. So we need to reemphasize our standards, be open to new possibilities such as the podcasts, and to constantly find new ways to be of use to our members. If we keep doing that, then we'll be the top writers' site on the net, and that would be rather fantastic!

Why did you decide to make Litopia private?

Litopia is only partly private. Anyone can join, in fact. They then have instant access to over half the Colony. Once you have been a Colony member for a month and have actively contributed to our collegiate life, you can apply to become a full member, which will give you access to even more areas, including the Pitch Room and the Houses. In order to qualify, you need to submit some sample work. This system works very well. It means that people who become full members are already known to the Colony, and are happy to uphold our sense of community. It also means that full members have been judged to be good writers in themselves, and not the deluded people you often see populating less well-regulated forums. That's the thing about writing—since almost everyone can do it, everyone thinks that they could dash off a quick book and make a fortune. They do not understand the blood, sweat and toil that go into honing the writer's craft. At Litopia, we do understand.

Final Thoughts From My Side of the Pond

When I think of sites like Litopia, Writer Beware, and The Absolute Write Water Cooler, I think of scrutiny—scrutiny of new agents or publishers and scrutiny with good writing. Gossip about a new publisher travels like wildfire, and it's more than likely to end up on one or all of these sites. "What have you heard?" is like chum in shark-infested waters, and the replies from a new publisher can initiate a feeding frenzy like none other. But it's necessary, and I applaud these sites for their vigilance in vetting new faces in the publishing industry. Any editor who can't handle having their feet put to the flames is invariably inept or hiding something.

Likewise, I applaud these sites for offering a safe place for authors to have their works in progress critiqued by their peers. As Peter said in his interview, writers tend to be solitary creatures, and it's the smart writer who surfaces with their work for a reality check. Dipping your toe into the dark waters to ask if your work is on the right track can be an intimidating experience, but it's the most valuable feedback you'll get, and it's all for free.

11: Publicists

Do I need a publicist?

The idea of "if I write it, people will come" went out with poodle skirts and saddle shoes. Nowadays, it's all about getting a book out into the world so people know it exists. This can be a touchy issue because it's an expense authors feel should be placed on the publisher's shoulders. However, in this age of belt tightening, very few authors are allotted any promotion dollars. And the publisher's in-house publicist can only do so much since they have many other authors to deal with. It is the publisher's responsibility to have their sales team pitch their lineup to the genre buyers, get the books distributed to the stores, get review copies out to the trade magazines, and send out publicity packages. With all that publishers do to get the book out into the marketplace, the first thing genre buyers still want to know is what the author is doing to create demand.

Genre buyers know that creating demand is what sells books and if the author isn't involved, they may decide against ordering the book. If no one knows your book exists, even though it's sitting on the store shelves, it's going to get shipped back to the publisher's warehouse within about eight weeks, where it will eventually take up residence in Remainder City.

Promotion is a huge undertaking, and many put these efforts into the hands of a publicist. Good, experienced publicists have the upper hand because they maintain relationships with all kinds of people, be they event planners for bookstores, the review editor of a major trade magazine, or station managers of radio shows. They put together professional promo packages and do all the follow-up calls. What's most important is that they help the author figure out what types of promotion are most appropriate for the book and the author. If an author is painfully shy, then it hardly makes sense to book speaking engagements for them. Rather, they might make a bigger splash writing articles for newspapers and specialty magazines. There are many ways to promote, and publicists are experts at ferreting out the best avenue for each book.

An example of this came through a conversation I had with an author who wrote a murder/mystery where a popular gardener is killed. She's with a small house with zero promo dollars budgeted for her book. She'd been going to all the mystery bookstores and having some success with her signings, but she wasn't reaching a big audience, and her sales were tepid. After talking with a publicist, they decided to go after the gardening community, which turned out to be a huge success. They had her do signings at a number of the large nurseries in her area. At the same time, the publicist got her on gardening radio shows and local cable TV appearances.

She became an "expert" in gardening tips and as word spread, so did demand for more appearances. The publicist also got her quite a few newspaper interviews in their gardening sections. Before they knew it, other reporters were asking to interview her and review her book. Long story short, her sales went through the roof, and her publisher responded by putting an ad in one of the big gardening magazines. Without her publicist, this author would have never had the time or energy to make contact with all the different venues required to make that full frontal assault, not to mention that she would have never considered the gardening aspects in the first place.

In the end, the only way to know if a publicist is right for you is to talk to one. Find out if you have some unique element that could create a new fad—like the knitter whose book is filled with patterns of naughty wear. Tell me that isn't ripe for a *Live With Regis and Kelly* appearance. It could be the difference between living in Remainder City or catching the red eye for Los Angeles to appear on *The Tonight Show*.

Anita Halton

A native of New York City, publicist Anita Halton has specialized in promoting books and authors for over twenty-five years. Building on experience in New York publishing houses, she opened her own literary publicity firm in San Francisco in 1986, and has worked since then in Northern and Southern California, handling both national and regional publicity campaigns.

Anita honed her professional skills at Little Brown and Company, as Publicity Director of Farrar, Straus & Giroux, and later as Associate Publicity Director of Charles Scribner's Sons, Atheneum Publishers, and Macmillan.

Anita has worked with Norman Mailer, Lillian Hellman, Susan Sontag, and John McPhee and launched books by bestselling authors Thomas Moore (*CARE OF THE SOUL*), James Redfield (*THE CELESTINE VISION* and *THE TENTH INSIGHT*), Larry Dossey, M.D. (*HEALING WORDS: The Power of Prayer and the Practice of Medicine*) and Jon Kabat-Zinn (*WHEREVER YOU GO, THERE YOU ARE*).

What is a publicist? What do they do? Who hires them, the author or the publisher?

A publicist is a publishing professional who gets the word out about your book. They work with broadcast, print, and online media to publicize your book. A publicist can be hired by either the publisher or author. The trend has been moving towards authors hiring their own publicists.

Are all publicists the same, or do they specialize? For instance, are some better at getting great reviews while others excel at getting their clients into the media?

Although some publicists specialize in electronic media (radio and TV) or online media, most do all. Some publicists do have specialties such as cookbooks, mysteries, business books or photography, but the majority handles all types of books. However, a number of independent publicists handle only non-fiction, and children's books are usually considered a specialty. As for reviews, I think they depend a lot on whether the book is a reviewer's type of book and whether it has been published before.

My book is expected to be released a year from now. When should I start my promotion?

You should start your research now. Active promotion starts about six months before publication date. You can:

* Research the name of independent book publicists through the Internet or by contacting associations of publishing professionals, such as the Independent Book Publishers Association (IBPA), or the Publishers' Publicity Association (PPA), or the Northern California Book Publicity and Marketing Association (NCBPMA). You can get referrals and interview publicists.

* Organize a database of your personal and professional contacts to let them know about your book and related events

* Clip or bookmark articles and blog writers on related topics

* Complete your author questionnaire, supplying your publisher with personal information and a background story on the book that can be used in promotion.

* Perfect a one or two sentence description of your book for marketing.

Since there are no guarantees as to whether my book is going to sell well, why do I want a publicist? Do some genres sell better under the direction of a publicist?

A publicist has contacts and experience that you don't have. All genres need publicists, but you are right in saying there are no guarantees. Publicists know reviewers, editors and producers who will take their calls and emails. Some publicists specialize in topics, such as children's books, or books related to health or business and have continual contact with the media in those fields. Their endorsement will often convince a reviewer or producer to pay attention to your book.

My publisher should be promoting my work, so why do I need to get out and work? I'd rather write.

In this day and age, selling your book is a very important part of the process. Gone are the days when an author could just write and leave the promotion up to the publisher. In fact, publishers seek authors who have platforms indicating that they are active in their community and know how to promote themselves and their work. A publisher's promotion only goes so far; they can get you a bookstore signing, but you need to build the audience.

An independent publicist acts as the author's advocate both with the publisher and the media.

What is the price range of a publicist?

The range is $2,500 to $50,000 or more, depending on what the responsibilities are and how big a commitment the author or publisher is making toward the book.

I have a fabulous book that would be perfect for Oprah. Can my publicist get me on her show?

Your publicist can't guarantee an Oprah appearance, but he or she can get it to the appropriate producer at the Oprah Show. The producers make the final decision.

A publicist develops pitches using concepts from the book. They offer show ideas, complete with possible guests. They relate your work to trends and breaking news.

What should I expect of my publicist? How do I determine whether they are doing a good job for me?

You should expect that your publicist will work closely with you and keep you informed every step of the way. You can ask for updates and whom they approached and what the responses are.

It's important that you and your publicist are on the same page as far as the goals for your campaign. Your contract with your publicist should clearly explain the campaign, including goals, length of time, fees, expenses, cancellation policy, and reporting method. If you are not entirely clear, discuss it further until you are. For example, does the campaign cover radio and television interviews as well as reviews and press interviews? Which outlets will be contacted? Does the campaign include both national and local media? If you have a limited budget, could your publicist tailor the campaign to fewer outlets leaving those that are likely to be most fruitful, but including selections from your "wish" list.

Be mindful also that there is a difference between exposure and sales. Media appearances do not always result in sales. What are your goals? Perhaps your goal is to be a more visible expert in your field.

My publicist told me I needed media training. What is media training, and is it really that important, and why is it a separate fee?

Your interview needs to be able to sell the book. A media trainer helps you prepare from sound-bytes to wardrobe. Since many media trainers are former producers or interviewers, they know what works on radio and TV.

Depending on the trainer and the package, media training can entail anywhere from one day to three. The training involves:

* Developing stories and details from your book that can engage an audience

* Honing responses to interviews of different lengths

* Practicing sound-bytes for short interviews

* Adjusting to the camera—learning where to look, how to sit, how to adjust your voice and reduce body movements.

* Watching videos of your performance

* Discussing appropriate attire

* Learning about different kinds of interviews and media

* Handling tough questions or negativity

Does the publicist talk to my publisher? Is that important?

The publicist should have a good relationship with your publisher to make sure you are not working at cross-purposes and also to get the materials needed.

I've just signed on with a publicist. Who is supposed to provide the publicist with books, my publisher or me?

It is ideal if the publisher will supply the books. If not, you will have to.

What do you expect from your clients? A website? Do you help with this?

I expect that my clients will be cooperative.

In today's world, authors need to have a website. In fact, your book needs its own website. Media and readers will look to the website to find out how to contact the author, read reviews, listen to interviews, read your bio. You will want to link your website to other sites that can be mutually beneficial.

In my experience most authors are cooperative. If they are not, it is usually because of a failure in communication. An initial phone conversation or better still, a personal meeting in the beginning of the project, is helpful, if not essential. The topic of consulting time needs to be addressed. I had one author who called me every day and talked for a long time until I mentioned that our contract limited consulting time to three hours. That being said, I find that email communication can be misleading, or abrupt, so picking up the phone is often important. I like regular conference calls every other week or so to make sure everything is on track.

If more than one publicist is involved in the project, it is very important that the boundaries be clarified.

I had one author who was very difficult to communicate with. She made a lot of publicity decisions without consulting me, and I felt undervalued.

In today's world, they need to have a website. I don't set up the website, but I can recommend people who do. I also provide content for the website.

What is the standard timeframe that a publicist works with an author?

Three to six months. The time frame can be extended when the campaign is working well and the client wants to extend the tour or the buzz.

Do publicists have personal relationships with the trade magazine reviewers and the media?

Yes. They do. Publicists do have many personal relationships with media. For example, when I was working with Thomas Moore, author of *CARE OF THE SOUL*, I met many interviewers and producers who were interested in spirituality. I've since worked on many books in spirituality and health, and continue to know some of them.

What are the most frustrating elements of working with a client?

When the expectations are unrealistic. We want our authors to be ambitious and grab for the stars, but we can't have them fall apart if we say that Oprah did not want them, or the producer hasn't responded to the latest pitch. I try to be versatile, and try many different avenues. I need to have the author trust that I have given it my best shot. Perhaps they don't have the same credentials as another author or we are working with a more limited budget.

Dreams, creativity, optimism, openness, communication, flexibility and realism can really make things happen.

Chip Jacobs is an example of an author I've liked working with. Although his book, *Wheeling the Deal*, has been challenging to publicize, Chip's energy, dedication and trust make it easy to want the project to be successful and to go many extra miles.

Annie Jennings - PR Specialist

Not all publicists were created the same. Annie Jennings PR is a national publicist specializing in promoting authors and experts to the media. Annie freely shares her publicity strategies with authors and experts so everyone can have access to PR strategies, both the basics and advanced PR thought, so they can share their messages with millions for the betterment of all.

Annie Jennings PR: 908.281.6201

www.anniejenningspr.com

What is a publicist? What do they do? Who hires them, the author or publisher?

A publicist publicizes you and your message. The ideal publicity is the expansion of your message so you can share your ideas, passion and message. Book publicity is different from book marketing and it is important to understand the difference between the two. Publicity is the sharing of your message in a socially relevant way while book marketing focuses more on the sales aspect of the campaign. The publicist helps you craft your message so it meets the desires and requirements of the media such as radio, TV, magazines, newspapers and various Internet sites and presents you to the media in a way that creates the best case scenario for secured media bookings.

A publicist can be hired by the author and/or the publisher. Many publicists offer a basic launch campaign for a certain period of time, such as three months. Once that time period is over, the author usually hires their own PR firm to continue the expansion of their message, their buzz on the author and the creation of national expert status.

Are all publicists the same, or do they specialize? For instance, are some better at getting great reviews while others excel at getting their clients into the media?

Publicists specialize in various areas and it is important to know what the publicist can deliver for you before you hire a publicist so you can match up your desired outcome with the publicist area of expertise. If you would like book reviews, you will want to hire a publicist who has experience in obtaining book reviews in your book's category. A publicist usually has relationships built up over the years with various outlets and it is essential to your overall success to hire a publicist with the media relationships in place that match your personal and publicity objectives. It is not unusual to hire more than one publicist as each publicist usually has a distinct area of expertise. The idea is to hire the publicist with the proven track record of success in your topic area and with your goals and objectives.

My book is expected to be released a year from now. When should I start my promotion?

It's a great idea to start to identify various target media outlets that you feel are right for you, your message and your book well in advance. Follow these periodicals, TV, radio shows, Internet sites, etc., so you are familiar with how they cover your topic over a period of time. This way, when you are ready to approach these media outlets for publicity you will know what they have already covered in your topic area. This knowledge of the history of your media outlet gives you an advantage as you have an informed idea of where they would most likely want to go next with your topic.

Be sure to collect articles and links to Internet articles so you have them for reference later.

Since there are no guarantees as to whether my book is going to sell well, why do I want a publicist? Do some genres sell better under the direction of a publicist?

Remember, hiring a publicist is about sharing your message, creating buzz about you and your book and the distribution of your message. The idea is to leverage your book into opportunities for yourself in terms of new clients, speaking events, national expert status, bigger book deals down the road and much more. Most authors use their book to build their platform rather than for increasing book sales. The fun of publicity is that you get to see and experience your book's message in motion. The focus should be on sharing your message, of experiencing your book alive and in motion and not on book sales.

My publisher should be promoting my work, so why do I need to get out and work? I'd rather write.

You are your book. You are the message of your book. Writing is just the beginning of living your dream of being an author, but sharing your message with others can be the ultimate gratifying experience for you. Keep in mind that readers love to connect with authors giving them a reason to want to purchase their book. Your goal is to engage your potential readers by giving them a preview of the material presented in the book. If they fall in love with you and your message, you most likely have a sale.

What is the price range of a publicist?

The important question to ask is, what is the guaranteed deliverable of the services you are purchasing? Hiring a publicist should be viewed as an investment and not an expense.

In looking at publicity as an investment, you'll want to earn an "ROI" that is, a return on your investment (what will you get back for the money you invested). Hire publicists who offer a guaranteed deliverable rather than simply the promise of trying to get you publicity and media placements. You want publicists who get you the results you are looking for, such as radio show interviews, TV show appearances, mentions in magazines or newspapers or on the Internet or you don't pay. Most authors are very disappointed when they purchase publicity services on the promise of a result that many times turns into a monthly report that says "we pitched this media list but everyone said no." This is an outcome that is not acceptable to you and does not help you share your message with others as you did not get any media outreach or the chance to experience your book in motion.

You can buy cheap when dealing with publicists but the true question is, can you buy better? Cheaper usually means less actual media outcome and return on investment for you. The ideal situation in publicity is to only work with publicists with a proven track record, who guarantee their work and only accept payment for secured media placements that actually take place. You should not pay for the process of "trying;" you should only pay for booked placements that air or print as presented by the publicist.

I have a fabulous book that would be perfect for Oprah. Can my publicist get me on her show?

In my experience, Oprah's team of producers knows what they want and they go after it. General pitching to Oprah is a good idea of course, as you want to be in the right place just in case it is the right time, however, it is best to assume you will not get booked on Oprah and go after being "everywhere at all times" using other media such as radio, other TV, magazine and newspaper mentions and Internet placements. The BIG advantage in the model is that you become extremely visible and socially relevant so when Oprah's producers are looking for a certain type of expert, they are sure to find you!

What should I expect of my publicist? How do I determine whether they are doing a good job for me?

The objectives of the publicist should be identified before you hire your publicist. You want secured media placements and want to know if the publicist can secure your desired media outcomes for you. You will know they are doing a good job if the placements, according to services you purchase, are being booked for you. If you are just getting reports that say everyone said "no," then you have purchased the wrong campaign for yourself. There is a place in the media for just about every author. The question is where the most appropriate outlet for you is and what the perfect publicity strategy for you is. Additionally your expectations should be clearly identified and attainable.

My publicist told me I needed media training. What is media training, is it really that important, and why is it a separate fee?

Media training helps you learn how to offer an excellent interview and experience for everyone involved—that is, for the show, the host, the viewer or listener and for yourself. Appearing on a radio show or a TV show is an honor and to be taken very seriously as many resources are involved in booking you on the show. You are expected to "perform," that is, to give them what they want and need which is a top quality interview that's packed with great and timely info and is entertaining as well. Providing a professional interview to the media is a skill set that can be taught and with practice, perfected.

Does the publicist talk to my publisher? Is that important?

It is a good idea for the publisher to connect with the publicist if the publicist is hired for a new book launch. This way, the publisher can share any secured media opportunities that they may have already booked, book reviews and their strategy, if any, that they have or will implement on behalf of the author. The author and publicist can decide on a logical course of action that takes into consideration the information shared by the publisher.

I've just signed on with a publicist. Who is supposed to provide the publicist with books, my publisher or me?

In my experience, the publisher has happily agreed to supply the publicist with a reasonable amount of books to complete the publicity campaign. You can check with your publisher on their policy or restrictions if any so you know if you might have to purchase books in advance for your publicist to use to implement your PR strategy.

What do you expect from your clients? A website? Do you help with this?

Clients should stay on top of any news that is in their area of expertise and be available for interviews that might be scheduled quickly. Rarely does the media schedule far in advance so flexibility is important or you might miss something BIG! The author should have a website that is optimized for the media. This type of site is called an author/expert media site and showcases the expert, their credentials, their relevant opinions and talking points, articles, a top quality demo (a top quality demo is an absolute must especially if you want to get booked on bigger, national TV shows).

Your author/expert media site should include a recent professional photo, an audio recording, links to any articles or mentions you have on the Internet, your book cover, book reviews and a list of publicity opportunities already secured. This site should not be promotional for the book because you are not trying to sell the producer or journalist your book. The site should be information-based as your objective is to provide the info the media needs to say YES to booking you!

What is the standard timeframe that a publicist works with an author?

The publicist should work with an author until the publicity objectives are achieved. If you put a time frame around your relationship and the publicist stops working for you, you can miss your BIG CHANCE. This is why retainer-based agreements are NOT GOOD for the authors as they secure the publicist for only a certain period of time, rather than a set of deliverables. With a Pay For Placement Publicity Program, where the author only pays for secured media events, the publicists are highly motivated to book you and quite frankly, never stop working for you.

Do publicists have personal relationships with the trade magazine reviewers and the media?

Publicists have professional relationships with the media built up over time. These relationships are important to your success in getting bookings as many in the media like to work with publicists they trust and have proven themselves to be dependable, knowledgeable, and have great experts over time. With this in mind, a good publicist will never book an unqualified expert with the media. By working with a publicist, the media saves a lot of time as publicists are able to provide the perfect author or expert for the media's objectives.

What are the most frustrating elements of working with a client?

Clients would do extremely well by combining publicity with marketing. Remember, publicity is the sharing and expansion of your message, the creation of national expert status for yourself via obtaining media placements on prominent media. Marketing integrates your publicity with your book or professional marketing objectives. This is a much broader view from the old thinking of "how many books did I sell" with the new thinking "how many lives can I change by sharing my message."

12: Websites

Put your best face forward

The effort to achieve notice for your book begins with a great book cover. Why? Because regardless what you may be told, everyone, and I do mean everyone, judges a book by its cover. If it's unimaginative with recognizable graphics and lousy colors, the book could gather dust. It's the goal of every publisher to create a cover that will leap into the hands of a customer with an itchy charge card.

If everyone is that anal about cover art, then it goes to reason that author websites are no different. Readers love going to author's websites. It's a great way to get to know the author better—what makes him/her tick, motivations for writing their book, pictures of the author trying to crank out 'Yankee Doodle Dandy' via their bellybutton, etc. On the other hand, it's disappointing to view an unattractive site that's dull, hard to navigate, or has little information.

A site doesn't have to reveal your inner demons (unless that excites you, or your personal life (save it for your blog). But it should be a crisp, clean site that is filled with reviews, awards, appearances, an excerpt of your book(s), where your book can be purchased, etc.

Review your websites. Dust them off if need be. Revamp if necessary. Your website is the face to you and your book. Your publisher has ensured that your book is wearing its Sunday finest, so it only goes to reason that your website should as well.

Cathy Scott – MBC Design

Cathy Scott is a one-person design firm. Her primary service is web design, development and maintenance, but she can also assist with brand positioning, logo, collateral design, photography and copy writing.

She has experience developing websites for a wide variety of small business and individuals. Her marquee site is Two Paddocks (www.twopaddocks.com), a New Zealand vineyard owned by actor Sam Neill and Cathy has been working with Mr. Neill for over ten years. The web design, fifty percent of the copy and most of the product photography is her work, so Ms. Scott was quite gratified to read the recent comments by British wine reviewer Jancis Robinson:

"I could burble on for hours—or metres—about the story of Two Paddocks but it is told much more eloquently on www.twopaddocks.com—one of the most agreeable and useful winery websites I have come across for some time."

Ms. Scott has designed and maintained several other sites including The Bicycle Club of Irvine, Booth Mitchel Strange (law firm), and Shawn's Studio Fitness (personal trainer).

Her training and experience are in all aspects of marketing communications. Her day job is Vice President of Corporate Communications for Western Digital, a hard drive manufacturer, and she maintains MBC Design to get back to what she loves; hands-on work with design and marketing for authors and small organizations. Because it's a second job, Ms. Scott keeps her client list very small and handles each client with personal care.

Why do authors need a custom made website for their books rather than a free downloadable template?

Embrace the Internet and use it to its fullest potential. You've poured your heart and soul into writing a great book, now you need to put that same kind of care and energy into marketing your book. The center of that marketing effort should be the Internet. Readers, booksellers and the press expect to find you on the web. You will be at a big disadvantage if you're not there.

To capture the look and feel of your book, to rise above the crowd, your website should be a unique design, not an overused template that thousands of others have used. This is your opportunity to express yourself and communicate why your book is different from the pack. Make your site uniquely your own, keep it fresh and interesting and you will attract many more readers than you would with a copycat website.

What kind of information should go on an author's website?

A content-rich, up-to-date, website is the most effective way to sell your books and keep reader coming back for more. There is some basic information you must have on your site and some nice-to-have stuff, too.

The basics:

* **About the book(s):** Position the book to your target audience. If you're a mystery or science fiction writer, you need to express that to your readers through the look and feel of your site. Include a short synopsis. It's a good idea to include some longer excerpts to show off your writing style.

* **Meet the author:** A short bio and photo is important to build credibility and establish a connection with your readers.

* **Contact information:** Post your email address. And if people write to you, answer immediately. Each new reader who likes you and your book spreads the word for you.

* **Where to buy information:** Add links to all online retailers carrying your book. Make sure you link directly to the page that sells the book, not to the retail home page. The fewer clicks to final purchase the better.

The extras:

* **Blog:** Keep this current with your thoughts and insights and you'll garner a wider and wider audience for your books.

* **Video:** promote your book with an interesting or timely video.

* **Reviews:** when the great reviews come in, post them on your site.

* **Merchandise:** If your book is particularly popular, you can sell hats, t-shirts and other promotional items.

* **Press area:** Make it easy for the press to promote your book with photos, cover art and synopses.

* **Links:** Post links to more information about the subject matter of your book. Find sites that talk about the location of your story, or provide background information about your narrative.

* **Email marketing:** Have your visitors sign up for your mailing list. Then send out a monthly newsletter or announcement about the next book in your series.

Do you make suggestions to the client as to what should be included on a website? For example, contests, Q&As, sample chapters, etc.

A good web designer must also be a good marketer. Look for designers with experience in designing websites for authors—someone who not only understands websites but also understands writers.

When I work with an author, I first learn as much as I can about the book and the author's marketing requirements. Then I recommend what the site design and content should be. It's not always necessary to meet face-to-face. In this Internet age you can accomplish a lot through email exchange.

Do you provide the author with several designs? How many?

Typically I will create more than one design, but not always. Sometimes I hit on something that I believe is a perfect solution to the site design. I always work with the author in several design rounds to make sure the design meets the author's vision.

Book covers are greatly impacted by color and fonts. Are websites the same? Why?

As a book cover is the face of your book, a website is your face to the world. It must be a professional design that communicates not only the look and feel of your book, but also your respect for your reader. Sloppy designs, clumsy navigation, weak graphics and color choices all put people off and turn them away from your site. People do judge a book by its cover and they judge an author by the professional quality of their website.

What is the average time you spend designing a website?

It usually takes about a month to design a great site and get it up on the web. Design time depends on the client's responsiveness in providing all the needed content.

What happens after you've completed the website? Do you just design the website and the author has to go find a company to host it, or do you do host the site and maintain it as well?

Designing a site is just the beginning. Once completed and approved, we need to get the site on the web. We do this through a web hosting company, which stores the website on their web servers and links the site with your domain name. Typically, I recommend low-cost hosting services that provide the types of services the author needs. If we're streaming video we need a host that offers that service, if not, we can use a less expensive host or hosting package. Sometimes my clients come to me with a web host already selected. No problem, I can work with any host as long as it provides the services we need.

Who buys the domain name?

A domain name is a way to identify and locate websites and resources connected to the Internet. No two websites can have the same domain name. Typically an author will use his or her name as their domain name, susiesmith.com, for example. There are many ways to obtain your domain name, and it may be cheaper than you think. You're not limited to purchasing names through a domain name registrar; you can get names through a hosting company or purchase an existing domain from an end-user or a reseller. I can help my clients acquire their domain name or they can buy it themselves.

What other fees are tied up with a website?

I charge for web design and development as a one-time expense. I also offer maintenance services which my clients can pay for monthly, or hourly. Hosting service is an additional cost that you should plan for. It typically costs between $15 and $25 per month. Domain names are leased annually and start at $45 per year with discounts for multiyear leases.

Can authors have their own email address, and do you handle this?

Once you own a domain name and subscribe to a hosting service you can have your own email address. In fact, you can have multiple email addresses using your domain. So Susie Smith, who owns susiesmith.com, can have susie@susiesmith.com as well. She can also have author@susiesmith.com and bob@susiesmith.com as well. I can help my clients set up their email addresses, or I can give instructions so they can do it themselves.

Can you make it possible for an author's website to appear at the top of a Google search?

Once your site is up on the web, you need to drive traffic to the site. The more people see your site the more effective it is a marketing tool. There are certain techniques to optimize a site for search engines. Make sure your Web designer includes website optimization as part of the design package. Beyond that, you can buy keywords in search engines like Google to make sure your site appears on the first page of a search.

Final Thoughts From My Side of the Pond

With much of the importance placed on blogs these days, many authors are forgoing websites. Personally, I think it's a mistake, since both are important. Sure, I know many blogs offer tabs that make them appear more website-like, but I think authors have more content freedom with a website. This is a great place to put up a sample chap of their writing, discuss other works in progress, include interesting tidbits that might be germane to readers of their book.

For example, I know a woman who wrote a gardening mystery, and she updates her site with various types of exotic plants. She has a "Murder by flower" month, and every week she includes some poisonous plant and talks about how to create the perfect murder. Her fans love it because her site is so colorful, yet she maintains that mystery flair of her books. She has more creative control with a website than a blog, and she uses that to full advantage with colorful pictures and such.

So many sites I look at appear to be created by a schizoid marmoset, with tons of text, wild graphics, and flash plug-ins belching out all over the index page. It confuses the already over-stimulated brain. Another thing that drives me nuts is the site whose link buttons are oh-so-clever and I have to actually try to figure out what they mean and where they are. Why would any author play Where's Waldo with their links? We don't all wear the same tinfoil hats, so authors are smart to keep it clean, crisp, and clear.

These days, promotion is a multi-faceted jewel, and every writer should include a great website in their tackle box. And, yes, I realize I mixed metaphors.

In conclusion

It is my hope these interviews have expanded your mind and given you new perspective about the publishing industry. Knowledge is one of the most important tools in your tackle box, and these folks are the very best in their business.

Section 2

The Submission Process

"Forget the bait, pass me the Maalox"

If authors could see how editors struggle through thousands of queries and make informed decisions based on teensy bits of information, they would have a clear understanding about why we think the way we do, how we work, and put to rest the controversy of whether we really do think at all. This would also explain our penchant for stiff drinks.

This section is about giving you a front row seat at our side of the desk in order to show you what floats editors' boats, what information we need to see, and how to present you and your work in the most professional manner.

Angler's Truth:

The idea is to not give an editor any reason
to reject your work other than it's simply not
right for them.

13: Before You Bait Your Hook You Need To. . .

Be a good Girl Scout

The whole trick to the query/submission process is preparation. I always tell writers at conferences to channel the Girl Scout motto— *Be Prepared*. An agent or editor may not ask you for a full synopsis right then and there, but that doesn't mean you won't need one at some point. It could be that you go from query letter, to a request for pages, to a full manuscript. But mark my words, you *will* need that synopsis eventually, and there is nothing worse than having to bang one out in a couple minutes. The professional has already written it up and revised a few hundred times.

Same goes for a log line or a promotion plan. You may think it's unnecessary and will cross that bridge when you come to it. Problem is, you never know when you're going to hit that bridge. If I ask for a synopsis to accompany requested pages (and I always do), then I'll take a dim view if the author says, "Can you hold on for a few days while I write the synopsis?" My answer will always be yes, but I'll also be putting a checkmark in the "You Made Me Cranky" column. It's not that I'm ill-tempered, but I always come to parties well prepared, and I expect the same of you. Don't blow it by not being a good Girl Scout.

Do an Ego Check

Here's the dictionary's definition of ego, what I call the "*it's all about me*" word:

The "I" or self of any person; a person as thinking, feeling, and willing, and distinguishing itself from the selves of others and from objects of its thought.

I have no problem with a hale and hearty ego provided its manufacture is in relative perspective to the rest of the bells and whistles that comprise our brains. A healthy ego begets confidence and conviction that any task can be accomplished, be it rewrites or promotion.

A healthy ego is all about balance, meaning their sense of self isn't undercooked over overcooked. The balanced ego writes with confidence but understand their words didn't come directly from the hands of the Great Cosmic Muffin. They are willing and happy to learn, and they accept critiques in a professional manner because they know it's *about the writing*, not them. They understand there is process to the query stage, and they learn how to do it right before jumping in with both feet. I adore these types of writers because they make my job so easy.

Conversely, it can be hard going if an author's sense of self is over- or under-cooked—especially in this business. The overcooked ego "it truly *is* all about me" author barrels through the query letter process without bothering to learn how to write one. They ignore the submissions guidelines and don't provide the information we request because, hey, those were written to keep out the tourists. Certainly not *ME!* They send what they want and expect a hasty reply in the preferred method of genuflection and enthusiastic praise. And of course, a contract. These types are usually the last to know that the publishing world got on nicely without them and will probably continue to do so. Rejection is a gargantuan shock to these types because they never consider the possibility.

The undercooked ego comes in two flavors; one who spends half their time apologizing to us during a meeting, or is so insecure that they can't accept rejection. This latter type is the wretched soul who responds to a rejection letter with colorful metaphors and invitations to perform all sorts of carnal acrobatics with barnyard animals. The apologist is scared of their shadow and feels guilty for taking up space and breathing air. I've been in meetings where I came close to ripping my eyelids off because the author kept apologizing whenever I made an editorial comment.

Don't forget that we're not just judging your writing; we're judging *you* as well. We want to know how you'll do during promotion of your book. If I have to worry that the apologist is going to turn into her shell during an interview, this doesn't help to promote the book. It does not bode well if the author writes to *Publisher's Weekly* and tells them they are a bloated codfish for the hatchet review they did on their book. (seen it; pinky swear)

I'm not suggesting authors need to have their dreams interpreted and submit to shock therapy, but self-analysis is not a bad thing. Publishing is tough and competitive. As authors, you will be rejected, scrutinized, discussed, tossed in the blender, and put in the spin and rinse cycle. It's far better to know up front whether you're incapable of critique or sorry that you walk on the planet among so much talent. Only through self-examination can you take steps to work through your fallibilities and attain balance and confidence. Hollywood may have plastic surgeons, but writers have Freud.

Consider this tidbit the golden lure in your literary tackle box.

14: Myth busting

Okay, now that we have Dr. Freud and the Girl Scouts out of the way, you can see how your tackle box has begun to fill up. The interviews in Section I gave you a good introduction to the numerous species of fish swimming in the pond and how they impact the publishing industry. But you're not an angler yet. You need to understand how to shiny up those rusty hooks and sinkers before you tie them to your fishing pole. There's a right way and a wrong way, and it's vital to know the difference.

The first step to presenting yourself in a professional manner is to first understand there is a lot of erroneous and conflicting information permeating the industry, which sends many authors into apoplexy.

* Am I expected to promote? Yes! No! . . . *yes*

* Should I include my promo plans in my query letter? Yes! No! . . .*not necessarily*

* Do I need to include a bio? Yes! No! . . . *absolutely*

* Do I have to know my readership? Yes! No! . . . *most definitely*

* Do editors care about genre? Yes! No! . . . *an unqualified yes*

One of the biggest pieces of erroneous information floating around is the idea that you're writing strictly for yourself, and you don't need to worry about anything or anyone else.

Angler's Myth:

"Forget about the marketplace, forget the audience, forget the genre, and focus on the writing."

I wince every time I hear this because it normally comes from the mouths of very big authors who bring in millions for their publisher. They have a proven, winning combination that appeals to the reading public.

But what about Joe or Jane Author who has no audience or prior experience whatsoever? Can they afford that same attitude? From where I sit, I vote no.

It's All About Understanding Your Readership

So why do you need to understand your readership? Well, we're going to ask, for starters. Are your readership teens with weight problems? Dog trainers? Motorcycle riders? Having a developed sense of your readers is simply smart business. You have to understand all of these elements in order to sell you and your story. So let's break these points down one at a time.

* Forget about the marketplace

* Forget the audience

* Forget the genre

* Focus on the writing

"Forget about the marketplace"

The "marketplace," simply put, is a place where products are bought and sold. Why should you care and how this impacts you?

Well, let's say the marketplace is filled with blueberry Twinkies (a crime against nature, in my opinion). All the vendors in the marketplace purchase boxes of Twinkies from the manufacturer. The trick is to order only the amount the vendor believes will sell because they realize the marketplace is a fickle mistress. In short, they don't want to get stuck with a full warehouse and no demand should buyers decide they don't like blueberry Twinkies.

Manufacturers know this as well, so they all watch the buying trends and see how crowded the marketplace is with blueberry Twinkies. In order to stay ahead of a heavily impacted market, one manufacturer may do something clever and add a unique element, tart multi-colored sprinkles, to their product. Their Twinkies' distinctive qualities separate them from the other manufacturers, thus enhancing their chances of succeeding.

If you write in an overexposed category, like chick lit, vampire YA, or divorce, and are trying to sell your "blueberry Twinkie" to an editor, then you need to be sure that your Twinkie (book) is different from all the other Twinkies (books) of the same flavor. For instance, I must receive about twenty surviving cancer/alcohol abuse/physical abuse/mental breakdown stories a month. This is a hugely impacted category, and I have to decide whether the marketplace can bear one more Twinkie (book) of this flavor. Unless it is distinctive and offers unique information that none of the other competing titles have, then I have to pass because I can't sell it. What is hot today can become cold three or four years later. Add to the fact that most books take roughly two years to hit the shelves, and suddenly your new hit could have a very short shelf life.

Avoid a rejection by knowing the market, which is every book in your genre—your competition—and tailoring your query letter to highlight your book's unique qualities.

To sum it up, if you forget about the marketplace, then you risk becoming redundant.

"Forget about the audience"

Writers who follow this advice fumble around a lot when we ask, "who is your intended audience?" And, yes, we do ask because we want to make sure there is a large enough audience to warrant publishing the book. Some books have a huge audience, like vampire romance novels or mystery cozies, while others attract a small specialty market—niche—such as aviation or transplanted Asians suffering culture shock. We have to know where your work fits.

So think about your audience. Is your work for the college kids who are scared about their future after graduation? Are they engineers? Dog groomers? Working professionals or stay-at-home moms? Students or retired postal workers?

My book is for everyone!

If you want to watch an editor implode, tell her that your book is for "everyone." I implode on a regular basis because I don't have "everyone" in my Rolodex, yet this makes up the bulk of the queries that cross my desk. It should be right there in your query: "This work is intended for the medical community, bird watchers, arborists, the Jewish community. . ."

If you can't define your audience, then how can you be sure you even *have* an audience? And if you don't know, then what is the probability of my wanting to review the work? As Austin Powers says, "throw me a frickin' bone."

Make sure you have an audience

Once last consideration is figuring out whether an audience for your book even exists. For example, I doubt there is an audience for the magic of tie-dye shoelaces or that novel about pygmy gremlins who take over Grand Central Station. So how does one go about figuring out if they have an audience? They are well-read in their genre. They look to see if there are any social trends that relate to their story—hmm, maybe there is an audience for that pygmy gremlin book.

Bounce your ideas off of friends and family and listen to their feedback. Join writer's groups. Getting advice and critiques from your fellow writers is a valuable tool for your tackle box. They are your sounding board, your reality check, and your audience. It's far better to know in the early stages of your story development that few will be interested in your book rather than writing it, querying it out for years, and collecting piles of rejection letters. Make sure you're on solid ground.

Angler's Truth:

Authors tend to be islands. Take a boat to reality every now and then and get your work critiqued by fellow writers.

"Forget about genre"

Forget the about the genre? Do it at your peril. We understand that writers hate to be pigeonholed and categorized, but, unfortunately, we live in a world where our books survive by being labeled and categorized. For instance, all our books have a BISAC (Book Industry Standards and Communications) code: www.bisg.org/index.html. The codes are assigned to books based on their content and are a must because they provide bookstores with the means to categorize, store, and shelve our books. You don't get more pigeonholed than that.

I see many authors get hung up in defining a genre:

* It's fantasy and mystery

* It's romance and chick lit

* It's a hybrid

A hybrid? There is no BISAC code for "hybrid." And don't suggest that I "choose" a genre for you. Argh! Don't make me guess because while most works are pretty easy to figure out, there is a surprising number that can cause confusion—like the time I was about to reject a work, even though I loved the writing because we don't publish YA. The author quickly clarified; oh no, this isn't YA, it's adult fiction. Ohhh . . . thinks I, that's a different story. Glad I asked. Not only did I not reject it, but we published it to critical acclaim, and Janice Eidus' *The War of the Rosens* has been a big hit. Protect yourself against a rejection letter; figure out what your genre is, and tell us.

"Focus on the writing "

In this, I agree. Absolutely focus on the writing because this is where your passion comes through. It's always, always, always about the writing. However, don't give an editor any reason to reject you other than the work isn't right for them. Be prepared, be smart, and keep one eye open to the other stuff.

Writing is a business, so treat is as such.

15: The Log Line

Okay, this is where the Girl Scout part comes in again. You've been duly warned about the necessity of needing tools *before* you begin casting your hook into the water, and this chapter will deal with helping you write them. We'll begin small—not because it's easier because it isn't—but it's the logical place to start.

The Log line

The log line is your one or two sentence overview of your story. It's that little something you whip out whenever anyone asks, "Hey, what's your book about?" It is also one of the most important tools in your tackle box because it is oftentimes the first face of your book, whether it's an editor, agent, a reviewer, a newspaper journalist, a radio talk show host, or a friend.

Don't mistake size for importance

You might be wondering what a log line has to do with the query process. Sometimes *everything*. If you're attending a writer's conference (something I highly recommend), you can be certain that conversation will always center on people's writing—whether you're at the bar, standing in the hallway, or at agent/editor pitch sessions. That someone standing next to you asking about your book could very well be an agent or editor. If you haven't created an effective log line, what do you do? I can say from hard experience that my eyes begin to glaze over when I see an author take a deep breath because this means I'm in for a ten minute blow-by-blow of their book. On the other hand, a great log line can bring about an offer to submit pages.

The idea is to start small and build on it—hello, Mr. Log line. This is your flavorful hors d'oeuvre that entices the listener to say, "ah, tell me more." The more prepared you are, the better able you are to suck in your listener.

Be an attention grabber

Everything that comes out of your mouth has to be designed to entice. You can be sure that I laughed myself silly with this:

"Alice Mae would have never been born had her mother not lost a poker game to Al Capone."

Talk about an attention grabber. Even with this weensy bit of information, I was hooked. The absolute best way to grab anyone's attention is to always, always, always reveal the conflict. It doesn't have to be huge, but it has to be implied, as it is with this example. Obviously something big happened during that poker game, and I want to know more.

Set the tone

Your log line is the precursor—a setup—to your story, so it should match in tone. If your book is a mystery, then your log line shouldn't be light and airy, but rather, more somber and moody.

Here's an example:

"*Japanese Maidens Busting Out* is about a modern American family who visit a traditional Japanese family."

It's ok. It gets the job done and tells us what it's about, but it has no zing, or tone. Is this a solemn indictment of culture clash? The title doesn't indicate this, so which is it? We noodled around with it, and came up with this:

"Cheeseburgers or Miso soup? *Japanese Maidens Busting Out* is a lighthearted culture clash between American relatives, equipped with Western weapons of mass corruption, and a conservative Japanese family."

Both are log lines, but which one makes you want to go out and buy the book? That's the tone you're looking for. Again, note the implications of conflict.

Log lines have a beginning, middle, and an end

Remember, your aim is to get us to ask for more information, so it's important to give us enough information at the outset. This is why you need to make sure your log line has a beginning, middle, and an end. How do you do this in one sentence, you gasp? It's as simplistic as, "I came, I saw, I went." The idea is to not leave the listener hanging.

Let's say we're back at that bar and an editor asks, "What's your book about?" Keep in mind that they're more than likely lacking sleep and hungry. The wine they're holding is a safety net to hide behind if things go awry.

Okay:

The Publisher is about an accidental publisher.

Who cares? This slip of information forces the editor to ask too many questions and more than likely, they'll nod politely, sip their wine, and move on. You're not engaging them. What does this person do that makes the story worthwhile? Why should we care? Where is this going? Try again.

Better:

The Publisher is about an accidental publisher has an odd stable of writers.

Ok, now you've offered up a bit more detail and introduced what sounds like could be the spark of a story. Very good. But the editor still has this "so what?" thing going on because she knows (hopes, assumes) there's more to it than this. What happens with these writers? Why did she take them on?

Best:

The Publisher is about an accidental publisher whose hands are full with five ladies in their mid-seventies, an internationally famous novelist, and a nosy reporter who is determined to expose their identities as writers of some of the hottest erotica to hit the shelves.

Ah ha. There it is; the beginning, middle, and end. Also included is the implied conflict of a reporter pitted against the publisher in a showdown. It sets about an interesting dynamic. Result: Tell me more. You can see that it's possible to say much with so little.

"I can't condense 70,000 words into two sentences."

Everyone knows our stories contain many characters and subplots, and the log line's job isn't about condensing all 70,000 words; it's about revealing your MAIN PLOT and YOUR MAIN CHARACTERS WHO PROPEL THAT PLOT.

Read my lips: Every single story has one major element that defines and drives the story. I've lost count of the many times I've listened to a five minute explanation of someone's story only to have no clue as to the plot. Reminds me of a conference I attended where I ended up sharing a wonderful chicken satay with an author while standing in a crowded bar. She went on for at least five or six minutes, and I could tell she could see my confusion. I kept asking questions to draw her out. Finally a light bulb lit over my head, and I burst out, "Oh, you're writing the five minute metaphysical mom." Her jaw went slack, and she stared at me. I could see it was a light bulb moment for her as well. Notice the beginning, middle, and implied end. For you parents out there, you can appreciate the implied conflict. It definitely has "tell me more" spice.

I can't say it enough; be the proverbial Girl Scout, and always be prepared. This little log line will be your lifeline throughout the life of your book because there will always be someone asking, "what's your book about?"

Remember, your job as a writer isn't completed just because you belched out 70,000 words. You still need to effectively represent and communicate those 70,000 words so you can snare one of those fish in the pond.

A quick word about writer's conferences

Since I've used writer's conferences as an example in this section, I want to recommend that all writers should attend at least one or two conferences in their career. Writers, by the merits of their hobby/job, are solitary creatures, and you need to surface for air, to take a few seminars and learn the ins and outs and the do's and don'ts of this industry. More people research buying a new car than they do the publishing industry, and I have seen the aftermath of sad stories and head-on collisions of, "if only I knew."

If you love writing, then honor your hard work by doing the research. Not only is the information vast and enlightening at conferences, but the networking can't be beat. I know many authors who have found agents or editors at conferences. There is always something to learn and people to know.

16:   The Pitch

Now that you have your log line, you're ready to work with more expanded information, heavier equipment. This is your pitch, which is a condensed synopsis anywhere from one to four short paragraphs. This will go in your query letter and also what you'll use when someone says, "tell me more."

Again, the idea is to entice an editor/agent/reviewer/interviewer to request your first chapters, or your book to review.

How do I start?

Just like the log line, the pitch has a beginning, middle, and an end. Since query letters are short, it's important to channel Joe Friday on *Dragnet* and keep it to, "Just the facts, ma'am." Stick to the central plot and the characters who propel the plot.

The ABCs of Pitchdom

Put this in your tackle box and never lose it. Like the log line, your pitch is your golden hook to catching a fish. Every pitch MUST:

Intro the characters—who's the protagonist? Who's the antagonist? What makes us empathize with them?

Intro the rudiments of the dilemma or conflict—it's the tension, the meat of the story where the protagonist stands to lose something

Present teasers or resolutions—don't give the ending here because it's more detail than we want right now. Save that for the synopsis.

Many authors get hung up in this, and I recommend that you begin by making bullet points next to each element. For **Intro the Characters**, list your protagonist and antagonist. List their qualities or attributes. Then go to **Intro the dilemma**, and do the same thing. List the tension, the conflict, and what the protagonist stands to lose. Same for **Present teasers**. Since you now have a list to work from, you can begin to build your pitch.

Now don't panic; let's go through it together using a sample.

Intro the characters—points of empathy:

* **Twist McPherson**: protagonist, young, successful, newly retired advertising executive, has too much free time, wants to write a novel.

* **Roz**: Twist's best friend, editor at a NY publishing house, wants to help Twist with her writing

* **Five genteel ladies in their mid-seventies:** been writing erotica e-books with an unusual quirk of taste and class, they write under nom de plumes, e-books sell well, ready to see their work in books.

* **Jack Crawford:** comes to Palm Springs to finish a book he doesn't want to write, looming deadline, famous John Grisham type. Ends up writing anonymously for Twist as well. Bloody hell! Watch out for those fireworks.

* **Carl Beckenham:** book reviewer/reporter for *The Chicago Times*. His department is in danger of closing, and he's looking for a big story to make a name for himself to save his job.

Intro the rudiments of the dilemma or conflict—the tension, meat of the story where the protag stands to lose something

* Twist can't get published and opens up her own publishing company in order to self-publish her book.

* She gets sidelined with five retired, genteel ladies who write hot, yet refined erotica under nom de plumes.

* She meets Jack, who's in the desert to finish his book, but instead writes for Twist as a way to break his writing block.

* As Jack and the ladies books grow more popular, Carl, smelling a good story, flies out to interview Twist and find out more about her and her anonymous authors.

Present the teasers or resolutions:

* Carl's incessant digging has Twist working overtime trying to shut him up, thus maintaining Jack's and her five ladies' anonymity.

Ok, now let's put it all together:

Twist McPherson, on permanent hiatus from the rat race, moves to Palm Springs and sets about writing the Great American Novel. Her timing couldn't be worse; the sour economy has publishers signing only the big blockbuster, like world class author Jack Crawford and his courtroom dramas. After one too many Harvey Wallbangers with her best friend Roz, Twist agrees to dust off her advertising talents and create her own publishing company.

During her weekly Mah Jong game with a group of saucy ladies, all in their 70s, Twist casually mentions her publishing plans. Before she can eat the olive out of her martini, Dirty Little Secrets, LLC is born, and Twist has a stable of five new writers who, under nom de plumes, have spent the past three years writing some of the hottest, yet refined erotica to hit the electronic bookshelves. As southern belle, Lucinda Du Pont, drawls over tea spiked with Jack Daniel's, "Smut sells, dear."

In the midst of cover designs and distribution, Twist—so named for her metaphorical gifts of rearranging the male anatomy during tough business negotiations—meets the mighty Jack Crawford, newly arrived to the desert to finish his faltering tenth book and meet his thrice-past-due deadline. He absolves his writer's block by writing for Twist under the name Marcella de la Prentiss.

It wouldn't have been so bad had *Chicago Times* book reviewer Carl Beckenham not smelled a story in the young new publisher who blasted onto the scene with her classy advertisements and sophisticated promotion. But Snarlin' Carl's nose for a hot story has him digging deeper into Twist's business to find out the identity of her writers, which threatens Jack's career and the ladies' dirty little secrets.

Whoa there . . . got Voice?

Before you begin any of this, don't forget the most important aspect: you. Writing a pitch or a synopsis is a lot like a fashion show where everyone primped for hours in an effort to look their absolute best, and the best way to look your best is to allow your voice come through. Some of the most memorable query letters I received were due to the author's distinct voice.

Voice is the term we use when describing an author's writing style; how they've combined syntax (how they strand together a sentence), flow, tone, character development, dialog. It's your literary fingerprint. It doesn't matter how short or long your writing is, always inject voice into it. More than anything, this is what we look for because it's what makes your writing come to life.

Let me take the pitch I wrote earlier and take out the "voice" so you'll see what I mean:

Voiceless Version:

Twist McPherson moves to Palm Springs to write a book. Publishers are only looking for big blockbusters, like the famous Jack Crawford and his courtroom dramas. Her best friend, Roz, suggests Twist open up her own company and publish her book. She tells her friends, all in their 70s, about her plans. She then finds out they have been secretly writing erotica as e-books. They form Dirty Little Secrets, LLC.

Jack Crawford comes to the desert to try to finish his book, which is late. Suffering from writer's block, he writes a couple of stories, which Twist publishes. Her company captures the attention of book reviewer/reporter Carl Beckenham, who is looking for a big story that will save the book review section of the *Chicago Times*. He looks to find out who her writers are, which threatens Jack's career and the ladies' well-kept secret.

Technically this is sound; it introduces the characters, the conflict, and teasers. But it's also pretty vanilla, and that's because there's no voice. It's as if a robot relayed this information. Who cares?

Voice is important because it sets the tone of the story while allowing the writer's style to come through. It is not necessary to say, "this is a lighthearted look at publishing gone horribly wrong," (as so many authors do) because your voice says it all. And you really want to avoid those kind of statements anyway because you're *telling* me rather than *showing* me.

And you know what? If a synopsis or pitch has a great voice, then we're willing to overlook a lot. Aspiring author, Matt Barlow has a pitch made from heaven that would have had me demanding pages. His is a prime example of voice:

Pitch for *FIVE MINUTES*:

I can see the future.

Great, right?

Not really.

Five minutes. That's what I get. Five minutes of the future.

Five minutes of fog so thick I can barely see, and, most often, vomit-inducing nausea to greet me when I come back to the present.

It's okay though. It's taken half my life for me to get a grip on this thing I call the Vision, but I've gotten used to it. Got a buddy to clean up after me. Got a girl. Well, she's a hooker, so I suppose I bought a girl. Even scraped out a decent little life finding the occasional winning slot machine.

At least, it was okay. Until I started seeing the murders.

Now, he broke all kinds of rules and didn't follow the ABCs of Pitchdom. But you know what? Who cares? He. Had. Voice. Do not take this tool of voice for granted; keep it in your tackle box because it's the difference between "yes, I want pages," and "no thanks."

Description vs. Detail—know the difference

Something else that will make us say "no thanks" is a query that's long on description and short on plot. Most of the queries I see lack some or all of the examples I explained above. Description lacks the specifics that editors need in order to make educated decisions as to whether we want to see more. I can do little with description, but I can do a lot with detail.

Example of description:

My book, *Clueless After All These Years*, is about my travails through six years of college. This is told in the first person and details how my parents forced me to attend an Ivy League school against my lifelong desire to be a food server at McDonalds. I talk about how my professors were idiots and the loose morals of my fraternity brothers and their dippy girlfriends.

I have only the most general idea of what the story is about, and none of the elements that propel this story along. This is filled with a picnic basket of "who cares?" Why should I care about six years of college? Why did the author's parents force him into college? Why did the author's aspirations reach no further than being a purveyor in the food industry? Why were the professors idiots? . . . and on and on.

Anything that forces me to ask more questions is something I'm going to immediately stop reading. If you don't tell us, we're not going to ask. We'll reject and move on. Yes, it sounds brutal but when our desks are filled with hundreds of queries, we have little choice but to make snap decisions. That's why it's so important to give us exactly what we need in as concise a manner as you can.

What is it I've been nagging? *Don't give an editor any reason to reject you other than it's not right for them.* This author gave me a huge reason to reject. For all I know it was a great piece of work, but it was so poorly communicated that I passed on it without a second thought. Don't forget, there are a lot of hooks floating around the pond, and we will only bite at the brightest one.

17: Author Bio

Creating Something From Nothing

Your Log line and Pitch are sitting comfortably in your tackle box, and the next tool you need is your biography. Whether you're writing fiction or nonfiction, I want to know:

* **A smattering about you / Why you wrote the book**

* **The book's unique qualities**

* **Connects with a specific audience**

* **If you have anything else in the pipeline, and your writing goals**

* **Publishing credits**

Among the elements that authors agonize over when writing a query letter is their biography. Most scream from the heights of flagpoles, "I don't HAVE a friggin' bio!"

Well, sure you do. Everyone does. What you mean is you don't have publishing credits. You're thinking that without a publishing history that you can't find an agent or editor. Sure, there are some editors and agents who only want published authors, but there are a large number who don't mind new writers. Before we can move to first base, we need to know something about you, and it's what you decide to say that makes a difference. Many make the common mistake of telling us stuff that's either cliché or of no interest. Here's an example of what I commonly see in query letters:

I write to relieve my stress as a corporate lawyer (plumber, mom, engineer, teacher, etc.). My writing puts me into a make-believe world where I can control the lives and stories of my characters. It's my goal to create plots filled with unique adventures and put my characters in situations that are filled with conflict—a mirror of everyday life. My creative writing class helps me improve my craft, so I can move closer to my real passion, building a writing career.

The problem I have with this is it screams "I'm a newbie writer." We're looking for a savvy writer, and this bio is pedestrian because it doesn't tell me anything I want to know. Just like writing, we want to avoid fluff, and this is fluff. It's a natural assumption that we all want to create great characters and plots, and we all have stress, so you're not telling me anything new or vital. Who cares? I'm glad you're taking writing classes, but this makes you sound like a work in progress. I don't want a work in progress, I want a pro.

Another type of bio I see is the "my kids" theme:

I wrote my novel because my seven-year-old twin boys inspired me. I read to them every night, and I thought it would be great to read them something that Daddy had written. My family thought *Twin Boys in TwinkieLand* would make for a great addition to the fantasy genre.

This is cliché, hobby stuff. Most of us don't care about your personal life and what elements drove you to write. We want to know what drove you to write *this* story. What elements did you feel were missing in the genre that your story could fill? We're looking at fundamentals about you that we can sell to the genre buyers and reviewers. We want to know that you're well-read in your genre because too many writers aren't, and they write stuff that's already been done over and over.

Here's an off the cuff example that works:

I wrote *Twinkies Take Manhattan* because Twinkies have made a huge comeback in the US snack market, and I saw this as a delightful way to portray America's favorite snack as a major character dealing with getting lost in a big city and how to find help. The child safety classes I teach in the elementary schools are a true inspiration because children tell me that getting lost is their biggest fear. This important topic isn't addressed in the current children's genre, and the use of a Twinkies character wraps sage advice in a very colorful package.

Notice that there is no mention of a lack of publishing credits, but rather I'm focusing on what I feel is the marketability and uniqueness of my story compared to everything else on the shelves. I'm trying to convey the existing popularity of my main character—anything that says "this is a book worth looking at." You're hyping your story while giving us a sense of who you are.

It doesn't matter that in my real life I crochet toilet paper doilies and have 1,000 cats that I've painstakingly potty-trained. Again, who cares? Focus on the story and why you wrote it. If you can't tell me why you wrote *that* story as compared to something else, then I'll suspect you're a hobbyist and will probably move on.

If you tell me that you just sat down one day and banged out this story because it was bursting inside of you, I guarantee that my eyes will glaze over. Why *this* story? I'm looking for the passion behind the words. I don't care if this idea came to you in a dream. If it did, then make it relevant to the marketplace, readers.

Why all the bugaboo about bios? It's as I said, we use this info to sell your book. The more exciting the author, the more exciting the book. "Exciting" equates to energized genre buyers filling out purchase orders. And that makes for a very joy-joy day for all.

It is possible to make something from nothing. Note that the "author" doesn't have a publishing credit and, instead, focuses on her close familiarity with her subject matter, her ready audience, and her ability to promote it. Smart stuff.

Angler's Truth:

Being published by a Print-on-Demand or vanity press is not . . .repeat, NOT, a publishing credit. Don't include this information. The only thing it says about you is that you either paid to be published or that you went with a publisher whose acceptance standards are below industry standards.

Platform: promoting something from nothing

The Tale of the Two surfer dudes -

And speaking of creating something from nothing, I want to say a brief word about the "P" word because it's an issue that will come up at some point. I'll discuss it in more detail in Chapter 25.

My motto is the sooner, the better because it shows that you're prepared. Most new writers lack a strong marketing platform—those elements that make you marketable, like the doctor who writes medical fiction or the cop who writes detective stories—so you have to dig a lot deeper to figure out the best ways to get the word out about your book.

I'm often threatened with flying wine glasses when I dare to bring up the "P" word while sitting at the bar during writer's conferences because it's the one of those things that gives writers apoplexy—like paying taxes. Note to self: never say the "P" word in the bar. Ever.

What is the "P" word? P-p-promotion. Now put down that glass! I'm tired of ducking from pouty chardonnay.

So I have this workshop on Promotion, and it's designed to help authors pull the elements from their books, or their lives, that will help create a platform where none seems to exist. I had this one guy—blond, wavy hair, deep tan, and said "dude" a lot. His book was science fiction, and his main characters were these two surfer dudes, a lot like him, I imagine. He had done the vanity press thing and wondered how to sell the book.

After a quick lesson in how his book would never be on store shelves, we set about making him memorable. Talk about a tall order. How on earth could we make lemonade out of this lemon? Science fiction? Surfer dudes? Oy, my burning ulcer. . .

We first looked at who he is; a surfer dude who's been surfing at the same beach all his life. He's well-known down there, so the first suggestion I made is that he set up a weenie roast on the beach and give away dogs and a free book to the first 50 surfers. Do this for the next few weekends.

I recommended that his next step should be to hit up the stores that are right next to the beach and see if they'd be willing to carry his book on consignment. After that, I recommended that he go to the skate/surfer stores in the area and do the same thing. Since those stores know him, I felt pretty sure they'd be willing to do this.

Since he was from my area, I was tickled pink to see an article in the local paper about his weenie roast and book giveaway. He even ranked a nice little interview out of it. My sons told me they saw his book in the surf shops, and that copies had sold.

Now, will this guy sell a gazillion copies and be reviewed by the *Los Angeles Times*? Probably not. But I'm sure he sold a few hundred units, and it was based solely on his ability to find a clever, unique way to use the "P" word to his advantage, and make people aware of its existence. If this guy can find the perfect wave, then I'm betting anyone can. Duuuude.

18: Word Count

"Ya want 150,000 or 79,000 words? You pick"

From a very accommodating author:

"I have a literary fiction of approximately 150,000 words. Should you like the story and find it salable, but are leery due to length, I can reduce the page content, or this manuscript could easily be converted to two books of approximately 320 pages each with a few revisions if you were agreeable; or remain one book of approximately 540 pages. I understand that the publishing world would prefer books in the 300 or so page range for economical reasons. If absolutely necessary, for publication purposes, this manuscript could be pared to a book of approximately 350 pages. As the author, of course, I would prefer not, but it could be done and I am willing to do so. . ."

It's really very nice the author is so willing to do whatever it takes to get the job done. Editors love anyone who says, "What can I do to help?"

However.

There are certain elements I don't want to be bothered with during a simple query, and word count is one of them. I DON'T WANT TO CHOOSE. That's your job.

Remember, you haven't sold me yet, so offering to carve up your manuscript like lamb chops strikes me as premature. See, this author is hoping that his willingness to make changes will mitigate the fact that he realizes his word count is too high. If he already knows this, then why try to sneak something in under my radar? He's blown his chance with me. And probably with anyone else he queried.

I know many agents and editors who literally stop reading the minute they see the word count. High word counts equal higher production costs and higher retail costs. The marketplace, in general, doesn't like big fat books, and this is why we're such bovines about word count.

If your novel has a high or a low word count, then you have some decisions to make. For the large word count, break it up into two novels and add to it, or get out a sharp scalpel. With the low count, consider developing the story in more detail. But don't send a query filled with caveats such as, "read this, but don't worry about the word count, 'cos I can fix that." Hello, if you can fix it, then do it before sending it out. Obviously this author knew better, and now, so do you!

Low Word Counts

On the flip side, low word counts are also a tough sell, and many of us have word count minimums on our submission guidelines. 40,000 words and lower fall into the novella category, and they're harder to sell because people want more bang for their buck. Their lower sales make them cost ineffective to produce. Market research tell us that most readers prefer a range between 60,000—90,000 words.

It's the market, baby

Remember, everything is market driven. If the buying public starts taking a shine to 30,000 or 200,000 word books, then, obviously, publishers will alter their submission guidelines to provide readers with what they want. Until that time, understand the constraints and work to stay within them because—what have I been saying?—you don't want to give an editor any reason to reject you other than your work isn't right for them.

Calculating your word count

If you don't know how to calculate your word count and you're using Microsoft Word, simply click the Tools tab in the toolbar and click on

Word Count. A little window will pop up that gives you all the statistics for your document. There are other calculations that are based on words per line, lines per page, but why work that hard?

19: The Snooze-less Query letter

The Art of Standing Out

Query letters aren't there to keep the tourists happy

I just tossed two submissions—unread—because the authors' cover letters were abysmal. They couldn't spell themselves out of a paper bag, and any knowledge of sentence structure was tossed under a bus. Adding to the mayhem was a lack of focus on their pitch, which boiled down to nothing but descriptions and no plot.

Editors and agents routinely receive heat for rejecting someone based on a lousy query letter. Authors complain that even if the query letter isn't up to par, the submission still deserves to be read. My comeback is that a query letter is the most important introduction of the author and their work, and if they can't get that small part right, then I will assume the rest is equally inferior. Given the stack of properly written letters and submissions that are reaching for my ceiling, I slice and dice out of necessity. Unfair, you shout?

Let's say you're the manager of La Fussy Restaurante de Yummy, and you need to hire a front desk receptionist. Two women walk in. One smells like week-old meatloaf, is wearing ripped leather, has safety pins stashed in her lips, ears, eyebrows, and nose, and sports a tattoo that says "Death to Twinkies." The other woman is wearing a conservative dress, nylons, sensible shoes, neatly styled hair, and smells like fresh flowers. Who do you think that manager is going to interview first? Even though Tattoo Lady could be the best person in the world, her appearance precedes her, and she'll be shown the door faster than the manager can utter, "Gastro demonics."

Thus is the case with a query letter, which precedes everything. In most cases the agent or editor requests pages based on that query letter. Like the restaurant manager, editors and agents will decline to interview anyone whose appearance is disheveled and unprofessional. A lousy appearance tells me that the author doesn't care or doesn't know enough to realize they are ignorant. Ignorance or apathy isn't a compelling defense or an effective method to catching my attention.

British author Brian Clegg shared some of his brilliance when discussing how he views a query.

Think:

* **Why should the editor care?**

* **Why is this book needed right now?**

* **What makes it different from other books out there on the subject?**

* **Who's going to read it?**

* **Why am I the right person to write it?**

I told Brian that I loved him. And I do. See, our tinfoil hats are rarely zeroed in on the same frequency as the author, and this means we can't divine these answers from a short paragraph pitching the joys of knitting toilet paper doilies.

Selling yourself and your manuscript is your job, and your "application" needs to be complete. It's not up to us to play 20 Questions in a game of email ping pong. And yet I've done this with incomplete queries, and

I grind my teeth while pounding out another Let's Flesh Out the Author email, wondering why they're making it so hard for me. They've whet my appetite enough to make me ask for more—which really bugs me because I should be asking for pages at this point instead of trying to find out all the pertinent details.

Why don't I ask for pages up front? Because if that toilet paper knitter is a grease monkey who fixes rust buckets for the local used car sales lot, I realize he's probably not the best person to have written this work, and he'll have little idea as to how to reach his readership. Why waste my time? On the other hand, if the author is the Grand Pooba of Knitters Anonymous and penned the now-famous 12-Step Program for Kitty Sweaters, then she has my attention because I know she's involved in the knitting community.

In short, I can't take the chance the author isn't the Grand Pooba, so I have to ask. Which wastes my time. I know, I know, who cares about wasting the time of an underpaid editor? But that same underpaid editor is the one who will say yay or nay to asking for pages. So fill out your "application"—the query letter—and tell us why you're the best person to have written your book, and why your book rocks. It can mean the difference between asking to see pages and sending out a form rejection letter. At the very least, it defines you as a pro.

Key Elements of a query letter

There are five basic elements that go into a query letter, all of which you've already written:

Log line - optional

Genre

Word count

Pitch

Bio

All that's left is to put the information into one letter. I included a sample query letter to give you a general idea of how it comes together. Now keep in mind that this isn't THE query letter to end all query letters. There are whole books given over to writing the perfect query letter, and I'm sure they're all great. But I can say that, sitting on this side of the desk, this is the type of information most of us like to see in order to make intelligent decisions.

Some editors want more, some less. You can't begin to make us all happy, so don't try. Rather, always read the publisher's submission guidelines—most are very concise about what they want to see.

Sample of Cover Letter

Dear Ms. Benevolent and Kindly Editor:

Twist McPherson, on permanent hiatus from the rat race, moves to Palm Springs and sets about writing the Great American Novel. Her timing couldn't be worse; the sour economy has publishers signing only the big blockbuster, like world class author Jack Crawford and his courtroom dramas. After one too many Harvey Wallbangers with her best friend Roz, Twist agrees to dust off her advertising talents and create her own publishing company.

During her weekly Mah Jong game with a group of saucy ladies, all in their 70s, Twist casually mentions her publishing plans. Before she can eat the olive out of her martini, Dirty Little Secrets, LLC is born, and Twist has a stable of five new writers who, under nom de plumes, have spent the past three years writing some of the hottest, yet refined erotica to hit the electronic bookshelves. As southern belle, Lucinda Du Pont, drawls over tea spiked with Jack Daniel's, "Smut sells, dear."

In the midst of cover designs and distribution, Twist—so named for her metaphorical gifts of rearranging the male anatomy during tough business negotiations—meets the mighty Jack Crawford, newly arrived to the desert to finish his faltering tenth book and meet his thrice-past-due deadline. He absolves his writer's block by writing for Twist under the name Marcella de la Prentiss.

It wouldn't have been so bad had *Chicago Times* book reviewer Carl Beckenham not smelled a story in the young new publisher who blasted onto the scene with her classy advertisements and sophisticated promotion. But Snarlin' Carl's nose for a hot story has him digging deeper into Twist's business to find out the identity of her writers, which threatens Jack's career and the ladies' dirty little secrets.

As editorial director for Behler Publications, I wrote *The Publisher* in order to give readers a behind-the-scenes peek of some of the insanity that takes place with a small trade press. There is a natural curiosity about professions that have a large impact on our society—medicine, law, politics—and while I'm certain the publishing industry won't influence world peace, ours is a world of escapism, and I'm betting readers would enjoy finding out how we make that happen—while maintaining our sanity.

The Publisher is a romantic comedy and complete at 75,000 words.

Thank you for your time.

Regards,

Brilliant Author

Sample of a horrible query letter

Never, EVER do this. Promise me . . . I could write a book just on query letters gone bad, but these samples will give you a good idea of what crosses agents' and editors' desks every day.

"If you're willing to invest fifteen minutes of your time reviewing the enclosed **self-published book**, I believe you'll be inspired to help me introduce it to a larger audience through a traditional publisher."

Angler's Truth:

Neversend a book to an editor unless they have requested it. Many editors don't review previously published books and usually state this in their submission guidelines.

Here is another disaster that was sent to me not too long ago:

"I apologize for deviating from the standard Query/Synopsis/Proposal paradigm the publishing industry imposes upon writers. I believe I'm entitled to this deviation for the following reasons:

Query Letter: I believe your time is too valuable to waste on the typical back and forth query letter process, I know mine is. A non-fiction query is best suited as a trial balloon for an author considering a project. The book that accompanied this letter indicates my project has advanced well beyond this stage.

Synopsis: I created a five-page chapter-by-chapter synopsis of this book and sent it to several agents last year. It was ignored. In reality I'd much rather prefer you read the first five pages of my book instead of the five-page synopsis

Proposal: Who am I to tell a literary professional how to do their job? I'm new to this business, so I'm asking you to help guide me through the publishing process. I understand another aspect of a Proposal is my opportunity to make promises about how hard I'll work to help promote my book. Instead of words, I've taken the action of sending you a copy of this book at my expense to demonstrate my commitment and belief in my project.

I've sent you this book because my research of Internet resources and trade publications indicates you're one of a limited number of publishers who would appreciate the potential for this book. If I'm mistaken, please feel free to pass it along to somebody you believe might be interested in either reading it or promoting it. I haven't included an SASE because I have no expectation or desire to have it returned to me. Please pass it along to anybody!'"

This letter is just wrong on so many levels I can barely see straight.

Assumption: Never assume to know what an editor wants. Those submission guidelines are there for a reason, and it's not to keep the tourists out. You *are* the tourist. Pay attention!

Going Rogue: If something didn't work for you in prior experiences, this isn't a valid reason to go rogue and make up your own rules. If an editor's submissions guidelines say, "One page synopsis," that is exactly what we mean. That doesn't mean, "Hey, lady, read my book instead." It's presumptuous. Authors are ill advised to write their own rules.

Requesting an editor's help: This is like putting a loaded gun to your head and asking me to pull the trigger. My first thoughts are, "Gee, let me shove aside my one hundred fifty query letters and get right on it for you. Oh, can I get you some tea?" Inviting me to do things the author's way has one result; a rejection letter. Earth to author . . . when you sit in my chair and sign my paycheck, then you can tell me what to do. Otherwise, I will stick to my way of doing things because it's logical and efficient.

Pass it around: This "if you don't want it, can you pass it around to other editors" schlock is just all kinds of wrong. Laziness is not an attractive characteristic. Do your own work, please.

Tone: The tone of this entire letter is one of "I don't care what you want, and I don't care to learn how to do things right." This author is destined to remain rejected and unpublished until it rains jelly beans. Don't be like this author. Act like a professional, and you'll never go wrong.

Tailor your query letter

Your query letter is a great template that can be easily tailored to publishers who cater to **specific criteria**. For example, all of our books are socially relevant personal journeys. The smart author tailors her query letter to point out the socially relevant elements of her story. This piques my interest because I can clearly see how her book fits in with our lineup. Smart stuff. Don't miss a great opportunity to appeal to a specific niche. This applies to agents who specialize as well.

It is vital to research the publisher.

Receiving queries for genres we don't publish has to be one of the biggest aggravations of our job because it's time consuming. We realize what happens; authors get a database of editors and race down the list faster than my daughter can change her hair color. They have no clue as to whom they are querying or what types of work they publish. All they know is that they "queried" fifty editors in the hopes that one of those is a "hit." To me, it's a form of spam, and most of the time I simply delete the query, or throw it into the trash—even if they sent an SASE. It's that irritating. Smart authors research **everyone** they query.

I don't care what you call me, just don't call me late for dinner.

Wrong! I do care. My name is listed very clearly on our submissions guidelines, and so are most other editors'. If their name isn't listed, find out. It may sound trite, but I really don't like being called "Dear Acquisitions Editor," "Dear Sir" (*Sir??*), "Hey there," or any other flavor of salutation. How do you like being addressed as "Dear Author"? I admit that our form rejection letters are addressed as Dear Author, but all our email correspondence uses the author's name. Do us the courtesy of using ours. We're silly that way.

20: The s-s-sy-sy-synopsis

So now you have the query letter tucked securely in your tackle box, and you should be feeling pretty great about yourself. But you're not done. At some point we'll need to see that synopsis, so you might as well get it done now, right? *RIGHT?*

Repeat After me—we must have a plot

At some point of the submission process, you will be asked to provide an editor with more than your pitch from your query letter. They want your full synopsis—the full detail. Some want it to accompany the query letter, others want it after they've requested to read some of your pages. Always be sure to read the submissions guidelines. In any event, it's a guarantee that you need a full synopsis sitting in your tackle box because it encompasses a lot more detail of your story.

Just as the pitch is an extended version of your log line, the synopsis is an extended version of your pitch. You should be prepared to write a one, two, and three page synopsis, all of which are based on the preferences of the editor or agent in question.

Before I get into the elements of what we like to see synopses, I want to pass along some tips.

* **Pay attention to length.** If an editor's submissions guidelines request a one page synopsis, that means A ONE PAGE SYNOPSIS. Editors and agents aren't likely to read anything longer than what they asked for, so don't tempt fate.

* **Include the ending or final resolution.** This is not Christmas. We need the ending, plain and simple. Don't be coy and offer a cliffhanger: "Does Bertha find her man and save the world? Read the book and find out!" Argh! I haven't even read the first three chapters, and already you're making me cranky.

It's not as tough as it seems, yet many make it so hard

As submissions cross my desk, I can often be found biting my nails over the vast number of writers who don't understand how to write an effective synopsis. A synopsis has to be clear to the poor dolt who's reading it. I am that dolt. If I'm left scratching my head trying to figure out the storyline, I'm more likely to drown my confusion in a glass of wine and reach for a form rejection. I'll admit that I like the wine part, but I detest rejecting an author because they can't communicate effectively. Yet, day in and day out, I do just that.

I've had many writers tell me that they can blow out 90,000 words with a smile on their face, but they'd rather have root canal without aid of some serious drugs than write a synopsis. Huh? All you're doing is telling the aforementioned dolt (me) what your story is about.

I understand that it's difficult to put together a few short paragraphs that will part the clouds and make angels sing. But you *have, have, have* to tell me the guts of your story. Don't smoke my doors off with introducing secondary characters who have nothing to do with the main plot. The same can be said for many interweaving sub-plots; leave them out unless they are vital to the telling of the main story. These things make my, and my colleagues', eyes glaze over.

It's all about the Plot

A synopsis must contain a plot. I know that seems like an obvious thing to say, but I continue to be amazed at how many writers don't understand this—about 65% worth. A plot needs:

Exposition: this is the information that gives the setting, creates the tone, presents the characters, and presents other facts necessary to understanding the story.

Dilemma: this is what creates and defines the plot. This is the conflict to the story

Climax: the turning point when characters try to resolve the dilemma. It's the high point of the story for the reader that results in the highest interest and greatest emotion.

Resolution: the events that bring the story to a close, it rounds out and concludes the action.

This is not the time to be witty or worry about Voice — you got that across in your pitch. This truly is about "just the facts, ma'am."

If you tell me nothing gets resolved in your story, then you may want to revisit your story and buy a snooze alarm. Or buy it for me. The true tragedy is being rejected because the editor can't figure out what the story is about. If you can't communicate it, I'm not going to slog around trying to find it.

Just like the **pitch**, where you made bullet lists next to each element, do the same here. For Exposition, make a list of the setting, characters, and facts that help to understand the story. Remember that you have your Pitch to draw and expand upon. Do the same for the other elements, and it will be easier to build a synopsis and to stay on just the most important facts. Most importantly, understand that you will probably rewrite your synopsis at least fifty times, so take your time. Don't rush!

I included a sample synopsis so you can get a feel for how it comes together.

Sample Synopsis

All Twist McPherson wanted to do when she retired early from her job as an advertising executive was move to Palm Springs, live a quieter life, and write a book. But when the rejection notices begin piling up, and the economy forces publishers to look for only the big blockbusters, Twist's best friend, Roz, who is on vacation from her job as an editor for a large New York publishing house, suggests Twist publish the book herself.

Twist shares the news with her friends, five saucy ladies in their mid-seventies, at their weekly Mahjong game. Twist is shocked to find out the ladies are popular writers of some of the hottest, yet refined erotica to hit the e-book market in years. And now these fine ladies are ready to see their work in print. The result is Dirty Little Secrets, LLC is born, and the only stipulation is that they must always remain anonymous.

Twist meets one her neighbors, internationally known thriller writer, Jack Crawford, who came to the desert to finish his tenth book. Jack does far less writing and far more poking his heart into Twist's life, which includes breaking through his writer's block by writing some hot stories, which Twist begs him to publish under the name Marcella de la Prentiss.

Rave reviews and Twist's flashy promotion catches the attention of book reviewer and reporter, Carl Beckenham, who is in need of a big story to help save his book review section from the chopping block at the *Chicago Times*. He sees a brewing story about the little publisher who blasted onto the scene from nowhere with a stable of anonymous writers.

Carl is getting close to exposing her authors—especially Jack—and Twist, in a preemptive move, tells Carl she'll reveal her authors' identities at the Book Expo America in New York and offer him an exclusive interview if he backs off until then. Carl does exactly what she hopes he'll do, and continue the media buzz. Twist's last mountain to climb is to convince the ladies to come out of the closet in order to take the heat off Jack, who thanks to his "writing exercises," finished a brilliant manuscript and returned to New York.

Months later, Twist's booth at the BEA is surrounded by agents, publicists, reviewers and media. Cameras are poised and cell phones are put on standby as Twist waltzes out her five stars while she unfolds a large banner, "Old Ladies Do It With Refinement." The icing on the cake is when Twist exposes to the media that she is Marcella de la Prentiss, thus robbing Snarlin' Carl of his suspicions of Jack.

Through all the requests for interviews and offers for foreign rights, Jack appears through the crowd requesting an autograph of Twist's book. Inside are hotel reservations for a nice, dull vacation in Barstow.

This next one is not a synopsis; it's description. It's important to see the differences. This is not what any agent or editor wants to see because it doesn't tell us anything about the plot:

This manuscript is a gut-wrenching story of the love, agony and tragedy of a boy born into a world of poverty and hate in the Deep South. It is reminiscent of the classic style of literature. The story follows the lives of a brutal family that can't escape its own heredity and tells the story of The Boy who seeks to break the chain of ugliness that has been passed from generation to generation. His life is an introspective search for the goodness that he believes can ultimately prevail. The end to his search will leave you shocked.

This book is a rare glimpse into a world that will leave you breathless, wrapping you tight in its gritty existence. It is a story that will make you search your soul, thankful for the love you have in your own life, and grateful for the love you have to give.

At times it is heart warming; at times thought provoking; at times tragic—- but over all a deeply moving and memorable story, one you are not likely to soon forget.

Write something like this to an agent or editor, and we can never be friends.

In short, there are scads of books donated just to the discussion of writing the perfect synopsis, but I don't really think you need to make this a huge deal. We simply need to know your main characters, their dilemma (what they stand to lose), how they go about resolving their dilemma, and the final resolution. There. I just saved you $20.

21: Submissions Advice

Leave Your Gimmicks At Home

I opened up a submission the other week, and a tennis ball came rolling out. It rolled under my desk and got caught in the wires of my computer. I had to get on all fours to retrieve it. A spider had taken up residence there and darted across my hand in its race to safety. Freaking out, I smacked my head on my desk as I lurched for the security of my chair. Can you imagine my frame of mind when I finally got to the submission? The month before that, I received a chocolate bar which melted inside the envelope and attracted ants. The post office had to spray the entire mail bin, leaving one very unhappy post office worker and one chagrined editor.

This sad state of our media-driven world has leeched its bad self over to the publishing industry, and authors are under the impression that the more outrageous or unique the presentation, the better. Nothing could be further from the truth. Success deriving from stunts such as these is the exception, not the rule, and no one should confuse the two.

For every story we hear about how Jane Writer got the attention of an editor or agent by having a male stripper deliver the manuscript, or Joe Writer wrapping his manuscript in Christmas wrap, there are thousands whose submissions are dumped into the trash unread.

Why do they get tossed? Because we see it for exactly what it is; schlocky and desperate. Submissions 101 teaches a number of Golden Rules. Number 2 is "Never Look Desperate." Ever. That you're submitting or querying initiates a foregone conclusion that you want your work read.

But for crying out loud, keep a firm grasp on your dignity. Inserting tennis balls, chocolate, sticks of chewing gum, a package of Cheese Whiz, or a Micro Machine does not scream to me, "I'm a serious writer." It screams that you depend on gimmicks because your writing isn't up to standards. What's sad is this many not be the truth at all, but this is what you convey.

Look at it from my point of view; I'm not an ad person, I'm an editor. This means that the only product I review is the manuscript; not tie-in toys or food that you think is cute and will capture my attention. It's not cute. It's annoying and unprofessional. Is this the frame of mind you want an agent or editor to be in when they begin reading your cover letter? Sure, you may happen to find the one in a thousand editors who find this effective. But are you willing to take that chance?

Repeat after me: **What you have to sell is your writing. Only your writing.**

What's the Number 1 Rule in Submissions 101? Write a great book.

My recommendation is that you keep your gimmicks for friends and family and stick to presenting a professional demeanor . . . unless you have access to a male stripper . . . .

Do Not Fold, Spindle, or Mutilate

I had occasion to send a rejection letter out the other day and went searching for the author's SASE. In amongst the first thirty pages was this flowery, dainty little thing that smelled like lilacs. It was a lovely little 4 x 6 envelope, addressed to the author, complete with little hearts dotting the 'i's' in her name. Gracious!

I thought this really cute when I was a freshman in high school, but then I grew up. It felt inherently wrong to put a rejection letter into something so frilly and fluffy. This was a happy envelope that should hold happy things—not "Hello, your work isn't right for us." As I folded, spindled and mutilated the rejection letter into the tiny envelope, I swear I could see its little paper edges begin to curl and the little hearts deflate. Could be I need more coffee or a brain scan.

This stuff sets my teeth on edge. It's amateurish to include cutesy stuff with a professional correspondence. After all, you're trying to give the appearance of being a serious writer. This goes for excluding unique envelopes. One writer included a coconut as his return address envelope. Yes, it was stamped and everything. He drilled a hole in the top, and I was supposed to curl up my acceptance letter and drop it into the hole. He even included a baggie to protect my letter. Sadly, the poor coconut held a rejection letter. If only his writing had been as clever as his choice of envelopes.

Dear, dear authors, we know you're clever, but there are times when your artistic enthusiasm needs an enema. Put your talents into your writing, and keep the #10 envelopes as boring and dull as they can be.

Formatting

If the submission guidelines say to send the first three chapters—SEND THE FIRST THREE CHAPTERS. If they want "sample" chapters, they'll say so. Most of us want to start at the beginning because we want to see if you have the ability to grab a reader's attention at the get-go.

Every so often I get a submission that looks like a fourth grader pounded it out. I'm not talking about the writing, but the appearance. I've seen all kinds of cutesy fonts like Comic Sans or Vivaldi that the author obviously thought matched the cutesy of her story. Problem was, I couldn't read it, so cutesy got dumped.

There are a few who don't know that teensy margins make it possible to cram more words on the page, but it also makes my eyes work harder from left to right. Others, still, format their works without paragraph indentations and separate the paragraphs with an extra carriage return—like the formatting in the Interview Section of this book. This is fine for a manual, but not fiction or nonfiction.

Please, for the love of all that's holy, adhere to standard manuscript formatting. Editors the world over will thank you. If the submission came to me via email, I can always go in and reformat it, but it does make me cranky. If it's a hard copy, then I'm stuck. And cranky. If it's an over the top mess, I will probably be cranky enough to not bother reading it.

Query and Synopsis formatting:

* **Single space**—no extra carriage returns in between paragraphs

* **Times New Roman or Courier**—12 pt.

* **Indent all paragraphs**

* **Paper clip—no staples**

Manuscript formatting:

* **Double space**—no extra carriage returns in between paragraphs

* **Times New Roman or Courier**—12 pt.

* **Indent all paragraphs**

* **Clip pages together**—do NOT staple!

* **Include page numbers**—be sure to check the submission guidelines for this, as some editors don't want page numbers. If they don't say, include them. Reason being, if some bonehead drops your manuscript, they can put it back together—like the time I dumped one in the middle of La Guardia Airport.

* **Unless specifically requested, don't send any artwork or photographs**

So now that I've helped you shape your synopsis and helped you ensure your manuscript is properly formatted, all while scaring you witless with all the do's and don'ts, the time has arrived. Believe it or not, your tackle box has all the right goodies, and you're ready to cast your line into the pond and do you some fishin'.

22: Après le query/submission

Please Lie Down on the Couch

Editors assume many roles in the course of their underpaid jobs—mother confessor, coach, cheerleader, lion tamer, and, yes, psychiatrist. I'm going into shrink mode, so bear with me because this warrants being said.

We all know being a writer can be mentally exhausting. You've spent a long time writing and perfecting your manuscript, researching publishers or agents, preparing your log line, pitch, bio, and synopsis all with the intent of one goal; publication. You've cast out the fishing line, hoping you've represented your work clearly and invitingly enough to garner a nibble from one of us fish. Now you suddenly feel like a part of you is missing.

Welcome to *après le query*—after the query. This is the time where your hands are idle, and you begin to wonder, "am I good enough?" Maybe your previous works flamed out in a flurry of rejections, or this manuscript was such an intense experience that there is a palpable emptiness of not writing it anymore. Whatever the reason, you think you're going nuts because you don't feel like jumping into another project right away—which is what I recommend while you play the waiting game.

My advice? Give yourself a break. Cleanse your palate. As a friend of mine, William D. Webb, Jr. likes to say, "Once you've finished breakfast do you immediately start thinking about lunch, or do wait until you digest it a bit?"

He's right. I bet your "breakfast" was fabulous, so give yourself time to relive cooking it, plating it, and eating it. Savor every bite, take a lingering delight in the ingredients that combined together to make such a fabulous dish. Heck, with all that investment over the meal, it would be normal to feel a sense of loss. Do what William suggests and let the experience digest. Don't push the process, but rather, let your feelings of readiness to move on come in their own time.

And don't worry; you're allowed to feel like meatloaf every now and then. Writing is a tough business and the ego isn't surrounded by one of those really cool Star Trek shields. Set your phaser to stun, have a margarita, and begin writing a new book when you're ready because you need something that will help you keep your eyes off the calendar.

Remember that queries take time, and it's not unusual to wait four months to hear anything. Our desks are crowded, so diving into a new work is the healthiest diversion I can think of. Resist the temptation to contact the editor after a couple weeks. It's irksome to receive a phone call or email asking, "Didja get my query? Huh? Huh?" If three to four months have passed, then you are generally ok to contact the editor.

Okay, our therapy session is over. Get off the couch and go write another bestseller.

There are times when the fish bite a little faster than you may have planned. This is a good thing, right? Well, it is if your manuscript is actually *written*. Yes, you read that right. Written . . .

"Oops. Uh, you want it now?"

Are there any lovelier words to a novelist's ear than, "Please send me your full manuscript." You get out that fabulous bottle of wine and knock back a snootful to celebrate the moment.

You have arrived.

You rock the literary world.

Let them hear you roar.

Look out all you Pulitzer weenies, I'm coming, and I have attitude.

Sing to me, oh magic quill.

Oh hell.

Um. . .I haven't written the full manuscript.

You haven't written the manuscript?! Then why did you query me? Nonfiction is almost always bought on spec, but not fiction. Not to an editor. I only know of a handful of agents who occasionally accept unfinished fiction from a new author.

The reasons for this aberration vary. The common one I hear is that the author doesn't want to "waste the time writing the story if no one wants to read it." I may be warped, but this is not a real writer. Stories burn in our hearts and souls. They scream to come out. Writers don't say, "oh, hold on, dearie, I have a fabo idea, but let's see if an editor is interested in it first." Editors are like small children. When we want something, we want it five minutes ago. If I have to wait for a writer to actually bang out the story, I've already moved on. I'm over it.

The reason I'm over it is because I know the author is very good at writing a great query and proposal because they took a lot of time with it. Can the same be said for a rush writing job? I'm dubious. Why send out something that probably needs a lot more finessing and has a high probability of being rejected? It's always better to do it right the first time because—what am I always yammering on about?—you don't get a second chance to make a great first impression.

23: Rejection

Rejection letters bite. There is no getting around it. We hate sending them as much as you hate receiving them. If you receive a rejection letter, there is no need to write back thanking us for our time. It's nice, but unnecessary.

What is really out of line is the angry rejoinder from authors whose tempers and egos color their common sense. These are the authors who can't take rejection and write back with all the venom they can muster.

Everybody has a bellybutton

The key ingredient to remember is that rejections aren't personal. We don't know you and have no interest in crushing your dreams. Our opinions are like bellybuttons; everybody has one. Just because we offer up a critique of your work—which you should consider a free gift from an experienced perspective—doesn't mean that everyone else is going to feel the same way. What I find rejection-worthy may be gold to someone else. Remember, it only takes one person to see the magic in your writing. On the other hand, if you keep getting the same critiques over and over again, that's a strong indication something is inherently wrong with your work. Listen to the bellybuttons.

Do You Want to Look Like An Amateur?

Because of the tendency of a few who lash out, most of us have moved over to the form rejection letter instead of personalized critiques. As a writer myself, I'd opt for the personalized touch because I want to know how I can improve. I respect writers a great deal because they sit down and allow a piece of themselves to be exposed on paper. It's a very intimate thing writers do and, as an editor, I try to honor that by giving critiques where I feel comments are warranted. This can range from the savvy writer who shows potential, to the writer who hasn't researched how to put forth a cohesive synopsis.

However, with the advent of email comes the inevitable "hide behind the keyboard" mentality, and unfortunately, writers feel very comfortable firing back some extremely unprofessional comments. The usual fare has two main themes. The first (and #1 cause for rejection) are those who don't take the submission process seriously and either fail include the pertinent information we ask for and/or a synopsis that makes absolutely no sense. Like this guy:

I am very sorry that I repulsed you and that my method of marketing wreaks (the author's misspelling) with the odor of decaying flesh. I should have been more of a conformist and sent you a pleasant email with a manuscript attached. I'm very certain, had I have done that, I wouldn't have received any response from you whatsoever. So please do me a favor and share this horrid ordeal and unfortunate waste of your precious valuable time with everyone you know.

Um, well, okay, I will. Look, I'm all for breaking the rules. I wear white after Labor Day and rip off the "Do Not Remove Under Penalty of the Law" tags from my pillows. Sometimes I don't floss at night either. But if there is something I really, really want, then I follow the rules. As much as authors may hate the system, things aren't going to change when it comes to the old-fashioned query process because it works. If an author really wants to get noticed, I'm of the opinion that it's best to get noticed for the writing and not some bonehead stunt.

This wasn't a very good idea either

"Lady, you are rude and ignorant, and have no class. I experienced the "rigors" of reviews and publication over a book which reached international audiences in the biggest topic of our time, the end of (redacted). But then, you probably didn't have the courtesy to read the beginning of my cover letter, which listed the book. It had been called, by reviewers, a landmark study in (redacted). Have you ever written a book, well have you? Or have you experienced the rigors of five years in graduate school, obtaining a Ph.D? You have an ego which far exceeds your intellect. Try reading my first book if you can understand it."

You want to guess the gigantor faux pas I committed to warrant this reply?

I didn't put a salutation in my rejection letter. Really. Avoid this.

The second type of snarky emails I receive are those whose writing I've commented on because they show promise but have some fairly large problems—like blatant POV switches within a scene or developmental problems. I've been told all sorts of incredibly rude things and invited to do all sorts of interesting things—things that invariably included my dog or someone's Army boots. Interesting thought, but my dog simply doesn't go that way, and my son won't give up his Army boots.

The themes are the same in these cases—I "didn't get their work" or I don't know what I'm talking about. It's an interesting reaction from those who show a flair for writing because I expect better. Their tank-sized egos prevent them from seeing that I have no dog in their fight. I'm merely an experienced observer who likes their work but sees holes in their story. They're free to listen to my observations or leave it. It doesn't matter one whit to me.

This goes for those who tell me they're "high strung because I'm devoted to my art." Ah, bullpucky, they're cranky hackers plain and simple. I work with real professionals all the time, and they are without a doubt the most delightful people to work with because they understand the business. They don't need to puff up and strut about with their nostrils flaring because they're the real deal. They accept constructive critiques because they understand their value.

To that end, the writer who acts like a professional will either thank me for my comments and move on, or they don't write back at all. This is how it should be.

The best advice I can give to any writer is to maintain a businesslike appearance. Ask yourself how you want to be perceived. Do you want an editor to see that you're an undisciplined newbie who is going to complain about the nature of things? Does anyone actually believe the rude person will be a desired addition to anyone's publishing house?

The long and short of this is that writers often wonder why they get form letters, and this is why. It's the cranky few who blow it for everyone else who welcomes honest feedback.

While I do send out form rejection letters for the most part, I refuse to allow the rantings of a few turgid sons of diseased yaks to quiet my little red pen. It's giving them more power than they deserve. I'm willing to overlook them in order to help those whose goal is to be a writer. However, I took a page out of a fellow editor's book and added an extra message at the bottom of my submissions guidelines:

Please be advised: there are times when I comment on query letters as a way of helping you improve your pitch. If you have an over-inflated ego, believe your writing originates from the hands of the Great Cosmic Muffin, or you're just an ass, please state this at the top of your query, and I will refrain from helping you in any sense of the word and let you stab about like a blind man trying to fork a pea.

The submission process can bring out the bitterness in many. Just be sure you're not one of them.

24: "So why did you reject me?"

Now that you know how to behave, authors always want to know why they were rejected. It's the sixty-four million dollar question that rings a harsh tone in every editor's ears because the reasons are many. Entire books could be written about what tickles our ribs.

Arthur Levine wrote a wonderful piece about his personal tastes, likening great writing to the lovely appearance and fragrance of flowers. Neat metaphor. I'm more of an opera gal myself and liken a great story to hearing Placido Domingo hit the high notes in such a way that I'd swear I'm hearing that note for the very first time. And that's the crux of it—making editors feel like we're seeing this plot or character for the very first time even though we know good and well there are very few new notes being sung.

Face it; it's hard to be original in this day and age. There are only so many categories to exploit, and the trick is to be able to rehash things like coming of age, love, struggling attorneys, evil corporations, or war stories without sounding like you're singing someone else's song. Chances are the rejected story's "song" didn't offer unique and fresh notes.

We may have rejected you because you failed to meet any of the following criteria:

* **Did you grab me at the first page?** I see many stories start out slowly—too slowly. I'm yawning by the second page. Yes, I have the attention span of a gnat. So do many readers. I've had authors write back telling me, "If only you'd stuck with it, this book ROCKS." Yes, this is lovely, but it's gotta rock a whole lot sooner, and the beginning is a good place to start. Keep the reader turning the page.

* **Does each chapter have a reason for being there?** At first blush this falls into the "duhh" category. But I see this in nearly every rejection. Writers either get sidetracked with a subplot or fall in love with their writing to where they lose the thread. If you think you're guilty of this, tattoo the following on your forehead:

If a chapter doesn't reveal my plot, stick it in the garbage pot.   Yes, it's corny, but if it takes cornpone to make you a better writer, quit laughing.

* **Was your writing cliché?** I see this a lot. I'm thrilled to bits that Dan Brown made gazillions for *The Da Vinci Code*, but if I ever see another knock off of this book, I'm going to throw myself under a truck. People; Dan's already done it, you don't need to do it again. It's like a train wreck; stop gawking and move on. Sing a different song—your song. So many writers sit down to write a book and fall into the trap of channeling someone else's story. Sure, it's almost always unconscious, but editors sniff this out like a hound dog. Any time someone beta reads your work and says, "Hey this is like John Lescroart's new book," you need to worry. Like Dan, John's already done it. Do something else.

* **Is it authentic?** Meaning are the emotions of the characters in keeping with the story and, if not, is there sufficient backup justifying the behavior/emotion? For example, if a character's child was tragically killed, you are ill advised to have your character go grocery shopping and ponder what to make for dinner without having some

serious justification behind it. Yet I see this disconnected character development all the time.

* **Did you keep your eye on the main ball?** Writers often have lots of balls in the air which include the subplots and peripheral characters. Following a linear line can get dull and to spice up our stories, we inject subplots. Problem is, it can become easy to lose sight of the main ball, and it's impossible to discern the main plot.

Just the other day I rejected a very well written manuscript with wonderful potential. What killed it was the fact that I had no idea what the main theme and plot were. It took a twenty-five minute phone call with the agent and the author, and I was still no closer to a lit light bulb than when I started because they were so busy explaining ALL of the subplots. My sales team doesn't have twenty-five minutes in which to describe every nuance. This is as easy peasy as asking, "Hey, what's your book about?" If you can't figure it out, how on earth can I?

Another tattoo for your forehead:

If you can't explain your book in one or two sentences, you have a problem.

* **How was your punctuation and sentence structure?** I hate to even go there. Anyone who writes should know how to use proper punctuation, and I cringe every time I hear people claim that the editors will fix punctuation during editing. This is true to a point. Punctuation is a part of effective communication, and if a writer doesn't know where to put a comma, or has a plethora of exclamation points, this tells me they don't care enough about their craft to learn. If they don't care, why should I? Yes, yes, I've seen the argument that some of the Big Hooha Writers can't spell to save their souls. Great. I have yet to find those writers. Poor punctuation and poor writing usually go hand in hand in my world.

The theory of evolution

Of course there are many other reasons why Joe or Jane Writer got rejected. These are the highlights. Take comfort that writing is an evolutionary process. What you wrote last year is probably far worse than what you wrote this year. Think of where your writing will be next year. Maybe *this* work isn't right for publication and you needed to submit it out to learn that on your own. Most writers don't publish their first manuscripts, but their fourth, fifth, or sixth may enjoy some success. Consider the possibility that your writing needs more seasoning rather than taking it out on the editor.

There are no magic bullets in this crazy business. What strikes a discord to my ears may be an aria to someone else. Remember, it's about the writing—always the writing. Keep it real, write smart, and sing your own song.

Special Insights

Rejections are hard to classify because stories fail to launch for so many reasons, but a common thread seems to weave itself among my many rejections, and that is isolation.

Writer's Island

I think of writing as a long journey down an assembly line. First you have the birth of a story idea, and it quickly moves down the conveyor belt to the Excitement Phase. Sleep deprivation sets in as the author bangs out their words with glee. After a bit of a honeymoon, the work moves on down the line to Self Doubt. Here is where the writer begins to wonder if anyone will like their story or if it's better suited for kitty litter. The story can then take another trip down the conveyor belt to This Sucks, Why Did I Think I Could Write? or Hey, This Is Great!

The main problem I see here is that this assembly line is sitting on Writer's Island. When we write, we're surrounded by a metaphorical body of water that isolates us from the outside world. If we're not getting feedback, then it's easy to see how the assembly line can wreak havoc on our spirits. We either wallow in doubt and failure, or we operate under a false sense of success.

I've had to reject many authors because I could see they hadn't built a bridge off their particular island in order to talk with trusted friends or other writers to see if their story had legs. They are so enthralled with their story that they never consider whether it would be of interest to anyone else.

Agents or editors are invariably the first encounter for the Island Writer, and it can be a rude awakening. Of course, plot, conflict, resolution, and characters comprise the elements of interest, but you have to have a solid foundation in which to build your plot. This is where getting off the island can be of great benefit. This gives you the opportunity to talk to people you trust—be they friends or fellow writers. Ask them whether they think the story is interesting. They can be the catalyst that either spurs you on or confirms your fears. The important thing to know is which station you're headed for on the assembly line.

25: The Promotion plan

As allluded to in Chapter 17, nothing can strike fear or disdain more than the request for a promotion plan. You'll hear a range of opinions on the subject, depending upon who you talk to. Some will say, "The author's job is to write, the publisher's job is to sell." Sure, I agree with this—to a point. It's not the author's job to SELL. That's the publisher's job. But in this day and age of limited shelf space and a revolving door of books, the reality is that author promotion plays a key element to generating publicity. It's hard work and time consuming.

"If I write it, they will come."

They won't come if they don't know it exists. Authors would be surprised to learn that after the sales team finishes pitching a title, one of the first questions out of the genre buyer's mouth is, "What is the author doing to promote their book?" They want to know the author has an active plan for creating demand. Buying books is an investment, and genre buyers work on an extremely tight budget. This means they can only buy what they feel is going to sell. The stronger the author's promotion plan—their visibility—the more confident they are about projected demand for the book.

Book Signing Events

Most of the promotion plans I see are generic; the #1 being, "Bookstores are a great place." I counter that they *CAN* be a great promotional tool provided the author takes the right steps to ensure their success—as was seen in the interview with Changing Hands bookstore owner

Gayle Shanks' in Chapter 5. But signings can also be hollow places of loneliness and boredom if no one shows up. It's a crapshoot. I've seen well-known authors only sell one or two books at a signing even though the bookstores advertised the event. Those are four long hours you'll never get back. However, three towns over, that same author may sell 180 books. Because of the uncertainty of success, book signings shouldn't be your sole source of promotion, and editors will be unimpressed if that is all you offer. This is an idea of what they have in mind.

Sample promo plan:

* I am actively involved with a Reiki volunteer group at two of my local hospitals. They invited me to speak to medical personnel on a monthly basis.

* I am involved with giving Reiki treatments to the Wounded Warriors at Camp Pendleton and at my local VA hospital.

* The hospital gift shops have given their go-ahead to a book signing during peak visiting hours as well as offering to carry the book.

* I've spoken with the local alternative healing groups in my area, and they'll be joining together to throw me a book party as well as inviting me to speak at their various meetings and seminars around the country.

* I have contacted The American Holistic Nurses Association and will be writing a series of articles on how doctors' attitudes can affect patient care.

* The manager/owner of a popular restaurant has agreed to host a reading/signing of my book.

* I've contacted my local newspaper and they've agreed to write an article about how my book could be very influential to the way people look at the medical community.

* I give regular seminars and talks to churches that tie in to the major themes of the evolution of our medical care.

* I have spoken with a leading NY publicist and, based on my theme of the inclusion of alternative medicine in mainstream America, we have agreed to a radio, television, and Internet campaign.

No one knows your local area better than you

The idea of authors promoting in their local area is twofold; no one knows your hometown better than you, and this supports the national efforts your publisher is doing on your behalf. If, for example, we get a great *Library Journal* review on your book, that feeds out to all the libraries—including your hometown. If you're visible in your community, the librarians can't help but notice. This would be a great time to ask about their hosting a reading, signing event, or author talk for you. Perhaps the upcoming library event yields a newspaper interview. But you don't stop there. You seek out your audience in your area because you know where they are far better than anyone else.

Where do I begin? Picking the bones

"I write fiction, so how do I write a promotion plan?"

The bane of nearly every author is figuring out the promotional relevancy and viability of their manuscripts. Would it make you feel any better to know that we all wear wigs because we've pulled our hair out over the same issues? After all, a book can be sheer brilliance but without proper promotion, it'll gather dust in someone's warehouse. That's why we take it so seriously.

When we ask for a promo plan, we are asking for the hook(s)—those one or two relevant elements that can be pulled out and exploited by the publisher, distributor, sales team, and publicist to help generate demand for the book. This is why I had you define your readership at the beginning of Chapter 14. This is easy to do with nonfiction, but what about fiction?

You defined your readership by picking out the main aspects of your book that you felt would relate to a particular audience—like the gardener murder mystery. The author and her publicist went after the gardening community, and it took off from there. I've known authors who wracked their brains trying to define their readership. This is where your imagination comes in handy.

Remember the author I talked about in Ch. 17, the one who wrote the *Bill and Ted's Excellent Adventure* meets *Lord of the Rings* fantasy with two surfer dude main characters? This is a prime example of picking at the bones of your story in order to find the meat. He took a specific element (surfing) in his book that he could take to a specific audience and sell it. This helped his book grow legs to a much wider audience, and in the process he created a platform that got people talking.

Platform

Platform, simply put, is the way you reach readers. It's a network, and it's celebrity. It's exposure. And it sells books. Hollywood stars have a huge platform, and that is how they are able to bang out books with little discernable literary experience. Who doesn't want to know what Mr. Hollywood Actor With A Substance Abuse Problem is thinking?

Likewise, the author who has published major articles in magazines or newspapers has an established platform. So does the multi-published author. Your track record gives you bragging rights, and this usually garners publicity.

While Jane and Joe Author don't have the instant notoriety of the rich and famous or the previously published, they still have the ability to create an effective platform. One of the most effective platforms is "the expert." This can be the doctor who writes medical fiction, the cop who writes murder mysteries, or the lawyer who writes lawyer fiction. Their credentials are unimpeachable, and they can parlay their credentials to any number of media outlets.

But what if you're simply a surfer who likes to write fantasy? Well, my example author made it work pretty well by drawing upon what he knew; surfing. He distinguished himself by becoming an expert in how to stay in shape. He used his main characters from his book to highlight every point he made, thus keeping him and his book in the forefront.

A platform can be developed through any number of ways. Not everyone is willing to seek his inner hambone and do public speaking. Many authors create a platform through writing articles for magazines and newspapers. One of our authors is quite shy and the thought of public speaking puts him into a cold sweat. His book, however, is fabulous, so I suggested that he do book signings at the many Star Trek conventions around the country. He would be surrounded by like-minded people. It was such a success that we had to do a second printing.

When do I start working on my platform?

Answer: the minute an idea for a book pops into your head. Since you already know you'll be expected to promote, it makes sense to begin laying the groundwork. Is your main character in a wheelchair? If so, you could contact your local hospitals or VA hospitals and talk to their physical therapy departments. You could use some of that research to enhance your character's disability and also set up venues for future events should your book get published. Or you could write articles to health magazines or maybe become a regular contributor to a news column. The trick is to keep your platform in the back of your mind because at some point, it'll have to move it to the forefront.

What about a publicist?

I know many authors who use publicists, but be aware that some are ambivalent about working with fiction because of its more elusive real-life relevancy and difficulty in finding the target audience. If your intent is to hire a publicist, then help them out by knowing where and how to find your audience.

Remember, selling books is all about leverage. If you have a promotion plan that says you're actively engaged in helping create demand for your book, then you're miles ahead of the game.

In conclusion

I hope that by giving you a tour through a portion of our jobs you're better able to appreciate our seemingly arbitrary rules and have a clearer window into some of the delight and difficulty that fills our day. Empathy is an important tool in anyone's tackle box, and its two-way direction makes for a rich and satisfying relationship.

Section 3:

Publishers

Chumming the Waters

"Oboy, oboy, oboy! I've written 'The End,' let's get that pole in the water and catch us some fish!"

Whoa. Not so fast. You have some more goodies to put into your tackle box. I'm talking about publishers. And guess what? All publishers are not created equally, and you need to know the differences so you can make intelligent choices. Remember, always take care where you drop your fishing line because the fish biting the hook may not be the best fit for you.

Most writers fall into one of four categories:

Confident: You've written "The End" after editing and rewriting at least five hundred times. You're confident about your manuscript, you know your readership and the marketplace, and you're armed and dangerous with your promotional ideas. You're ready to find a publisher.

Hard to Sell: For a plethora of reasons, which may or may not have anything to do with your writing, your agent can't sell your work. This is not a happy time for you because your options are limited, and you may have lost your representation. You decide to strike out on your own and find a publisher.

Renegade: You're one of those authors who throw caution to the wind and make the conscious decision to go it alone, without an agent. (You folks scare me the most and if you read the Agent Interviews in Chapter 1, you know why.)

Rebound: You're unhappy with your publishing decisions and are now trying to find a different means of publication.

Regardless of the category, you're all in the same boat—you want to find a solid publisher. This is where many authors refer to publisher databases and start running down the list, blasting e-queries out at the speed of light. It isn't until you get further down the line that you realize not all publishers are created equally.

Commercial trade press?

Independent trade press?

Vanity? Print-on-Demand?

Shared equity?

Yikes! you scream in frustration. *What the hell am I doing?*

26: Publishers Are Not Created Equally

The 1900s gave birth to the New York publishers, who still dominate the industry to this day. However, recent improvements in desktop publishing and the advent of digital printing have given way to many changes within the industry, and the idea of "being published" has taken on a whole new meaning—along with a lot of confusion. Because these variations have a huge impact on your book's placement within the marketplace, it's vital that you understand exactly who the players are, the foundations of those players, and most importantly, how they can influence your success.

It all started with. . .

Influencing criteria

There are decisive factors that shape and define the success of any business. With the evolution of the publishing industry, these accepted standards of measurement are the catalyst when comparing and contrasting the newer kids on the block. In a perfect world, these elements, whose genesis come from the original big publishers, define a solid publisher:

Cash flow: Publishing is hideously expensive, and it is imperative publishers have plenty of cash flow to keep them afloat. Publishers don't see remuneration of sales for about six months. In the meantime, they still have expenditures for advances, editing, cover art, interior design, print runs, warehousing, advertising, marketing, and promotion.

Knowledge: This is a lousy industry for on-the-job training because everything moves at lightning speed. This is a "you snooze, you lose" business, and publishers have to know what they're doing in order to get their books out to the marketplace. Mistakes happen with every publisher. "I didn't know" shouldn't be one of them.

Editing, cover design, interior design: Besides print runs, these three are the biggest production cash outlays due to their labor intense requirements. The idea of "you get what you pay for" is a truism. These elements are the face of your book, and they have to be of superior quality.

Print runs: We need physical stock in order to make a sale, and this means print runs. Print runs have two flavors: web based (offset) and digital. Web based printing is cost effective starting at 1,000 units up. Digital printing is great for small print runs. The size of the print runs are normally predicated upon how many units (books) are sold at pre-sales (meaning what the sales teams sell to the genre buyers before the book is actually published), and how well they expect the book to sell over its lifetime.

Distribution: This is the lifeblood for every publisher. You can have a product all shiny and ready to sell. But if you don't have a means of getting your books sold to the marketplace, then you'll be out of business within months. There is a lot of confusion surrounding distribution because it has different meanings.

*   **Warehouse wholesalers:** Ingram/Baker and Taylor/Brodart fall into this category. They are centralized warehouses that fulfill and distribute books wholesale to libraries and bookstores. They don't have sales teams who sell directly to the bookstores' genre buyers.

*   **Independent Distribution:** These are book distributors whose sales teams actively go out and pitch titles for their clients, who are made up of independent publishers.

* **Commercial trade publishing distribution:** This refers to the Big Gun publishers and any publisher who has their own in-house sales team.

Catalogues: Publishers print up catalogues for every season to reflect their upcoming new titles. These go out to bookstores, genre buyers, reviewers, and libraries. You can't do business with any store without them asking to see your catalogue, which has the ISBN, retail price, book description, and discounting information.

Return policy: Publishers have return policies, which stipulate that bookstores may return unsold stock after a period of time, usually 90 days.

Retail price: Publishers price their books in order to stay competitive with the marketplace. That's why it's important to get the best printing deal, because it reflects on the retail price. Otherwise, it eats into the publisher's profit margin.

Reviews: Publishers send out Advanced Reader Copies (ARCs) of their upcoming releases to all the trade magazines and online sites in order to garner reviews. These reviews can be very helpful in the marketing and promotion process.

Marketing, promotion: In addition to sending upcoming releases out for review, publishers send out hundreds of media packages to radio, print, and television media to announce their upcoming new releases.

Reputation: This is based on the regard in which the publisher is held within the industry; are they honest, have they continued to conduct their business with integrity.

27:   The Players

Since these criteria define the ability to get books produced and marketed, let's take a look at how they impact those who employ them.

Trade publishing

When anyone thinks about publishing, they first think about the large conglomerate publishers in New York because they've been around the longest. They are the genesis, the Big Bang of the publishing world. They are Simon and Schuster, Random House, etc. Their size and growth has dominated and influenced what people read for over a hundred years. The criteria in the previous section are a by-product of the commercial publisher, and all other types of publishers are compared to those standards. In short, they remain the brass ring for every author's reach, and the gold standard of every other solid publisher.

Since they wrote the original book on publishing, this means that they pay writers advances against future earnings and assume all financial responsibilities (and risk) for the titles they buy. They assume all major aspects of editing, cover design, national distribution, reviews, marketing, advertising, and promotion.

Because these commercial presses are owned by mega corporations, they have a large cash flow, and their print runs average in the tens of thousands to the millions, and they will release hundreds of books every year. However, this is a double edged sword, as Jerry Simmons discussed in Chapter 3, and the large numbers require them to move more product to larger audiences, forcing them toward the blockbuster model. This shift has given rise to the independent trade publisher, who works on a smaller scale.

Independent trade publishing

These publishers are the same as their big brothers, the conglomerate publishers, and work in the same manner with the exception that their cash flow has fewer zeroes. Predictably, this impacts their ability to produce on the same massive level as their much larger brethren. In a word, they publish in smaller volumes and work very smart. That means, in order to stay viable within the marketplace, they put their money into ensuring that their books are returnable, they print catalogues, market and promote their new releases, price their titles in keeping with the marketplace norms, have national distribution, and get their books out for national review.

Here are some other elements that define the independent publisher.

* **Fewer released titles:** Since the indie press has fewer editors and other employees, they release fewer titles per year. Instead of published titles in the high hundreds, they may publish between 25-75 titles a year.

* **Print runs:** Average print runs are much smaller—2,500—10,000 units. On the up side, this means they don't require massive 100,000 unit sales to consider a title a success.

* **Specialize:** Unless the indie publisher is very big—Ten Speed Press, Sourcebooks—many indie presses specialize in a genre or niche because their editing teams aren't large enough to do justice to all genres, as with the commercial publishers. Instead, they may concentrate one genre; romance, horror, mystery, memoir, nonfiction, etc. The importance of this is that they have an intimate knowledge of their audience and marketplace. They know how and to whom to sell their books.

* **Distribution:** Most indie presses are too small to have their own distribution arm, so they sign on with independent distributors who represent, pitch to genre buyers, and distribute their books on the publisher's behalf (Ch. 7). Another choice is the indie publisher contracts with a larger publisher who will distribute for them. This is how they get their books on the bookstore and library shelves.

* **Marketing, promotion:** This is a huge money burner, and most independent presses have to put their money where they feel they'll get the most bang for their buck. This usually takes place in the form of sending out hundreds of ARCs to reviewers, all media formats, and to their distributor's sales teams. They also coordinate book events and appearances for their authors and targeted print ads.

* **Reputation:** Since the independent publisher doesn't have a huge name backing them up, they have to create and maintain their reputation based solely on their continued sales success, producing consistently great books, and honest business dealings, or they risk becoming yesterday's news. Reputation is Gossip's twin sister in this industry, and I've seen indie publishers burst on the scene with a huge, glittery splash and garner all sorts of attention and adulation. But as time passes, the chinks start to show, and the shiny new image begins to tarnish when the gossip machine kicks in. Editors and agents aren't the only loose-lipped members of the industry; authors are a valuable litmus test in gauging the reputation and abilities of a publisher because, in nearly all cases, the gossip is real. Do yourself a favor and keep your ear close to the ground. Where there's smoke, there's usually a fire close behind.

28: Print-on-Demand-POD

Here is where things get a bit confusing:

* **Publishing:** Print-on-Demand, simply put, is a publisher who prints books based on demand, meaning physical orders.

* **Digital:** Print-on-Demand, simply put, is a printing technology where short runs are printed up digitally in numbers smaller than 1,000. This allows for good quality books (depending upon the digital printer) to be printed for a reasonable price. Publishers use this technology for printing ARCs (advanced reader copies) to send to reviewers and sales teams. Another use is printing up backlist titles that are still active but not in huge demand. The advantage to this is that fewer backlist titles are taken out of print.

So which is it? Is Print-on-Demand a publishing plan or printing technology? Both, actually. Confused? It's ok, so is most of the industry, and here's why:

The printing process vs. the publisher

A large portion of a publisher's cash flow is taken up in print runs, which normally run into the mid-thousands for just one title. This traditionally limited the publishing industry to those who had a large enough bank account in order to pay for those print runs and the means to get them to market. But with the advent of digital printing, that component was no longer an issue, and this opened the floodgates for a new breed of publisher whose philosophy is "we'll only print books against physical orders."

It was a brash, innovative idea. Fewer trees would be cut down, less waste, only print what someone has physically paid for. Sounds like a good idea, right? In reality, the Print-on-Demand idea adversely affected the author in unforeseen ways due to the fact that these new publishers had less operating cash than standard publishers. And the biggest problem was that authors were unaware that this could render their books obsolete.

The Print-on-Demand (POD) Business Model

The lack of cash flow creates a domino effect that impacts the quality of the book at every level of production.

Quality Product

The lifeblood of any publisher is to create a winning book, and that comes via a great manuscript, editing, cover design, and interior design, and it requires a whole lotta cash. The POD business model is based on author volume (they accept a higher number of authors than standard publishers, which I'll discuss later in the chapter), and a modest budget. Insufficient working capital translates to the inability to hire experienced editors, which easily runs in the thousands for every title. The result is poorly edited manuscripts by inexperienced editors. The same goes for cover designs, which also go into the thousands. There isn't money to pay for the best designers, royalty based artwork, graphics, or photo shoots, so cover designs can be all over the place. Some are great, others are amateurish. Some covers are recycled repeatedly on other books.

If you don't have a quality product, then how is it going to sell?

Risk:

Due to the lack of proper funding, the POD publisher lacks the ability to shoulder much risk. Too much risk, and they'll go out of business. So the question is, how can they diminish their risk?

* **Distribution:** A logical option to diminishing their risk would be to distribute their books, right? Books in the stores means higher possibility for sales. However, this requires sales teams—which they can't afford. The next option is to see about being taken on by an independent distributor so their sales teams can pitch their books to the genre buyers. The problem is that distributors won't accept POD publishers due to the lack of sufficient print runs.

* **Sell to the stores:** If they can't get a distributor, another option to diminishing their risk would be to get direct sales of their books into the stores. In order to make this happen, the POD publisher must send a book and sell sheet to the small press department at the store chain's corporate headquarters, where they review the book and decide whether to purchase any copies for distribution to their stores or just enter the title into their database—which means a customer can come in and order the book. If the POD fails to do this, the book won't get into the chain's database, and this means no sales. This also means no author events because the stores can't order the books unless they're in the database.

* **Returns:** Believe it or not, there is risk to the POD by having stores buy their books. Let's say a buyer decides to order 1500 units of a title. This requires a print run. Even if the publisher takes the book to offset (which they would in order to get better pricing), it would cost them roughly $3,500. Since publishers can wait four to six months to get paid for their sales, this cash outlay will more than likely create a financial burden for the POD

publisher and affect their ability to produce new books. And this is assuming those books will stay sold. The dark side to this scenario is, what goes out can invariably come back in returns of unsold titles. Returns are the bane of every publisher, but for the POD, it can ruin them in months because they paid for a large print run that they couldn't afford and it didn't sell.

When PODs first came on the scene, they had a no-return policy because print runs were expensive, and they couldn't afford a warehouse of unsold books. But in an attempt to keep pace with the trade publishers and diminish the negative reputation swirling around the POD business model, more and more companies gave into pressure and began accepting returns—thus increasing their risk. Given their circumstances—low cash flow, newly instituted return policies, and deep bookstore discounting—PODs had to ask themselves just how badly they really wanted to be in the stores. As a result, some PODs rewrote their return policies that were so extreme it was nearly impossible for stores to return unsold stock. But at least they could claim to authors and industry watchdogs that they did, indeed, have a return policy. The flip side to that was that if stores couldn't return the books, they weren't going to order them, either.

As time went on, and shelf space being tight, bookstores realized POD books didn't sell as well and declined to shelve them. The only way POD books would see the inside of a bookstore was through author events—provided the bookstores could order them—and special orders.

But there are other concerns that plague the POD business model:

* **Pricing:** At the same time PODs began establishing return policies, they realized they had to make their retail prices competitive, which was difficult to do because digital printing is more expensive. But buyers balked at their higher than normal prices, so they were forced to lower their prices. The decrease in profit margin resulted in more risk for the POD.

* **Reviews**—Everyone is always looking for "street cred"—that little extra mileage that says someone very cool and important thinks a book rocks. Reviews give our books that kind of oomph. If it comes down to two books that look equally interesting and are of the same category, who's going to get the sale—the one that says Ann Rule or *Library Journal* thought this book is the bee's knees, or the one that has nothing more than cover art, title, and author? I'm betting on Ann Rule and *Library Journal*. However, the trade magazines quickly learned about the lower quality in POD books, and they refused to review them. This puts the POD on a lower rung of the ladder.

* **Marketing**—Marketing is vital to publishers. This is how we get word out about our new releases and stir up demand. As with everything else, it takes money. We send out hundreds of Advanced Reader Copies to libraries, bookstores, reviewers, and anyone who we feel has a big enough mouth to talk up the book. Marketing can also take the form of print and media advertising. POD companies, on average, don't have a marketing budget, and this translates to zero marketing. If people aren't aware a book exists, then how will it ever sell?

In short, that is some pretty huge risk . . . for the author.

So the main options that reduce the risk for trade publishing don't work in the POD publishing business plan because they lack the means in which to play on the same ball field. POD companies need guarantees to stay financially viable. Problem is, there are no guarantees in publishing because publishers are beholden to a fickle buying public. With no distribution and no store placement, there is only one way to reduce the risk, and that's to sell to the only existing marketplace left—the authors.

Authors as sales force

Authors are the POD's one reliable and consistent sales outlet, other than friends and family, that guarantee the publisher has no risk and no inventory. Authors need those books in order to market, promote, and sell. As an inducement to authors, many PODs structure their author discounts based on the amount of units they are willing to buy. The more books authors purchase, the deeper their discount. This is particularly beneficial to the publisher because there is no concern about returns and authors usually buy in larger quantities to get the deeper discount. Those direct sales increase their profit margin. And since the author is buying the books, no royalties are due.

On top of the authors' necessity to have their own stock, they have the added expense of marketing and promotion without the support of their publisher because they simply don't have the money. Authors are on their own for every aspect of selling their books. They are the POD's unpaid sales force.

Volume business

As I mentioned earlier, PODs are successful by doing a volume business, and their primary sales are based on selling to their authors. This means they need a lot of authors in their lineup to buy their books. Problem is, not every author has enough money to buy their own books, so this becomes a numbers game. They need assurance that they have a large enough "inventory" who will make up for those authors who don't buy their own books. Since they need a constant stream of authors, their acceptance percentages are much higher than standard publishing, which is around .5 to 1% of all submissions. With the higher acceptance ratios come lower quality manuscripts. But it doesn't really matter because the POD marketplace is aimed at the author, not the public.

There are only a few pieces of kryptonite that can level a POD:

* Returns

* Lower retail prices

* Unsold print runs

* Not signing enough new authors on a regular basis

* Authors not buying their own books

Disclosure

Now, none of this an arrestable offense. It's merely a different method of publishing, and it can be a viable option for hard to place niche books or giving new life to out of print titles. However, PODs get into trouble for routinely failing to divulge what they can and can't provide for their authors, and this is why they tend to draw the ire and disdain of the publishing industry. Authors sign on the dotted line, and only when it's too late do they realize the uphill battle that awaits them.

The Dark Side

Publishing is filled with many successes and heartbreaks. Sadly, the heartbreaks come from the POD end of the business.

"I had no idea. I thought they were a small press."

I'm a writer, so I know what it's like to pour my soul into a story morning, noon and night. I know what it's like to agonize over character development and arc placement. I know what it's like at the end of the day to have respected people in the business say, "Hey, Price, I think you really have something here."

So does it seem right that all the hard work we pour into our writing ultimately dribbles down into a steaming pipe of oblivion? Of course not. But that's exactly what happened to a friend of mine.

When her book was published, she jumped into promotion with both feet. Her subject matter was bursting with all sorts of different promotional paths, so she hired a publicist and had visions of book signings dancing in her head.

It never happened. Stores looked up her title in their computers and saw that the book was non-returnable, and the retail price was too high.

Undaunted, she convinced several stores in her area to read the book and made them promise that if they liked what they saw, they'd agree to a signing. She'd provide the books.

They read it and loved it. Yahoo! They were so impressed that they ordered fifty copies for their stores. Her signings went off without a hitch, and she ended up outselling a well-known author whose signing was the same day.

But POD giveth and POD taketh away. The store called the author and informed her they couldn't shelve the unsold books because the publisher hadn't sent her title into the corporate buyers in New York. Her title wasn't listed in their corporate database. The books remained in the boxes and were never unpacked, and she had to buy them back from the store.

And the publicist? She bolted after finding out that no matter what she did to promote her client, the books would never hit the stores.

It was the same scenario every time she had a book signing; she had to order all her own books and lug them to every signing.

Who made out? The publisher. Why? Because the author was the origin of sale, not the bookstore. There was no risk to the publisher, and all the financial risk was placed on the author.

Broke and unable to obtain more signings, her only choice was to hawk her book in other ways. In and of itself, this is fine. Many well-published authors do the very same thing. The difference is that their efforts are in conjunction with the publisher's own national marketing plans.

After a year, she asked to be released from her contract, taking the tact that she wasn't aware of any these problems before she signed the contract. The publisher refused. The author got a literary attorney with the intent of suing. The lawyer said she didn't have a solid enough case that would hold up in court.

She looked at me with tears in here eyes. "I had no idea. They never told me I'd be all alone. They told me my book would be in the bookstores."

"No," I said. "I'd bet any amount of money they told you your book would be *available* in bookstores—meaning customers could special order your book."

"I didn't know."

Nightmare On Madison Avenue

While most of the PODs result in an author's book having a hard time seeing the light of day, there is another side of the coin: Success.

"What's that you, say, Price? Success? You're mad! Since when is success a problem?"

Obviously it's not a problem when a publisher is set up to meet the demand that's been created by theirs and their authors promotional efforts.

Case in point:

An author contacted me asking if I'd consider taking on her book. Her story tumbled out in an emotional rush.

Her book had caught the attention of a major sports chain, and they wanted 20,000 units in three month's time to coincide with some sports hoopteedoo. She spent that night celebrating with an expensive bottle of wine and caviar. She'd done it. She hit the big time. The next morning, while nursing a hangover, she contacted her publisher with the fabulous news, expecting they'd name a day of the week after her. They hemmed, they hawed, and . . . dumped her.

That's right. They dumped her. The reason they cited was "not a successful title."

The author was dumbfounded. As I explained earlier, PODs aren't equipped to handle huge orders like this because the printing costs alone are very high, and they most certainly didn't want to face any returns. The only option they gave her was for her to buy those 20,000 units and sell them direct to the sports chain. She didn't have that kind of money, so the "logical" choice for them was to dump the author lest she try to be successful again. Who needs that kind of grief?

Suddenly without a publisher, the author was left hanging in the wind. The sporting hoopteedoo happened without her. They found another book to promote at their event, and that author is becoming quite a name in the sports world. This author aches at the thought that it could have been her.

"I had no idea," she said in a quiet voice.

"Is POD a good thing or a bad thing?"

As I've said before, POD can be a good method of publication depending upon your goals and circumstances, AND provided you're fully aware of their limitations. The other side of this particular coin is that there is a lot of room for abuse due to ambiguity and the authors' gullibility. Simply put, many authors aren't aware, and this has caused untold heartache.

Websites - look for the signs:

Look at publishers' websites carefully—especially the About Us page. Who are they trying to attract—authors or buyers? Standard publishers don't donate webspace trying to attract authors; their focus is on selling books to bookstores and libraries.

Nearly all POD websites will call themselves independent publishers or small presses, which is where the confusion begins. Their sites may be filled with variations of the following:

* We are looking for the many great unknown authors who are just waiting for the opportunity to break into print

* We care more about the author than the conglomerates

* We are here to fill the void of untapped talent that is looked over by the big publishers

* We're saving trees

* We are a small press—while technically correct, this gives the impression they are a small *commercial* press that has a sales force.

Some websites are quite well written and lack the usual hyperbole, so you need to know what you're looking for. One of the most revealing statements is that they sell directly to the bookstores and libraries. This indicates they don't have a sales force or an independent distributor to pitch their lineup to the genre buyers. There are other telling statements that can clue you in to a POD:

"Why of course we have distribution"

Authors are getting smarter and realize the key to getting sales is distribution. In response, PODs use this classic line:

Our books are distributed through Ingram and Baker & Taylor. Both companies comprise the largest distribution network in the world. POD or Print-on-Demand is a term to describe a printing process and should not be confused with distribution. All titles are available worldwide.

As I have mentioned before, Ingram and Baker & Taylor are warehouse wholesalers, not distributors. They don't have sales teams who pitch their catalogue to genre buyers. PODs want to give the appearance of having distribution, and Ingram and B&T do not qualify. This only means that the titles are AVAILABLE for ordering wholesale to stores and libraries.

We don't need no steenkin' distribution

Yes, PODs are nothing if not inconsistent. A friend of mine asked a POD about independent distributors, and their response was that a distributor would "take too much of a cut of the sale price" and after all, "the money should go to the author." What this really means is that the POD can't afford a distributor because they require money, advertising, sufficient print runs, and discounting. Given their short cash flow, they can't afford to discount anything.

"We're here to give the author a chance."

Publishing will never be mistaken for the Great Benevolent Society. We base our businesses solely on the belief that we can get a large number of people to buy quality books, and we employ all the right people to ensure that our books reach the store shelves. Giving authors a chance does not play into the notion of making money. This is a vanity statement, used to make the author feel good about themselves and their publisher.

"POD means digital printing, and all publishers use this. There's no difference between us."

This gives the impression that the only differences between commercial publishing and Print-on-Demand is the use of digital printing, and that they are being unfairly labeled. As I've explained before, trade publishers and PODs have vastly different business models, something that gets swept under the metaphorical carpet.

Contracts:

Should you get so far as to be offered a contract, pay particular attention to the royalty payments. They can say something like this:

Net sales are defined as the Total Dollar amount that is actually received by the Publisher from the wholesale or retail sale of the Work **minus** the Total Dollar amount of any Returns of the Work and **all costs associated with the sale**. Wholesale amounts vary with each wholesaler/distributor.

This means that the publisher has free reign to dip into as much of your royalties as they want in the name of "associated costs." The sky is the limit, and you could literally receive pennies on the dollar in royalties. This is NOT standard, so don't fall for it. If they can't define those "costs associated with sales" then they're looking for one thing; lining their pockets at your expense.

Be especially diligent because many PODs have a copy of their contract on their website, and it might not match the one authors receive.

Are all PODs really bad?

No, they aren't. There are some very respectable PODs that concentrate on out-of-print titles or niche genres. Some work very hard to market and promote their titles. But make no mistake about it; this business plan relies on heavy author support. Without the authors driving sales, PODs have a harder time staying in business because they lack distribution and marketing teams.

There are POD companies out there who are honestly trying to do the very best with what they have. They admit to miniscule print runs and lack of marketing. Their abilities are severely limited, but that doesn't mean they're trying to steal your dog and wear your new shoes while you're at work. I know a number of people who are very happy with their POD publisher. They offer appropriate author discounts to purchase their own books but also recognize the restrictions by staying with them.

It is possible to sell a lot of books with a POD publisher, but it will take a great deal of elbow grease. If you know this going in, then you won't suffer buyer's remorse later.

Author copies

"Is it necessary to buy your own books if I'm with a POD?"

No. But keep in mind that you need to do something to create demand so readers know your book exists, and this requires sending out a lot of free copies. Since the POD publisher isn't going to do this in enough numbers to make a difference, the responsibility rests on the authors' shoulders to purchase plenty of books to send out. Some authors are natural marketers and can sell sand to Arabs. The thing to ask yourself is, can you? And do you have the money to send out hundreds of books and possibly hire a publicist?

Do the research, analyze your personality type, and analyze the intent of your book.

29: Questions every writer should ask a publisher before querying

Before you inject your morning cuppa directly into your veins, before you freebase that jelly donut, before you brush your teeth . . . research, research, research BEFORE you query!

I've seen thousands of queries from trusting souls who know nothing about us. They didn't know whether we were scammers or the next best thing to sliced bread. All I would have had to do is say, "This is the best thing I've read since the last submission. Wanna contract?" and they would have jumped. This, frankly, scares the bejabbers out of me.

Writers, please, know who you're dealing with BEFORE you submit. Once you've signed on the dotted line, they own you, and the next number of years can be wonderful or dreadful. The desire to be published should not overrule good business practices.

It reminds me of a few years ago when I returned home to see my kitchen and breakfast nook flooded in two inches of water. I panicked, as any self-respecting woman would, and called the biggest ad that screamed promises of being at my home within minutes. They stopped the flood and proceeded to suggest all sorts of things that were in dire need of fixing or my house would explode. Having just jump-started my heart, I agreed to their generous offer of $1500 to make my life complete. Hubby wasn't nearly as amused. I'd been scammed. Thankfully we charged it, and they never got paid.

But what about you? You won't have the luxury of calling the credit card company and saying that you made a mistake and your publisher is an idiot. Lawyers have a very difficult time winning court cases against publishers. Your only protection is to know who you're dealing with.

I've included a number of questions that should give you a good idea as to the type of publisher you're talking to.

* **What kind of a publisher are you?** Are you a commercial press, vanity, or POD? Be very careful. Many PODs will tell you they are a small press, and this gives the impression they are a small *commercial* publisher. As you have learned, there is a big difference. Vanity publishers have a harder time fooling anyone because they require money up front. But at that, the smaller vanity presses aren't always forthcoming until you get to the contract stage and they whip out this little tidbit of "which publishing package would you like?"

* **Who distributes your books?** If they say Ingram, Baker & Taylor, then you know you're dealing with a POD or vanity press. If they say Midpoint, BluSky Media Group, IPG, Consortium, then you're dealing with a commercial press.

* **Are your books listed in the bookstores' databases?** If they say yes, then call up a bookstore and have them look up a few of the publisher's released titles. If they say they don't have it listed in their database, this means that no one can buy or even order your book through the bookstore.

* **What kind of editing do you provide?** Better be developmental and copy editing, or walk away. Ask them what standard they use—for instance, we go by *Chicago Manual of Style*.

* **Do you do print runs?** On average, how big? If not, why? Would they consider doing a print run for you? If not, why?

* **Do you send out galleys to reviewers?** If so, how many and to whom? If they don't mention the usual suspects—*Publishers Weekly, Kirkus, Blooomsbury, Booklist, Library Journal, New York Review of Books* etc. this is a giveaway because these folks don't review POD books.

* **Are your books returnable?** Ask if it's a standard return policy. Again, be very careful. I know of some PODs who say they have a return policy but in reality, it's so restrictive that most bookstores won't order their books. A standard return policy where the book is returned to either Ingram, Baker & Taylor, or the publisher's distributor within a three-four month time.

* **Are your books competitively priced?** This is easy to check by going to any of the online bookstores.

* **And lastly, ask around.** It's as simple as asking, "Hey anybody heard about Haveievergottadealforyou Publishing?" You're bound to get feedback. Never, never, ever assume everything is okay with a publisher. Talk to their authors. Just because they're friendly and appear to be very concerned with you and your book doesn't mean they are what you're looking for. You have worked your fingers off writing your novel—treat it with the respect it's due.

30: Vanity/Subsidy Publication

Pay to Play

The definition of a vanity press from dictionary.com is "a printing house that specializes in publishing books for which the authors pay all or most of the costs."

This particular horse goes by many different names: shared responsibility publishing, cooperative publishing, joint venture publishing, or subsidy publishing. Whatever they call themselves, they are all the same thing— the author pays the publisher to take complete control of producing a book.

The problem with some of these descriptions is that they give the impression the publisher is sharing the risk with the author in terms of marketing and promotion, and this is not the case. The author shoulders most or all the expense and all of the risk of generating demand.

Vanity publication is NOT self-published

There are many vanity presses that refer to the author as being **"self-published,"** and this is incorrect terminology. Self-publishing is when an author sets up his own publishing company and conveys that name in all references to the book, including the book spine and copyright page. The ISBN is purchased in the name of that company, and that company, of course, assumes control of every physical and financial aspect of production, sales, and distribution. All rights are reserved in the name of the publisher.

Self-publishing can be a very viable publishing credit, as seen through Brunonia Barry's *The Lace Reader*, published through their company, Flap Jacket. They had great distribution, a great marketing plan, and a great publicist. Through their hard work and great distribution, the book sold extremely well. So well, in fact, Harper Collins picked it up for $2 million. The sky is the limit with self-publishing, and I've read many fantastic books from authors who took this route. Mind you, self-publishing is not for anyone suffering a weak bladder, high blood pressure, a drinking problem, or heart trouble. Self-publishing is a full time job.

Vanity presses, on the other hand, make all the production decisions with respect to the final product based on the package the author purchased. The printing rights are the property of the vanity publisher. They purchase the ISBN in their company's name, and it's their name that goes on the copyright page. This is an important distinction.

You are either self-published, or you are published by a vanity press. There is no gray area.

How vanity works

Vanity publishers offer service packages that range in price. Authors can always add extra à la carte features such as proofreading, editing, press releases, entering books into book contests, promotional opportunities, and so on. It's important to note that vanity books are not refundable, so genre buyers won't stock them.

Is vanity publishing bad?

Many authors have given up trying to find an agent or have a stack of rejections. They're frustrated and tired. More than anything, they want to be a published author, and this is where vanity publishing can look attractive. On the face of it, there is nothing wrong with paying someone to publish your book. But it also depends on your goals for you, as a writer, and for your book.

Perhaps you're a hobbyist writer and aren't looking for anything more than money well-spent on the personal pleasure of seeing your book in print rather than seeing a return on an investment. I knew of a woman whose husband bought her a vanity package as a birthday present. I thought that was about the cleverest birthday gift I'd seen in a long time. She was thrilled to pieces. I also knew a man who was a gifted speaker on a very niche subject. He needed product for back of the room sales. For him, vanity publishing was the perfect solution.

But if you're looking to be a serious writer, keep in mind the strikes against you.

* **You get what you pay for:** if you're looking for quality editing, cover design, interior layout, and marketing then you best look elsewhere. Vanity publishing takes the maximum amount of money and produces a book with the least amount of work. There is no incentive to create a quality product because they aren't burdened with any risk. They already got their money.

* **Not a publishing credit:** Acceptance isn't based on talent, but rather the size of your checkbook. For this reason, the industry doesn't regard these books as a valid publishing credit. It's important to note that the first publishing rights are now gone.

* **It's not about the author:** Vanity publishers are very good at complimenting authors. Why do you think it's called "vanity"? They'll tell the author how marvelous their writing is and present them with all their various packages. It's about making the sale.

Define your goals before you research publishers

As you can see in this section, not all publishers are the same. Now that you understand what each of these "fish" in the pond do to get your book out to market, this will make chumming the waters easier, right? Wrong. You must first decide the goals for your book.

We've all heard the saying that you don't bring a peashooter to a war. Likewise, you want to make sure your target matches your literary artillery.

Hobbyist writer

If your writing is a fun hobby, then your target isn't Random House. Your promotional net probably doesn't expect to expand beyond selling to friends and family, and you more than likely recognize that your writing isn't award winning quality. For you, the act of writing scratches an artistic itch, and you're happy to sell a few copies here and there.

Professional speaker

These are the writers who give speeches or conduct seminars for a living and invariably need complimentary product to sell at the back of the room. Public speaking is how you promote your work—this is your platform—and your end all, be all isn't wrapped up in having a bookstore presence. Random House may not be your target either.

Serious writer

You're the writer who feels your story has a solid spot in the marketplace, and you're willing to put some major time into your writing career. Your intent is to be on the store shelves and available in every venue. You're a serious writer with serious plans, and you're willing to work on creating a platform that will support your book. The idea of rejection is frustrating, but you're experienced enough to understand that you have a good product, so you don't let the rejections get you down.

Exhausted and frustrated

These are the newer authors who know very little about the industry. They jumped into writing their first book and are determined to see that first book in print. Come hell or high water. They may have had their work critiqued a little bit, but for the most part they've been hanging out on Writer's Island (pg. 268) for too long, and they are looking for a short cut. This group is the most susceptible to poor publishing choices because they don't fully understand the consequences of their decisions and end up sad, broke, and disillusioned.

If you're exhausted and frustrated, at least understand the goals for your book. Is your book for friends and family? Regional? Back of the room sales—seminars? By taking the time to analyze your book's goals and reading *this* book, you'll avoid the most heartbreaking utterances I've ever heard: "I had no idea."

Chumming the waters is fine, but avoid the sharks.

Section 4:

The Writer's Survival Style Guide

"Why did you reject my manuscript?"

There isn't a writer alive who doesn't wonder this, and it's doubly frustrating because we rarely give a reason. Time doesn't allow for a detailed critique. And then there are the reprisals to deal with. These are the ones who don't take well to rejection and fire back nastygrams inviting us to do all sorts of things with our favorite barnyard animal. They ruin it for everyone else.

So the form rejection letter stares back at you, and you have no idea whether the agent or editor didn't like the story, the point of view, the pace, the characters, the plot, your writing style, *WHAT*? If you only knew, you'd fix it, right?

Manuscripts are rejected for a whole host of reasons, but a big ticket item is the repeated violation of the rules of writing, which almost always renders a manuscript dead on arrival. Regardless of what you're writing, an editor or agent will reject your manuscript if you have repeated POV switches or overuse clichés. What have I been saying throughout this whole book? Never give an agent or editor any reason to reject your manuscript other than it isn't right for them. In my way of thinking, it's a federal crime to have to reject a manuscript because the author can't spell worth a tinker's damn or writes in a passive voice, especially if the story is good.

I can hear you asking, "Won't the editor fix all this?" The answer is no, they won't. Sure, editors do make editorial changes and demand rewrites, but they won't go in and restructure an entire manuscript. There simply isn't that kind of time. Besides, it's a buyer's market, and there are too many good, savvy writers out there to have to put up with an author who can't spell.

I had an author come unhinged when I rejected his manuscript because his entire story was written in the passive voice. "Why can't you fix it?" he demanded. We won't fix it because it's assumed authors know the finer nuances of grammar and rules of writing. After all, these are the writer's tools. It's like having a plumber come fix my sink without the benefit of his plumbing tools. Stupid, no?

The problem is knowing the pitfalls that result in a speedy rejection. In order to determine this, I ordered up a manuscript autopsy to define the various causes of death.

This section is your personal Writer's Survival Style Guide—the last piece of equipment that goes into your tackle box.

31: When a manuscript feels sick

The scene: Dr. Editor's exam room, which consists of a comfy leather couch and matching chair, some leafy green things that Dr. Editor tries not to kill, and gentle backlighting that highlights the new fish tank where three piranha pace back and forth in search of fresh meat. A smoky song from Aretha Franklin plays softly in the background.

Dr. Editor: (opens the door and greets a tattered and frayed manuscript) Come on in and have a seat. You look horrible. What's ailing you?

Troubled Manuscript: I don't feel well. My pages have been turned so many times, I feel like a Japanese fan. And my words? Ach, don't even go there. They've been changed around so much, that I don't feel like me anymore. I still have a story in here, don't I, doc?

Dr. Editor: I can't know this until I do an exam. (she pulls out her magic red pen and begins to inject the pointy end into the patient)

Troubled Manuscript: (recoiling in fear) No! No! Not the red pen!

Dr. Editor: Relax, it'll only sting a little bit. I have to do this to make the proper diagnosis. Ah, yes, I see some problems already. Here is a case of the "wasies." and its evil twin sister, the "hadies." See here, you have a ton of "was seen," "was given," "had said," "had forgotten." There is a place for "was" and "had," but not in front of a verb, if you can avoid it.

Reason being is there is a tendency to overuse them, and they weaken the verb into anonymity. "was seen" now becomes "saw." "Had forgotten" becomes "forgot." And so on. Here, let me give you an example.

"She **had** seen the boy licking the chocolate fudgie sundae from the window of the ice cream shop and **was** trying to remember the humiliation she **had** felt when she stole a fudgie sundae."

Let's take out the wasies and hadies.

"She saw the boy licking the chocolate fudgie sundae from the window of the ice cream shop and tried to remember the humiliation she felt when she stole a fudgie sundae."

See how it puts the action where it belongs and makes the sentence sound stronger?

Troubled Manuscript: Oh, my little pages look all red now! What am I going to do?

Dr. Editor: A way to make life a bit easier would be to do a universal search and find in Word for "had" and "was," and correct the ones that are sitting in front of a verb. (Dr. Editor looks deeper with her magic red pen) Okay, you're going to need a colonoscopy.

Troubled Manuscript: *WHAT??*

Dr. Editor: It won't hurt very much. But see here, you have a lot of colons and semi-colons. These are good for teaching or reference manuals, even nonfiction if you keep them to a minimum. You, my pulpy little friend, are fiction, and colons and semicolons have few places on your pages unless absolutely necessary. Fiction is about flow and pace. Colons and semi-colons are about brevity, and they can interfere with the natural flow of fiction. Here, let me give you a refresher course:

* **Colon:** used to emphasize a series of elements or a list of whatever preceded the colon. The first word after the colon is lower case unless it introduces a speech in dialog.

Example:

I was sad and reached for my favorite comfort foods: chocolate, Twinkies, and a bag of potato chips.

Change to:

In my sadness, I needed my best friends, my comfort foods, and knew the pantry was filled with chocolate, Twinkies, and potato chips.

* **Semicolon:** stronger than a comma but weaker than a period. The most common use is between two independent clauses not joined by a conjunction like "and" or "but."

Example:

She hates watching soppy love movies in public; her nose runs and her eyes swell up like she's been stung by a bee.

Change to:

She hates watching soppy love movies in public because her nose runs and her eyes swell up like she's been stung by a bee.

See how this invites more exposition and character development? That isn't to say that you can't use colons and semicolons, but be careful and mindful of your flow and overusing them. If, for example, you're writing in a minimalist style, this could work quite well. But you have to be aware of them in order to intelligently break the rules.

Troubled Manuscript: Okay, I guess the colonscopy didn't hurt too much. Is there anything else?

Dr. Editor: 'Fraid so. You suffer from what I call Transitional Paragraph-iotis.

Troubled Manuscript: Sounds serious.

Dr. Editor: It is. You lack proper transitions from one paragraph to the next. This can send an otherwise good story into septic shock. Each paragraph needs a transitional sentence to set up the next paragraph.

Example:

I watched the gopher leave his hidey hole to steal my peanut butter sandwich. He wore a triumphant little grin as he cleaned jelly off his twitchy little whiskers. I was enraged and hungry. From that moment on, I declared a fatwah on all gophers.

Beth's disdain of rabbits came from a childhood memory when the neighbor's white lop eared bunny stole all her Easter eggs. . . blah, blah, blah

You can see there is no transition between the first and second paragraph. You're talking about gophers and peanut butter sandwiches then you suddenly switch to Beth hating rabbits. It makes the reader wonder about the tie-in between the two paragraphs. One thing you never want to do is take your reader out of your story to re-read the passage again because they're wondering what they missed.

Example:

I watched the gopher leave his hidey hole to steal my peanut butter sandwich. He wore a triumphant little grin as he cleaned the jelly off his twitchy little whiskers. I was enraged and hungry. From that moment on, I declared a fatwah on all gophers. **But as much as I hated gophers, nothing could compare to my friend Beth, who believed that all rabbits should be rounded up and sent to Mars.**

Beth's disdain of rabbits came from a childhood memory when the neighbor's white lop eared bunny stole all her Easter eggs. . .blah, blah, blah

See how the transitional sentence (bolded) now gives the second paragraph clarity? (At this point Troubled Manuscript breaks into tears) Look, I know it's tough to hear all this, but out of all your ailments, this is the worst, and it will require you to go through every single sentence and paragraph in order to make sure you have properly set up each new paragraph.

Troubled Manuscript: (wiping eyes) I-I'm not ready for publication, am I? (Dr. Editor shakes her head) Are you sure there isn't a vaccination you can give me?

Dr. Editor: Sorry, there aren't any easy fixes in writing. Knowing what the mistakes are and how to avoid them is the best medicine. However, finding them and recognizing them is quite another. For this, I may send you over to my good friend, Independent Editor Sam Spyglass, and have your eyes checked.

~~~

This story suggests that a manuscript can be filled with great characters and an engrossing plot, and still get rejected. Why? Because it's an editing nightmare. The realities are that only the author's best work should be submitted. Long gone are the days where an editor will hand feed an author, sentence by sentence, in order to make the manuscript publish-ready. The costs of doing so are prohibitive and time consuming. Wonderful manuscripts are rejected every day by simple blunders that kill the story. Take punctuation, for instance. Talk about the potential for a nightmare. . .

32: Punctuation Beerfest

Comma: (slams down a half-full mug in a seedy bar that's inside an equally seedy manuscript) Yessiree, now that I think about it, and that's only because I'm half-tanked, this beer, even though it's too warm, is the best I've had in a long time.

Exclamation Point: Oh! I love this beer!! I haven't had this since I was in college! We drank too much and got thrown out of the bar for dancing on the tables!! Imagine that!

Ellipsis thought about the last time he'd had beer . . . and thought some more . . . realizing he was allergic to beer . . . it made him turn green around his dots.

Adverb: This beer is so astoundingly horrible. It tastes amazingly like dirty sock water. How can you drink this absolutely achingly awful swill?

Em Dash: When I hold my glass—like so—I swear I can see tiny grains of sand floating around—how gross—

Cliché: You all are so, like, five minutes ago. You're all three sheets to the wind, so I'm gonna make like a tree and leave. Besides, absence makes the heart grow fonder.

Evil Editor: (bursting through the door) STOP! You're all leaving. Now.

Em Dash: Why—don't you love us anymore—I thought we were friends—

Evil Editor: You all serve a purpose, but you need to be put on a serious diet. Punctuation sucks writers into taking shortcuts rather than relying on their writing. This results in dry or overwritten prose. **Comma**, four of you in one sentence is too much. They need to broken up into smaller sentences, and you need to make like Houdini and disappear.

Cliché: I heard that! You're a girl after my heart, but you don't need to get all bent out of shape.

Evil Editor: Exclamation Point, you are a buzz kill because I see you all the time. We rely on you to signify excitement. But just like my box of Twinkies, if I see too much of you, I get sick of you because you've lost your importance. **Adverb**, you are a modifier on crack and the root of all overwriting. Whenever I see you and your best friend, **Exclamation Point**, in the same manuscript over and over again, I want to scream. You're over the top.

Adverb: (sobbing) I'm so totally achingly sorry. I totally had no idea I was abusively horrible.

Evil Editors: And you, **Cliché**, you make my eyes roll to the back of my head with your overused expressions. Sure, at one time your little utterances were witty or sage, but now that everyone uses you, you're no longer novel and distinct.

Cliché: (breaking down) I'm nothing more than yesterday's news? I'm all dressed up and nowhere to go?

Evil Editor: (*casts a warning glance at Em Dash and Ellipsis, who are holding hands and trying to sneak out of the bar*) Not so fast, you two.

Em Dash: Ahhh—

Ellipsis: We . . . uh . . . weren't trying to sneak . . .

Evil Editor: You two are equally guilty in ruining good writing because of the tendency to overuse yourselves. Sure, sometimes dialog does need to be cut off or indicate two characters interrupting each other. When I see too much of you, then I know the writer is relying on you rather than writing a complete sentence. So gather up your things and hit the gym, you overweight punctuation nightmares. You are meant to make reading easier and clearer. You were never meant to take the place of writing.

~~~

Time and time again, I've rejected manuscripts for improper/ overuse of punctuation. It's time consuming for a copy editor to go in and fix all the transgressions. Punctuation overkill is the sign of an unschooled writer. Since agents and don't have the time to perform on the job training, we reject these outright.

I want to be clear that there is nothing wrong with being a *new* writer, but you never want an editor to think you don't know what you're doing. It is one of the fastest ways to get a one-way ticket back to the fishing pond. But there are other ways as well . . . .

33: Submission Autopsy

Part 1 - Show vs. Tell

I always think of Show vs. Tell as the old Spy vs. Spy from *Mad Magazine*. One wears white (the good spy) and the other wears black (the evil spy). It's the perfect place to begin a manuscript autopsy.

~~~

The setting: In the operating room. A manuscript autopsy is being performed by the eminent Dr. Editor and her ever-faithful helper, Overworked Intern.

Overworked Intern: Dr. Editor, I've wheeled in the patient for further examination. I've looked and looked, but I can't find any cause of death.

Dr. Editor: Ah, the deceased; Submission 101—yes, yes, I'm familiar with the patient. Well, not this one, particularly, but I've seen the signs many times, and in many of those cases, the death was senseless.

Overworked Intern: You mean you know the cause of death? But you haven't even begun the autopsy.

Dr. Editor: I don't know the exact cause of death, my dear intern, and that's why we must perform an autopsy. But I can see in the chart that this was an acute case where the covers of the manuscript were too far apart.

Overworked Intern: You mean . . .

Dr. Editor: Yes. Death by Dullitis. Let's pick up the scalpel and investigate, shall we? (sounds of the buzzsaw and grunting fill the small operating room) Ah ha, see this, Intern? (Dr. Editor yanks on a misplaced verb and dangling participle) Here's our first clue; massive hemorrhaging between **Show vs. Tell**.

Overworked Intern: This is just so sad.

Dr. Editor: Indeed. What happened here is that there was too much **telling** and little **showing**. This puts a barrier between the reader and the story and the characters. When you *tell*, you lack passion, like reading a history book.

Overworked Intern: What do you mean?

Dr. Editor: I'll give you a quickie example.

Tell: "Blutto Bovine was fat, but he loved 31 Flavors."

The end result is that I have to draw my own opinion as to what fat means. Now, this sentence alone, isn't bad, but if an entire manuscript is written like this, I'm forced into my own head rather than being in the story. It's lazy writing and uninteresting. Let's spice up that same sentence with some show.

Show: "The cracks in the sidewalks widened an extra millimeter every time Blutto Bovine made his midday trek to 31 Flavors to order a double scoop of Double Fudge Maraschino Cherry. He always made a point of eating it quickly to avoid staining the only shirt that could cover his fleshy belly that hung over his belt like a root beer float. "

Overworked Intern: Isn't that longer?

Dr. Editor: Of course it is. But in those two sentences, we've gleaned the enormity of Blutto's girth, his favorite ice cream, his schedule, and his lack of wardrobe. And, we've done this with a very visual picture.

Overworked Intern: Do you think this patient simply didn't know how to show?

Dr. Editor: It's possible. But ignorance isn't an excuse for causality in death, my dear Intern. Just as in real life, our writing should utilize all our senses—smell, sound, sight, taste, touch. They bring a story to life. After all, a muddy pond can be just a muddy pond, or it can smell like a dusty attic on a winter day. Take your pick. This poor patient suffered the consequences.

Overworked Intern: So is the hemorrhaging between **Show vs. Tell** the cause of death, Dr, Editor?

Dr. Editor: It doesn't appear so. (Dr. Editor cuts out an intransitive verb and gasps) Oh my holy liver, it looks like there's a lot more going on. It's so sad, so tragic.

Overworked Intern: What, Dr. Editor? What?

Dr. Editor: (sniffling loudly) The patient is filled with Fluffitis and Backstoryosis. . . .

Special Note:

Backstory and fluff have huge potential as manuscript killers. If you continually interrupt your story in order go back in time and fill me in on circumstances that took place before the story began, then I'm going to get out a form rejection letter because you're boring me. If you find yourself continually reverting to your backstory, then think about writing that book first. Sometimes there really is a story that's itching to get out first, and excessive backstory may be used as a good litmus test for just such an occasion.

Fluff is an equal opportunity offender because it slips into writing so easily that the author is rarely aware of it. If you're constantly adding unnecessary tidbits with the intent of adding color and depth to your characters, then tread carefully because fluff is a lot like chocolate—too much can give you a stomach ache.

34: Submission Autopsy

Part 2 - Backstory, Fluff and Good Intentions

The setting: In the operating room. A manuscript autopsy is being performed by the eminent Dr. Editor and her ever-faithful helper, Overworked Intern. The suspected causes of death appear to be an acute case of Show vs. Tell. However, further explorations reveal other possible causes, the latest of which is Fluffitis and Backstoryosis.

Overworked Intern: Fluffitis and Backstoryosis? I'm not familiar with these terms, Dr. Editor.

Dr. Editor: Unfortunately **Fluff and Backstory** are the number one killers of all manuscripts because they tend to team up and destroy all the healthy writing. The result is that the reader falls asleep due to terminal boredom and/or confusion. I've seen cases where the backstory was so severe that I forgot the original plot. Those are the worst, and we normally isolate those in the EPC Unit because they're so infectious.

Overworked Intern: EPC Unit?

Dr. Editor: Eternal Pile of Crap. The only way to circumvent Fluff and Backstory is to put them on a severe diet.

Overworked Intern: What exactly is Fluff?

Dr. Editor: Fluff is the little inconsequential stuff that, when properly done, can round out a chapter or a character very nicely but has nothing to do with the plot. For example, it's the quick sidebar to explain that the hopelessly rich Margarita Von Aldenbald was nicknamed Lampie during an inebriated foray into a trucker bar where she commenced to dancing on the tables wearing nothing but a lampshade while singing "I'm An Oscar Meyer Wiener." It goes to development and adds richness to the story. It can be a lot of fun **if used in small doses**.

Overworked Intern: But?

Dr. Editor: But overdo Fluff, and you veer the train off the tracks. And I see this all too often among new manuscripts who are so in love with their own writing that they forget they have a story to tell. Now, if Fluff isn't too overdone, we're normally lucky enough to edit it out with a surgical strike of our mighty red pens. If it's metastasized throughout the entire manuscript, the standard medical procedure is to rip the guts out of the manuscript and rebuild it. I liken it to eating a Hershey bar after it's fallen in the gutter—I could do it, but why? I just throw it away and get another one. So goes it with the overfluffed manuscript. There are always other manuscripts waiting to be read.

Overworked Intern: So what about Backstory?

Dr. Editor: Same type of atrocities going on with Backstory and can have the effect of a bucket of warm spit. Like Fluff, Backstory is good in small doses. Backstory, when done properly, lends necessary background to a character or a situation in order for the story to progress with clarity. It's a small trip back in time.

Overworked Intern: Doctor, how will I recognize Backstory?

Dr. Editor: Let's say that you see a story that has pink Martians threatening to invade, and the only person who can save Earth is the head cheerleader from Bucktooth High. She's discovered that her sneezes are toxic to the little pink Martians. Problem is, every time she sneezes part of her luxurious blond hair falls out, so she has this dilemma: sneeze and save the world, don't sneeze and keep her hair. There's your action and your story. Now, a tiny bit of Backstory could detail how she was teased as a kid because her hair was a ratty mess until she hit puberty when it grew in thick and became the envy of every girl on campus. Even though it's Backstory, it goes to motive and character development, and explains why she's so freaked about sneezing. This is effective Backstory.

However, you can go too far. Let's say that Backstory yammers on about how Tommy Zitface used to pop the cheerleader's bra strap as his immature way of telling her he had a mad crush on her and wanted to take her to the "Dance With a Dog Social" that Friday night, now you're treading into Who Gives a Rat's Hiney land. It has nothing to do with the plot at hand and adds zip to the story.

As with Fluff, we treat Backstory the same way if it hasn't metastasized too much. We excise the tumor with a surgical strike with our mighty red pens. Luckily, the bleeding is normally minimal. But also like Fluff, if it spread itself throughout the entire manuscript, we normally have to pronounce it DOA—Dead on Arrival. And we always, always, always attach a Do Not Resuscitate order to it.

Overworked Intern: So Fluff and Backstory are lethal.

Dr. Editor: Oh my yes. I've seen them kill the tension of a story many times. I've read stories where I was on the edge of my seat. Then Backstory or Fluff came along and killed every bit of it. And what's really sad is that the manuscript has built-in antibodies that are often ignored.

Overworked Intern: Antibodies? So there's actually hope.

Dr. Editor: Absolutely. The **Intent** antibody lurks inside every single manuscript and is designed to kill anything that ruins a story. **Intent** is always asking, "What are you trying to say? What is your intent? What is the point of this sentence, this chapter?"

You see, every line and every chapter must have a reason for being there, and **Intent** works in the background much like the antivirus program on our computers. It pops up whenever Fluff and Backstory rear their ugly heads and signals a warning sign. But, alas, just like the popups on our computers, we turn them off all too often because they're irritating. The result is that Fluff and Backstory are free to wield their damage.

Overworked Intern: And that results in . . .

Dr. Editor: Yes. The dreaded Rejection Death Notice.

Overworked Intern: So Fluff and Backstory is what killed this manuscript, right, Dr. Editor?

Dr. Editor: I'm not sure. The autopsy isn't completed yet. Ah ha, see? Look there, past the sentence fragment and misplaced story arc . . . I think I see . . . oh dear, Dialogal tagococcus . . . .

35: Submission Autopsy

Part 3 - Dialog tags

The setting: In the operating room. A manuscript autopsy is being performed by the eminent Dr. Editor and her ever-faithful helper, Overworked Intern. Immediate cause of death has been determined to be an acute case of Dullitis—the covers of the manuscript were too far apart. Contributing causes are slowly being uncovered in this autopsy. So far, the patient suffered from massive hemorrhaging between **Show vs. Tell, Fluffitis and Backstoryosis**, and the latest - **Dialog tagococcus.**

Dr. Editor: (clucking sounds fill the operating room) Ah, such a pity. Dialog tagococcus, or its more commonly recognized form, the dialog tag, is an insidious little beast because most manuscripts have no idea of their existence. They're like little viruses that suck the life out of a story. If their numbers are kept to a minimum, they're fairly benign. The problem with dialog tags is that they're most virulent when put into the body of an immature manuscript. They colonize and prevent richness and flavor of the writing to propagate.

Overworked Intern: How so, Dr. Editor?

Dr. Editor: I'll give you an example:

"What does that cloud look like to you?" asked Bobby.

"I dunno," I said. "It looks like a kid sucking on a helium balloon."

"You ever sucked on a helium balloon?" Bobby asked.

"Sure," I said, "every time one of my sisters has a birthday. I stick a fork in the biggest one and recite the Pledge of Allegiance."

Overworked Intern: Seems okay to me. What's wrong with it?

Dr. Editor: It's lifeless, like they're talking heads. Let's see what happens when I take the dialog tags out:

Bobby looked over at me through quizzical brown eyes. "What does that cloud look like to you?"

I squinted on what looked like a giant bag cotton balls in the sky and shrugged. "I dunno." Bending my head sideways, I focused on one tiny cloud. "It looks like a kid sucking on a helium balloon."

Bobby laughed and punched my arm. "You ever sucked on a helium balloon?"

"Sure, every time one of my sisters has a birthday. I stick a fork in the biggest one and recite the Pledge of Allegiance."

Okay, it's not Faust, but it breaks up the monotony and gives them dimension. Instead of relying on a dialog tag to signify a speaker, try assigning an action to the character; a scratch of the nose, bite of a candy bar. When you decrease the use of dialog tags, the writing is opened up to a whole new world of communication and, in the process, a richer story.

Overworked Intern: Does this mean that all dialog tags should be irradiated?

Dr. Editor: No, not at all. Everything should be done in moderation, unlike that box of Twinkies you ate at lunch. Obviously we need tags to signify who's doing the talking when there are more than two characters in a scene. But too often dialog tags tend to create this ka-thunk, ka-thunk cadence, and it detracts from the dialog. It's off-putting to read a lovely piece of dialog and finish it off with, "he said." Clunk.

Overworked Intern: Does this go for saying things like, "he intoned," "he gasped," "he wheezed"?

Dr. Editor: Argh! These are some of the worst offenders because dialog tagococcus joins forces with **Show vs. Tell** and creates a mess. By using anything other than "said," you're assigning more importance to the tag than you are the dialog. It sticks out much like your pink paisley blouse with that red striped skirt. If a character gasps while speaking, then the manuscript has to jolly well *show* that, not *tell* it. Don't cheap out.

Example:

"I can't believe you ate my entire box of Twinkies," I gasped.

Now, let's try it again:

I clutched my throat and staggered toward the empty box—the very box I'd been saving to bribe the traffic judge. "I can't believe you ate my entire box of Twinkies."

Or:

I looked at the empty box and gasped. "I can't believe you ate my entire box of Twinkies."

Overworked Editor: Yes, but, Doctor, you use a lot more words to say what I could with two words.

Doctor Editor: This is true. But in the process, the reader better understands the depth of the character's angst. The long and short of it is to never take short cuts when telling a story. Words are a manuscript's only tools, and these poor patients suffocate under the weight of their own dryness and single dimension.

Overworked Editor: So this is what killed the patient? Dialog tagococcus?

Doctor Editor: Still not sure. I haven't gotten to the last third of the manuscript yet. Hand me the retractors and let's see what's lurking behind this prepositional phrase. Eeek! Point of Viewicemia. Oh, I really hoped to avoid this beast . . .

36: Submission Autopsy

Part 4 - Point of View

The setting: In the operating room. A manuscript autopsy is being performed by the eminent Dr. Editor and her ever-faithful helper, Overworked Intern. Immediate cause of death has yet to be determined, but contributing causes are mounting. So far, the patient suffered from massive hemorrhaging between **Show vs. Tell, Fluffitis and Backstoryosis, Dialog tagococcal,** and the latest—**Point of Viewicemia.**

Dr. Editor: Quick, Intern, my smelling salts! I've met the beast, and it's going to be a tug of war to extract this out of the manuscript.

Overworked Intern: Why, doctor? After all, the manuscript is dead, so what difference does it make?

Dr. Editor: Bite your tongue and wash your mouth out with Draino. My dear Intern, have you learned nothing? If I extract Point of Viewicemia without care, there will be nothing left of this poor manuscript to bury. No matter how horribly a manuscript died, it deserves a smidge of dignity. Hand me the buzz saw. No, no, the tiny one (a puff of smoke rises from the bowels of the manuscript, leaving an acrid odor wafting about the operating room).

Overworked Intern: Gah, what's that smell?

Dr. Editor: Sorry. Plug your nose. It's an infected First Person Point of View (POV). It tends to give off a rancid stench when it sits right next to the Limited Omniscient POV. Oh my, look here, you can see the lesions that were left by the Objective POV.

Overworked Intern: First Person , Limited Omniscient, Objective points of view. I'm confused.

Dr. Editor: Yes, yes, so was this manuscript. You see, what happened is this manuscript was slowly strangled by combating points of view. Look at this paragraph; it's written in the Objective point of view and right next to it is another paragraph written in the First Person point of view.

Overworked Intern: (blinking with bewilderment) Objective? First Person?

Dr. Editor: Say, just where did you get your MFA from anyway? Dr. Scholl's? Come on, think!

Objective—look it up in the dictionary. Objectivity is based on facts, things that are external—like action or dialog, not internal—like thoughts or feelings. Simply put, the reader can't see anything other than through the dialog or action. You never get into anyone's head.

First Person, on the other hand is where the story unfolds through the eyes of the narrator, and it's only his thoughts and impressions we get to see. Keep in mind that this point of view isn't necessarily the truth because you're limited to this one person's perceptions.

Overworked Intern: Tricky stuff.

Dr. Editor: It's that and a bag of chips, I tell you. And there's more than just these two points of view. There's **Third Person Objective, Limited Omniscient,** and a few others that I can't possibly go into or I'd never finish this autopsy. Suffice it to say that when a manuscript mixes points of view together, it creates a toxic smell that'll frizz your hair. My problem isn't what POV the manuscript used but rather that it stays consistent. Lookie here, I'll pull out this one offender and read it to you:

I couldn't believe that I'd won the Hot Bellybutton Contest. My competition was sooo tough this year. That snobby Marcia Mammary had a bellybutton tuck last summer, and I'm pretty sure Rosie Pinkgut used all her clothing allowance on a personal trainer. I hadn't done anything other than oiling my bellybutton down every night and keeping it lint free.

Marcia looked at the new winner and curled her lip. "Nice crown, O-Ring. Who cares about a stupid contest anyway? Especially since Brad Meathead asked me to the beach this weekend." She tossed her hair and gave the new queen a flip of her middle finger.

Rosie couldn't believe what she was hearing. She felt her temper rise to the boiling point. Brad was **her** boyfriend, and who did that loosey goosey Marcia think she was kidding with that innocent act? No one wanted to win the Hot Bellybutton Contest more than anyone she'd ever known. *Marcia, however, knew that Rosie was, in fact, planning on stealing Brad away at the Cotillion this weekend. Good luck with that, she thought.*

Can you count the POVs, Editorial Intern?

Overworked Intern: Um, **First Person** in the first paragraph, the second paragraph is **Third Person Objective**, and the last one is **Third Person Omniscient.**

Dr. Editor: Exactamundo. Now, remember, I don't give one whit which POV the manuscript is in - but that it freaking stays in one POV.

Overworked Intern: But what happens when you want to have a story with more than one character's point of view?

Dr. Editor: Sure, this happens in just about every manuscript. A story can get boring if we're in one person's head all the time. The trick is to keep one point of view **per scene.** If the manuscript wants to get into someone else's head, then there needs to be a scene switch. You can't, can't, can't be in Marcia and Rosie's head in the same scene. This is called head hopping. This is usually the work of a new writer. Truth is, very few manuscripts can pull this off effectively, so the common recommendation is "don't try it." Ever.

Overworked Intern: Is there anything else you see in there?

Dr. Editor: Wait, pull aside that modifier and exclamation point. Ah, geez, the final insult. This manuscript went into the point of view of a very minor character.

Overworked Intern: Why?

Dr. Editor: Good question. There are very few valid reasons for a story to be seen through the eyes of a minor character. The action is with the main characters, so that's where the focus must remain. It's illogical to elevate minor characters who add nothing to the plot. It derails the strength of the narrative and adds to the confusion.

Overworked Intern: Doctor, you're taking off your gloves. Does this mean—

Dr. Editor: Yes, Editorial Intern, I'm finished with the autopsy. This was one of the toughest autopsies I've done in a long time.

Overworked Intern: So have you determined an exact cause of death?

Dr. Editor: I have. It was a conflagration of **Show vs. Tell, Fluffitis and Backstoryosis, Dialog tagococcal,** and **Point of Viewicemia.** It's amazing the entire manuscript didn't explode into a ball of fire. I've heard of this happening. You remember Miss Snark? The story on the street is that her office blew up in a raging inferno from one of these kinds of manuscripts, and that's why she closed down her blog. Beware, Intern. Recognize the signs of Manuscript Extreme Dullitis. You blow up my office, and it's coming out of your paycheck.

~~~

Later that night, Editorial Intern crept back into the operating room. She was still confused about the POV's—especially Third Person. So she pulled out Dr. Editor's medical malpractice manual and read . . . .

Objective Point of View: This is, in a word; detached. The writer tells what happens without revealing anything more than can be inferred from the action and dialogue. The reader never knows a character's emotions or inner dialog.

Third Person: Can be omniscient or limited.

Omniscient means that the narrator knows all the thougths and feelings of all the characters.

Limited means that the story is limited to the thoughts and feelings of one character.

First Person: The story unfolds through the "I" of the story. This can be limiting because that "I" may not be reliable or trustworthy. Also, the emotions can only be felt through one character.

Editorial Intern closed the manual and decided she needed to start drinking. Heavily.

37: Physical description in blocks of text

Watch Those Bosoms. . .

Judy noticed the woman was tall, blond, and had a healthy bosom. She wore expensive jewelry as though she'd been born in it. Her nails were manicured to fine points and sported blood-red polish. The woman's clothing was woven from the finest linens and silk that money could buy. Her black sweater offset the woman's straight teeth.

I admit to a bias against physical descriptions that take up blocks of text like this. It derails the story. Here you have your reader's mouth watering with action, and *SCREEEEECH* . . . let's stop the story and take a brief time out while we get a description of what the character looks like.

To me, these text blocks show a lack of agility and imagination because they're all tell and no show. It's like a menu, dry and flat. Action—Obligatory Description of one character—Action—Obligatory Description of next character. Ka-thunk ka-thunk.

It's easier on the eye when writers weave in a few descriptions while keeping the story where it belongs—firmly entrenched in the action. Descriptions, in general, are a personal choice. Some authors prefer to leave their characters' features up their readers' imaginations. Others want to fill in every nitty gritty detail. I'm ok either way; but I do not like seeing text blocks. Show your writing chops by adding bits of description here and there.

Judy walked over to the snoring woman laying face down in the gutter and pulled the near-empty bottle of Jack Daniel's from her jeweled-encrusted fingers. She shielded the woman's body from the water that splashed up from a passing car. *Could this be the senator's missing wife? I'm betting someone will pitch a fit when they see mud and dog poop stains covering her Donna Karan slacks and sweater.* She tenderly brushed the thick, blond hair from the woman's face and noticed a finely manicured nail indelicately inserted in her nose. "Helloooo," Judy whispered into a diamond-studded ear. "Anyone home?"

So it won't win this year's Pulitzer, but you see that it's possible to give full descriptions while keeping the action going. Descriptions are great because they give us a frame of reference. In this case, it gives us a visual of the woman's stature and, well, lack thereof. Descriptive text blocks are something I see a lot in submissions, and my reaction is always the same; ka-thunk.

And while I'm bleating on about descriptions, be careful these descriptions make sense. For instance, in the example I used, I listed "a healthy bosom." First off, who uses that term anymore? Sounds like something my grannie would have said right before clucking her tongue. Yet I just read a "healthy bosom" description—in the book of a very well-published author. For shame. Made me go "eww."

Keep in mind that if you have a character observing another character, as I do above, ask yourself whether that observation makes sense. For example, does it make sense to have Judy, a woman, take notice of this woman's "healthy bosom"? Not unless she's gay or it's a foreshadowing that those bosoms are going to see some action fairly soon.

I recommend that you avoid the text block description. It's clunky and almost acts like a quickie commercial break.

38: Survival Style Guide

The stories in Chapters 31—37 highlight just a few of the many things that can kill a manuscript. I've put together a list of goodies to watch for and avoid in your own writing so you can avoid an unleashing of the angry red pen. Remember, you never want your work to be rejected for any other reason than it's not right for that agent or editor.

Exclamation points:

Rule 1- avoid them. Never rely on punctuation to do the job that your writing should be doing. Emotion should be conveyed through dialogue, action, and description. I've seen works that were filled with so many exclamation points that they ended up having the opposite effect.

Example:

* Zelda tried the door; it was locked!

* Zelda broke out into a cold sweat as her hands tugged at the doorknob. "Oh, dear God, it's locked."

The writer has conveyed fear and panic through words in the second sentence and, in the process, enriched the story. If you shouldn't use one mark, then it's obvious you should never use two, as in, *Did he think I was kidding??* or *How dare you say that!!*

Capitalization:

Using capitalization is a new-writer tendency and should be avoided with the same consideration as exclamation points. Since capitalized words translate as shouting, it's unnecessary to create this redundancy when your action or dialog has already created this effect of urgency.

Example:

She grabbed the TV remote from her husband's hands and flung it across the room while screaming, "I'VE TOLD YOU A MILLION TIMES THAT I HATE FOOTBALL!"

She's already screaming, so avoid the redundancy with the capitalization.

In the case of this example, "Hey, beautiful, let's go," you don't capitalize the word "beautiful." You only capitalize words that are titles used as substitutes for names. When you say something like "Hey, Senator" you capitalize "senator." When you say "Hey, Mom," you capitalize "mom." When you say "Please, sir, come with me" you don't capitalize "sir."

POV/POV shifts:

This topic was pretty well discussed in the Manuscript Autopsy Series, but just to reiterate; multiple points of view in the same paragraph or scene are confusing and distracting to us. Until you have the same status as Larry McMurtry, author of *Lonesome Dove* and *The Last Picture Show*, who changes point of view every other sentence, you need to follow the rules by staying with one point of view to a scene. If you need to change your point of view within a chapter, separate it with a scene break; signified by an extra carriage return.

Backstory:

As I wrote about in the Manuscript Autopsy, backstory can kill a good story because of its tendency to derail the progression of the plot. It's the same as slamming on the brakes to your car when you're headed to McDonald's for a Big Mac. You want that burger; you can taste the secret sauce and, oh, the fries, salty and hot—then WHAM! you have to slam on the brakes because there's tons of traffic ahead of you. Creeping along, you sense the burger and fries are slipping through your fingers because it's taking forever to get there. Backstory has the same effect. If your story is so filled with events and people that aren't relevant to your current story, then you need to take your foot off the brakes and find a more direct route to McDonald's.

Italics:

Italics signify a number of things: inner thought, a foreign word, a letter within the story, emphasize a word, or the dreaded dream sequence. Try to avoid putting large passages in italics because it's harder to read.

Examples:

* Inner thought without the attributes of speech: *I'm in deep trouble.*

* When you use attributes of speech, **do not** italicize inner thought: I'm in deep trouble, she told herself.

* Foreign words should be in italics, except for foreign words adopted by English speakers and used regularly. For example, the word "macho" is Spanish, but has become a part of American English slang to mean masculine. Do not put it in italics. "Adios, amigo" should be in italics.

* Emphasis of a word: "She did *what?*"

Italics also have other uses. The following items are italicized:

Titles of:

* books

* magazines

* journals

* newspapers

* films

* TV shows

* long musical pieces

* radio programs

* plays

* long poems

* software programs

* albums

* paintings

* sculptures

* dances

* ships

* trains

* aircraft

* spacecraft

* opera

Setting the scene:

Writers, oddly enough, often forget to set the scene in their chapters, or the beginning of their stories. We're a tactile bunch, and we need to know where we are in order to get our bearings. After all, we're probably going to scratch our heads if your main character rides to work on a horse— unless you live in Montana. Most of us drive cars. Ohhhh, this takes place in the Old West? Ah, important stuff. What does your setting look like, what smells might we encounter? Are we in an office with week-old ham and cheese sandwiches next to the radiator, or in a meadow just after a soft rain? What time period are we in? Day of the week? What is the weather like? Is there a breeze, or is the sun beating down on the back of your character's neck? Is your character sitting on a crate or rich Corinthian leather? Appeal to all our senses when you set your scene, and this will make it easier to immerse ourselves in your world.

Adverbs:

It is a fact that agents and editors seek out a writer's dependence on adverbs like heat-seeking missiles because of their tendency to dilute the verb. I tend to think of them as blood-sucking leeches that devour the vitality out of writing. It's the lazy man's version of trying to kick it up a notch. Verbs are the backbone of a sentence. They create the action and set the tone. Sticking an adverb into a sentence is like putting on too much make-up that hides a peaches and cream skin.

Now don't get me wrong. Adverbs are lovely little creatures provided they come out to play in moderation and stay in their neighborhood— like places where brevity is the name of the game.

Novel writing is a wild neighborhood, and the Neighborhood Watch crowd has their phasers set to vaporize if a manuscript depends on too many adverbs. Why? Adverbs "tell," they don't "show." And this is the crux of novel writing—showing.

There's a far cry between, "He ran slowly," and "His corpulent body prevented his legs from moving faster than a snail's pace."

As an editor, I want to "see" the story, and sentence two offers me an unambiguous picture.

I can hear the voices of discontent; "But aren't we looking for an economy of words in our writing?" Yes, of course you are, and adverbs provide this. After all, why take a paragraph when you can say it in a sentence? I agree but with a caveat; don't economize with your words at the expense of your writing. If it takes a longer sentence to convey a point, then use it. A writer can't communicate "he smiled happily" with the same precision as he can by injecting a nice piece of dialog (showing), "I couldn't be happier if I were twins."

As novelist Ray Wong says, "Adverbs most often become placeholders, vague and dull." Hip hip hooRay.

Adverbs are a lot like chocolate—one bite, and you can't put the candy bar down. Before you know it, your manuscript is filled with adverbs, and the wonderful world you created from your imagination comes out dull and lifeless. If you're going to use an adverb, by golly, they better know how to behave themselves and not attempt to take over the neighborhood.

Qualifiers:

Qualifiers are words or sentence elements that limit or qualifies another word, a phrase, or a clause. They're "Twinkie" words, it's meaning taken from junk food, which has little or no substance or nutrition.

Example:

* It **seems** that he was **very** sad.

* He was **basically** left without a car after the accident.

* The woman was **really** angry at the gas attendant.

This is weak, wishy washy writing, and agents and editors are looking for strong, decisive, confident writing. Qualifiers clutter the page, slow the story, and have no meaning in fiction. If something is *completely* devastating, then it can't be *more* devastating than devastating. If a character is *pretty* nice, I wonder what you mean. If the character is nice because he serves dinners to the homeless, then say so. This isn't to say you can't use qualifiers, because in dialogue they are acceptable, but if you do use them in narrative, use them judiciously. Remember to **show** as often as possible and be specific, be bold, be definite.

Avoid overwriting by limiting the use of qualifiers. My nominations for Twinkie awards are:

* really

* completely

* probably

* various

* needless to say

* quite

* definitely

* a lot

* perfectly

* actually

* usually

* pretty

* very

* certainly

* mostly

* frequently

* generally

* essentially

* sort of

* just

* to say the least

Most are good words, yet they have been spoiled by excessive and careless use until they have become hollow.

Active/Passive voice:

Agents and editors are always looking for strong writing, and this comes from active voice. Think of it this way; do you like your significant other to say, "Oh, I don't care what movie we go to; anything's fine with me," or would you like them to be certain? It's that way with writing as well. Active voice is when the subject of the sentence performs the action. It's strong and decisive. Passive voice is when the action of the verb is done to the subject. **Simply put: it's the difference between doing and having something done to you.**

Example:

Active: Fergus took control of the car.

Passive: The car **was controlled** by Fergus.

Active: The lime fizzie turned Blutto's tongue green.

Passive: Blutto's tongue **was turned** green by the lime fizzie.

Passive voice isn't grammatically wrong, but rather, it's a stylistic choice that yields uninteresting, comatose results.

Writing Dialogue:

I know this seems elementary, but I see a lot of dialog that isn't formatted correctly, and I get confused as to who is doing the talking. Write each person's spoken words, however brief, as a separate paragraph.

Example:

Underpaid Editor grabbed the blender.

"Margaritas for everyone."

Overworked Intern tossed the slush pile into the air.

"Whoopie doo!"

While I'm a sucker for a good margarita (and I do make the best in the world), this is a case of incorrect dialog formatting. I just finished reading a submission where the writer had formatted every bit of her dialog in this manner. I was constantly confused as to who was talking; and no, it wasn't because of the margaritas.

I have a lot of people asking me how to know when to keep the sentences as one paragraph. Simple. You have a lead-in sentence, and the dialog. The lead-in sentence matches the character's action with the upcoming dialog, so it belongs in the same paragraph, as seen here:

Example:

Underpaid Editor grabbed the blender. "Margaritas for everyone."

Overworked Intern tossed the slush pile into the air. "Whoopie doo!"

If one person's speech goes on for more than one paragraph, then use quotation marks to open the speech, and at the beginning of each new paragraph. To close the speech, use quotation marks at the end of the final paragraph.

Quotation marks:

In American usage, single quotation marks are used only for quoted words and phrases within quotations.

Example:

Angela had the nerve to tell me "When I saw 'BYOB' on your invitation, I assumed it meant 'Bring Your Old Boyfriend'."

If this is a case of the narrator talking to someone and she says, "The kids were always saying 'write a check,' so I did." then single quotes are used. The British, on the other hand, do the opposite and use the single quotes to denote dialog.

British Example:

Angela had the nerve to tell me 'When I saw "BYOB" on your invitation, I assumed it meant "Bring Your Old Boyfriend".'

In cases where quotes are used but aren't part of the speech, put the punctuation on the outside.

Example:

Didn't he say he'd "be back with bells on"?

Quotation marks are also used to enclose:

* chapters of books

* articles in newspapers

* radio episodes

* songs

* short stories

* articles in magazines

* sections in newspapers

* short poems

* TV episodes

* articles in journals

Em Dash:

Use the **em dash** to create a break in the sentence, for example a long sentence that already has commas in it. They can break up clauses, a word, or a phrase—or you can use them at the end of a sentence to separate it from the rest of the sentence. Be careful not to overload your story with em dashes. They make for hard reading after a while.

En dash:

Is the width of a typesetter's letter "N," means "through"—as in referring to dates or numbers: June 23–25 or pages 17–24.

Ellipsis:

Ellipses are handy little beggars to let the reader know when you're quoting someone and want to omit some text from a sentence.

Example:

"The World Shuffleboard Tournament was attended by thirty countries, five were from the U.S., and was a rousing success in 'board management'."

Now becomes:

"The World Shuffleboard Tournament was attended by thirty countries . . . and was a rousing success in 'board management'."

If the omission comes at the end of a sentence, you'll place your period as you normally would and add the ellipsis, which would total four dots. Be sure to keep a space between your period and the ellipsis.

Pause in flow: The ellipsis is also used to indicate a pause in a sentence, including dialog.

Example:

I thought I told Galinda to meet me at Murph's Margaritas . . . or did I?

"Should I buy that hot little red dress or the chaste green one? I wonder . . . ." (note the fourth dot to signify the end of the sentence)

Be careful of the ellipsis. They are seductive to new writers because it's a natural desire to want to use them for pauses in speech. The problem is that the manuscript ends up looking like a dot convention, and I've tossed many a manuscript for this over-dependence on ellipses. If you have a lot of pausing in a dialog passage, don't depend on punctuation to bail you out. Signify those pauses through your writing.

Hyphens:

Messing up hyphen usage has never been a reason for rejection, but not understanding their use does mark a writer as being undereducated. Since hyphens aren't used a whole lot in literature, they can be an indicator as to the depth and breadth of someone's writing chops. Sneaky Petes, aren't we? Here are the most common uses of hyphens in fiction and nonfiction:

Compound Modifiers: This is a fifty-dollar term that means the words are modifying a noun.

Example:

She is a **first-time** novelist.

My beagle is an **equal-opportunity** face licker.

This is the **third-floor** apartment.

Ambiguity: Hyphens are also used to eliminate ambiguity. These aren't mandatory, but rather, they are used in order to make for easier, clearer reading.

Example:

My secretary's lobotomy made her brain-addled but also more compliant.

Swearing at your editor is a sure-fire way to find yourself looking for a new editor.

Numbers: The last rule you should be aware of about hyphens is numbers and ages.

Example:

I remember when I was **twenty-five**, lo those many years ago.

Now that Joe Author won a Pulitzer, he behaves like a **five-year-old**.

Colon:

The colon follows an independent clause (a complete statement) and introduces one of the following three things: a defining example, a list, or a quotation.

Examples:

She had only one person to blame: her mother.

A new menace threatens Hollywood: a Botox shortage.

I was depressed and reached for my favorite comfort foods: peanut butter, ice cream, a bag of potato chips, and a chocolate martini.

The title of one of her poems signified Bertha Crabtree's feelings about losing the Homerville Baking Championship: "No One Makes Banana Cream Pie Like I Do."

Semicolons:

Semicolons are stronger than a comma but weaker than a period. The most common use is between two independent clauses not joined by a conjunction like "and" or "but" (See Comma Splices);

Example:

I'm dying to see *Star Wars* before it leaves town; I'm told the three hours it takes to watch this movie passes very quickly.

Semicolons are also used, instead of commas, to separate items in lengthy, complex lists.

Example:

It's vital to have all the right goodies when renting movies; for example, ice cream, microwave popcorn, diet pop, and Maalox all make for a perfect evening.

Classically, colons and semicolons were exclusive fare for nonfiction, but we see them creeping into fiction as an interesting stylistic choice. Just don't overdo, as it can become tedious.

Apostrophes:

Apostrophes are used to show possession, **not plurals**. I see this far more than I should. Now, blowing this won't result in a rejection letter, but it will mark you as not possessing . . . get it *possessing* . . . all the tools of your trade.

It's correct to write:

I'm leaving for four weeks' vacation.

I adore all of my authors' books.

However—"I have three **title's** up on the *Los Angeles Times* bestseller list." will earn you a rap on the knuckles by a cranky editor.

And what about those pesky names that end in "s"? Yes, I know your teachers in grade school and high school told you the possessive of Charles is Charles' **but it is not.** In fiction, it's Charles's, Damaris's, Willis's, and so on.

Contractions:

Use contractions when writing fiction. Say "don't" instead of "do not" and "can't" instead of "cannot" and so forth. Contractions signal informal writing, which translates as friendly writing. Anything else is academic and tedious to read. However, don't say something like this; "I've new shoes in the box" because that isn't how we speak. In this case, you would say, "I have new shoes in the box."

North, South, East, West:

Capitalize points of the compass when they designate geographical parts of the country.

For example:

* Southern States, out West, the Northwest, Midwestern States.

* The South has increased its manufactures.

* Election returns from the East are eagerly waited.

* The North took a stand on the question.

* Orders credited to Eastern sources were in evidence.

Do not capitalize when merely used for direction

For example:

* In the colonies to the north and south of her, giant rabbits edited troublesome manuscripts.

* She was facing south when the pink bunny dropped his red marker.

* The rabbits preferred to make their home west of the Rockies and south of Colorado border.

The Government Printing Office Style Manual presents the following on Army, Navy, and Air Force:

* Capitalize U.S. Army, French Army, the Army, Army Establishment, the Navy, Navy, Navy officers or Naval officers (you get the idea), but NOT Lee's army or the armies of the Russian republics.

Dialog tags:

As you read in the Manuscript Autopsy, dialog tags are used to denote who is doing the talking. Many new writers take this to the extreme and follow every line of dialog with a tag. Drives me buggy. I also go buggy when writers seek to avoid using "said," thinking that it's boring. Instead, I see things like:

* He snorted

* He laughed

* He threatened

* He guzzled

* He burped

* He cried

* He yelled

* He wheezed

* He paused

Blah, blah . . .

Only one thing should be going on with dialog tags: identify the speaker. But too often, writers use dialog tags as a crutch to reveal emotion, hence the above examples. Or they don't realize the tags are unnecessary—especially when two people are talking. Passages of dialog that has a "he said" after it creates a ka-thunk ka-thunk pace.

"Blah, blah, blah, blah," he said.

"Blah, blah, blah, blah," she said.

-yawn-

It's unnecessary and unimaginative. Rather than using a dialog tag, use action to indicate who is doing the talking.

Example:

Overworked and Underpaid Editor stood in the middle of the office and stared at the floor, now littered with envelopes and tip sheets. "Overpaid and Underworked Assistant, get in here immediately and clean up this abomination."

Overpaid and Underworked Assistant cringed in the darkness of the closet where she'd been having a major makeout session with the computer technician who'd arrived to reboot her hard drive. Reboot her hard drive, indeed. "Coming, boss."

No tags. Instead, I used this passage to set the scene while still identifying who is doing the speaking. This adds flavor to a potentially boring scene. I'm not saying that you won't use dialog tags, especially when there are three or more characters talking. Sometimes you need a more rapid fire pace. But if writers avoid overusing the "he said, she said" tags, this goes a long way to avoiding ka-thunk.

Special note about "pause." Don't say "he paused, "she paused," "they paused," or any version of pause. A change in scene or dialogue naturally signals a pause. If a character stops talking, that's a pause.

Sex and cursing:

Cursing doesn't equal drama, and sexually explicit scenes don't equal erotica. There is an art to creating tension and drama. If you don't know how to create tension and drama, read *The DaVinci Code*. Dan Brown knows how to create both and that's why his book is selling like umbrellas in a downpour.

Unless you're writing erotica, sex scenes and sexually charged passages have a common thread: less is more. When an editor tells you the sex scene is raw, clinical, or offensive, believe her. Put your heroine in the kitchen in the moonlight in a transparent nightgown, rather than on the kitchen floor naked with her legs pointing east and west.

Your characters may be heathens, but if the writing is explicit, we may call you the heathen as well. That's human nature. We know how to separate the writer from the narrator, but readers don't always afford the same benevolence. You can still have the scene, but whether it works depends on how you write it. If you don't know how to write a sex scene that will keep us reaching for a cold shower and a cigarette, find and read sex scenes by the great writers. Some of what you find will be steamy and some will be graphic, but the greatest scenes will seduce you with few words and no description of the sex act.

If you aren't famous yet, stay away from sexually direct scenes. I'm not sure you're aspiring to be Henry Miller, but if you are, give it up. Henry isn't shocking anymore, though some still call him crude. Until you're so famous you can chance being labeled a swine, don't take the risk. Learn how to write sex scenes so they entice and enthrall us.

Comma splice:

When you have two independent clauses (complete, stand-alone sentences), you have a choice; to *join* them or *separate* them. A comma splice is a sentence where two independent clauses are joined together in one sentence and separated with a comma and no conjunction. These are also called run-on sentences, and I've seen enough doozies to curl my hair.

Example:

I adore Twinkies, I eat one after every meal.

Technically, this is incorrect writing, so there are means by which to make those two independent clauses come together happily enough to make any writing coach sing from the tree tops. Yes, you can use these **in moderation** because it can mix up the pace, which keeps the reader engaged.

Conjunctions: these are your little connectors that combine independent clauses together: and, but, or, nor, yet, and so.

Example:

I adore Twinkies, **so** I eat one after every meal. (notice the comma is still there to separate the two independent clauses.)

Punctuation: This is what I usually call "the end game" because you're using punctuation at the end of the first independent clause to separate it from the one that follows.

Example:

I adore Twinkies! I eat one after every meal. (exclamation point/broke it up into two sentences)

Example:

I adore Twinkies. I eat one after every meal. (period/broke it up into two sentences)

Example:

I adore Twinkies; I eat one after every meal. (semicolon)

These are pretty easy to flesh out. But many of us write sentences that contain several independent clauses, and things can get dicey. And confusing

Example:

I adore Twinkies, I eat one after every meal, they give me a great sugar high.

Now you can see where editors or agents blink a few times before rereading the sentence. These run-on sentences are hobby/hacker stuff and create a clunky cadence. Let's fix this up.

Example:

I adore Twinkies, **so** I eat one after every meal **because** they give me a great sugar high.

This example brings me into that handy little word **"because."** You'll note that whenever you use "because" there is no comma after the first independent clause. Use "because" when you have an expression of cause and effect.

Example:

I love my wicked red pen because it scares the willies out of writers.

We screamed for joy because our author's book made the bestseller's list.

I love my job because I meet the most wonderful people.

Comma splices aren't all bad

Okay, so I can hear you screaming in frustration; "is there ever a time comma splices aren't denizens of evil?" Fear not because, actually, there is.

Example:

That's not just a Twinkie, it's food from the Gods.

Those aren't shoes, baby, they're Ferragamos.

Punctuating these sentences with a semicolon would be like using semi-dried Elmer's Glue to hold the space shuttle together. It's too strong for the sentence.

Comma splices that won't make me scream

If the two clauses are short and the subject matter is the same in both clauses, then you probably aren't committing any rash acts of literary bioterrorism.

Example:

I saw that hot red car, I bought it.

I saw the banquet table, my stomach growled, I ate like a pig.

If you have two pretty short clauses that present a negative/positive contrast. This can also take the form of a question.

Examples:

This is my Twinkie, that is my main course.

I'm not getting fat, I'm redistributing my body mass.

I'm going to the gym, I'm not headed for the beach.

My bikini is too small, isn't it?

You've been to that bar, haven't you?

Heh, heh, got you with those last two, didn't I? Believe it or not, those very recognizable sentences meet the criteria of a comma splice.

Look, agents and editors aren't real sticklers for the two sentence comma splice *PROVIDED* it isn't overdone. Like my love for chocolate, everything should be done in moderation. Comma splices create a minimalist style, which can be very effective. But it can also make for choppy writing, which translates as unprofessional writing, which translates as a writer who doesn't know how to write. All great writing has rhythm. Read your work out loud to see if it has rhythm. If it doesn't, you are a choppy writer. Choppy writing is not read. Avoid it.

Mr. Independent Clause meets Ms. Fragment:

This makes me crazy because it's just plain ugly writing and forces me to do a double take. If I do a double take, that means I have to reread the sentence. If I have to reread the sentence, then I get cranky. If I get cranky, I'll probably reach for a rejection letter. Sadly, I see this type of writing often enough to give it dishonorable mention.

Example:

A stretch of gray sky opened up (independent clause), the skeletal branches of a dead tree reaching for heavens. (fragment)

A lion roared (independent clause), the windswept savannah growing cold. (fragment)

These are the sentences that leave me saying, "HUH?" Not only is the second half of the sentence a fragment, but it's unrelated to the independent clause. These read like a short circuit because they don't have anything in common. If you write like this, I'll be forced to call the law on you. Pinky promise.

Comma usage:

Learn how to use them. I'm not going to go into a long diatribe for all the uses for a comma, but I will implore you to understand its uses.

Commas are our friends, believe it or not. They can be all that's protecting an innocent sentence from obscurity. I will say that the most common abuses are the following examples:

Example:

Next Tuesday, **which happens to be my secretary's birthday**, is the only day I'm available to talk to you.

There always needs to be a comma **separating a clause** from the rest of the sentence. Remove those commas, and the sentence becomes a mish mash.

Example:

This bar serves great drinks. The bartender, *on the other hand,* is a real jerk.

There always needs to be commas surrounding the **phrase** so that it doesn't read like a run-on sentence.

Example:

I love your writing. In this case, *however*, you are lacking a marketable plot.

You always need commas surrounding an **adverb** like *after all, but, however, nevertheless, nonetheless, notwithstanding, though, that said, still*, etc.

Lastly, use commas to separate three or more items.

Example:

The things I love most about skiing are the hot guys, the wind in my hair, and hot buttered rums.

Stereotype:

Stereotype is an inflexible and oversimplified perception of characteristics that are typical of a person or group. It's cliché's ugly twin sister. Don't write to stereotype because it's unimaginative and lazy. All white males are not out to get women and people of color; all blondes are not airheads; all Spanish speakers are not alike culturally; all women of color are not exotic; and all people from the Middle East are not Muslims. While you can write a character with some stereotypical characteristics, you run the risk of boring us senseless or being labeled narrow minded. We are familiar with every stereotype on the planet, so show us something new. You don't want agents or editors bored out of their skulls, so avoid the same old dribble. You want us to embrace your work, not send out form rejection letters.

Correct Word Usage:

I'm a big proponent of authors expanding their vocabulary because it makes for richer writing. But please be sure you use those new words correctly. Words are our tools, and we take a dim view of writers who misuse the tools of their trade. Use online resources like Dictionary.com or Merriam-Webster.com. Better yet, subscribe to it. It's cheap, and you'll be able to see examples of sentences using the word(s) you're curious about. I lifted the following sentence from an actual submission.

Example:

Jenny didn't know for certain, but guessed by her brother's **demure** that he was guilty.

The word the author should have used is **demeanor**. **Demure** is an adjective and has an entirely different meaning. Sadly, the author went on to make other blatant errors, and I quit reading.

Research:

If you give a character a disease you don't have, research the disease. If your story takes place in Brooklyn, New York, but you live in Tiny Town, Mississippi, and have never visited Brooklyn, much less New York, do the research. Readers will call you on misinformation and write angry letters to your publisher if you are wrong—and worse, they'll ask for a refund. If you have a British character during the War of 1812, for example, make sure your character refers to it as The Napoleonic Wars. If you have a character who has a disease, say, Multiple Sclerosis, then you better be an expert in MS and know all the symptoms, medicines, the stages of MS, and what your character is able (or not able) to do.

Point of View:

This determines the person whose the story is viewed through, and narrative voice, which determines how it is expressed to the audience. They are the narrator, and it's through their eyes in which we see the story. There are four main points of view that are used in writing:

Omniscient and Limited Omniscient Points of View

A narrator who knows everything about all the characters is all knowing, or omniscient. A narrator whose knowledge is limited to one character, either major or minor, has a limited omniscient point of view.

First Person Point of View

The voice/narrator is part of the action of the story, and the story is told through their eyes only. Remember—just because we're seeing the story unfold through this POV doesn't mean that it's trustworthy. This means that other events may be taking place outside of that character's purview.

Objective Point of View

The writer tells what's going on without getting into any character's head. This POV is nothing more than a detached observer.

Third Person Point of View

This is an outside voice/narrator. They aren't participating in the action as one of the characters, but we know exactly how the characters feel.

When creating your story, take the time to think about these issues because it could determine which POV is best suited for your story:

* Through whose eyes do you want your story to unfold? What voice gives the story the most strength?

* Who seems to have the biggest voice in your story? For instance, there are stories where the protagonist isn't the biggest voice, and being inside his head may destroy the framework of your story.

* How does the point of view affect your responses to the characters?

* How is your story affected by how much the narrator knows and how objective he/she is?

To that end, I've seen manuscripts where one character is written in First Person, and all the other characters are Third Person. There are very few writers who can pull this off, however, and I don't recommend it.

Characters:

There exists one last element that is a part of your Survival Style Guide, and that is your characters.

39: Watchful Writing

Mind Your Characters

Manuscripts seem to come in two forms; those that contain characters so real you can smell their aftershave, and those whose characters are as flat as my last attempt at baking a cake. Since characters are what move the plot along, make them vibrant and three dimensional.

Most of the authors I've talked to regarding character development have a single common thread; they invariably extrapolate bits and pieces from real people. They have a ready-made palette in which to draw upon. How many times have we heard that truth is stranger than fiction? Same goes for characters. Some of the colorful people I've written about in my own writing actually exist in some form or another.

Great character development shouldn't be overlooked because they are the conduit through which your story is told.

* **Do they have a quirk?** I have a gorgeous character with the mouth of a truck driver. She can't say anything without adding a colorful metaphor. What makes her likeable is that she's a closet softie for pregnant mothers (she's an OB/GYN) and is fiercely loyal to the few she considers good friends. This isn't what defines her, per se, but it does make her memorable. In reality, she's a composite of about four people I know. And none of them know this.

* **Personality traits:** Personality traits add depth. Are they shy, outspoken, demanding, argumentative, loving, inquisitive, smart? Think of the people you know in your life and see if you can't assign your characters some added depth. A lack of depth is one of my biggest problems with manuscripts because so many of them are lacking. The writer simply has them delivering dialog, and I have no way of getting a bead on that character's personality, what makes them tick.

* **Physical description:** There are a couple of schools of thought on description. I discussed text blocks of description in Ch. 37. Some writers go way overboard in writing a physical description, right down to the whiteness of teeth and whether they shave their armpits. Some readers like to have description left up to their own imagination. Whatever the writer's personal tastes regarding this matter, the trick is not to give a description all at once like a shopping list. Dole it out in tidbits. Things like this drive me nutso:

She had a mane of thick, golden hair and startling blue eyes. Her long fingers sported equally long nails that were painted a deep green. Her feet were huge, and she could barely squeeze into the size 12 Ferragamos. She was tall, had a tiny waist and slender hips . . . blah, blah, blah.

The idea is that these sentences aren't that bad if they are offered piecemeal. Try putting a sentence here on one page, a sentence there a few pages or chapters later—just enough to give the reader a general layout of the character. Shoving them into one paragraph slows down the narrative because you've stepped outside the story much like a commercial: "scuse me while I do the obligatory description here before I bring you back to your regularly scheduled book." A useful way of adding a physical description without the reader being aware of it is to apply it with an action.

This sentence:

Her long fingers sported equally long nails that were painted a deep green.

Now becomes:

Her long fingers wrapped around his neck in one easy movement. Blood stained her painted fingernails, creating a holiday pattern of crimson red and deep green.

* **Plausibility**—If your character is shy, retiring, and is very short, they have to behave in the manner of a shy, retiring, short person. This character isn't going to stand up in the front of a classroom of eighth graders, leap onto a desk and belt out a rousing rendition of "I'm A Little Teapot." Yet I see this type of writing all the time, and it's because the writer hasn't completely fleshed out their characters. They aren't living, breathing entities, and this breeds mistakes and inconsistent writing. If you're going to write with characters (and who isn't?), then you have to make them your best friends and know how they will react.

In short, much of what we write about in the fictional world comes from our imaginations. But we need to draw upon the real world in order to put our stories into perspective so that our characters leap off the page and hold us hostage.

This Survival Style Guide is a quick, down, and dirty reference that is geared to stay by your side while you're writing your bestseller. Let it be your constant companion so you can avoid becoming a rejection statistic.

40: Do Miracles Happen?

You've read all of the insider interviews, read what excites us, taken the Survival Style Guide to heart, and you're wondering about your chances of being published. Do miracles happen—especially in these tough economic times? Miracles happen every day for new writers. I realize this sounds hollow, especially if you've just wallpapered your bathroom with your rejection letters, but let me give you a case in point.

Not too long ago, I blogged about the importance of agents, and this set off a bevy of frustrated comments from many authors. One poster caught my eye because her heartfelt observations encapsulated everything I've heard over the years. I was more than happy to allow her a forum in which to beat her fists into the sky because I think she represents many writers:

Poster: I had a "high profile, top of the line, well known" agent and, needless to say, I wasn't treated very well. He made it very clear that I was not high on his priority list, and after only seven submissions to the major houses (one submission where he didn't even get the name of my book right) he decided not to represent me anymore. Here I am, back at the beginning; frustrated, a little angry, and obviously feeling hopeless. Although I received rejections, they were quite favorable. Most liked the book but didn't feel it "right for their house." I'm new, never published, and I wonder daily why he didn't work his way down the line. I was considering doing submissions myself until I saw this blog. Do I keep going with the agent thing or do it myself? I realize every yahoo from here to China wants a book published and agents filter these people out but, how far should a writer go to achieve publication?

I'm going to play the devil's advocate for a moment with your comment:

Where is it written that life offers guarantees of fairness and the nice guy always finishes first? This is a business about making money by publishing marketable literature, and you have to treat this as a business.

Something like this tends to really demean the publishing industry. I can't seem to get published, writing what I believe to be enjoyable novels that send a strong, realistic, message to society on topics most would prefer to not read about. In an **enjoyable way**, they give the reader countless information on how **to protect themselves, and their children, from people like him.** OJ, and the Goldman family, both had agents in like one day? Obviously, and taking into consideration what I do in my "day job," something like this really floors me.

I can write enjoyable novels, and not get published. If I go out tomorrow and commit some heinous act; publishers will be beating down my door. I understand that most of the publishers, and agents, don't agree with the book but I felt the need to rant like a lunatic about it anyway. It's extremely frustrating.

Sorry, but the unspoken "anything goes" rule in the biz sometimes gets to the best of us.

What exactly is "marketable literature"?

Me: "Marketable literature" is that vague-assed manuscript that any particular publisher or agent may feel will sell well. I say vague-assed because what's marketable to me may not be marketable to Jane Editor or Joe Agent. It's subjective, and yes, for a writer, this revelation sucks stale Twinkie cream.

Poster: And, clearly, sometimes the nice guy not only doesn't finish first; he comes in dead last.

Me: Dead last of what? Nice guy who writes brilliant stuff has a higher chance of eventually being recognized. And at that, what's brilliant? It's in the eye of the beholder, and that would be the agent or editor.

The question is when to give up. I'd say that if Nice Guy has been rejected by about a hundred outstanding agents and editors, he may not have such a brilliant work. That's why writers can't be islands. They have to be a part of a writing community that will offer unbiased crits of the work.

Poster: As you can imagine how frustrating it is for struggling authors who spend years perfecting their novels and have countless doors slammed in their faces to see the biggest headline in the book industry is about an animal who got away with murder. OJ. (There, I said it . . . ugh)

Me: There's no doubt about it, a ton of perceived crap gets pubbed. Why? Because it sells. The more voyeuristic and dysfunctional it is, sometimes the better it sells.

We have several titles that have been optioned for films only to be dumped. These are brilliant pieces of works that have the capacity to become classics. When I see the dregs coming out of Hollywood, I moan. So, yes, I understand your angst and sympathize. On the other hand, a lot of great work is also getting pubbed, so, believe it or not, there is a balance.

Poster: As I said before, this demeans the publishing industry.

Me: I don't believe this. Publishers are in the business to make money, so we gravitate toward works we think will sell. I'm not saying that there aren't those who push the envelope, like the OJ drivel, but that's really the way of Man—to push the envelope before someone stops and says, "enough!" For the most part, publishers reflect on what readers want. They'll put out new types of works to test the waters and evaluate the response. If it sells, you'll be apt to see those types of genres flooding the market the very next season. Alas, the birth of chick lit and teen lit.

Poster: I can't seem to get published, writing what I believe to be enjoyable novels that send a strong, realistic, message to society on topics most would prefer to not read about.

Me: I haven't read your work, and I don't know how many agents and editors you've submitted to, but if it's hundreds, it's possible you need some outside help to give you an honest critique.

And don't worry; you're allowed to feel like meatloaf every now and then. Writing is a tough business and the ego isn't surrounded by one of those really cool Star Trek shields. So, set your phaser to stun, have a margarita, and begin writing a new book.

This author wasn't done with me. She wrote back a few days later:

Poster: What would I do without you? My day of feeling like a leftover three-day old meatloaf has passed . . . I love someone like you to "tell it like it is" and throw me back into reality. Tell me to quit my whining, bitching, and move forward!! You are right 100%. I apologize for the waste of space. As for the publishers, I only had passed through seven and, although rejected, they had many positive things to say. I jumped into the sea of despair due to circumstances of the day beyond my control.

What is the ultimate humorous ending to this week? Other than falling on my face in front of a restaurant full with people (I wasn't even drinking) I opened my mail this afternoon and had an offer for rep from an agent. I actually felt myself laugh away five weeks of stress. I'm being careful this time around and not jumping into a contract, giving myself time to think about the offer in full.

Regardless, a weight has been lifted . . . many margaritas are being consumed in Ohio this weekend. One of which is being "cheered" to Lynn in Cali. Thanks for everything, lady!

~~~

The story doesn't end there. Stacy Dittrich, who was ready to drink Draino, ended up being represented by a wonderful agent, Claire Gerus, and won a multi-book deal with Dorchester and Kaplan for her CeeCee Gallagher series, and several other books.

Cinderella story, you say? I met Stacy at Book Expo America in Los Angeles, and she is no Cinderella. She kept with her writing, found solace where she could, and didn't give up. New writers are signed to publishers every day, so yes, as far as I'm concerned—and I'm sure Stacy would agree with me—miracles *do* happen provided you have all the right tools in your tackle box. Stacy's tackle box was lined in gold, and I couldn't be happier for her if I were twins.

Conclusion

So that's it, my fine fisher folk. You've had a personal tour of our side of the pond, and your tackle box is full with the wisdom and advice from some of the best minds in the publishing industry. We've told you what turns our heads in the murky waters of queries and submissions, and we've alerted you to what makes our teeth grind and what makes us sing with delight.

The rest is up to you. There are no guarantees in this crazy world of publishing because we are at the whims of so many volatile elements. The economy and reader tastes ebb and flow like the tide. There is no doubt there will be rejections, but *The Writer's Essential Tackle Box* was written to keep smart writers on top of their game, educating you to the pitfalls, and staying ahead of the rest of the fishermen crowding the shores so those rejections will be fewer and farther between.

May your writing be bright, may your words flow with ease, and may your fishing pole always remain creative, shiny, and wonderful.

- Lynn Price and the beagle